CASE STUDIES IN
CULTURAL ANTHROPOLOGY

GENERAL EDITORS

George and Louise Spindler

STANFORD UNIVERSITY

THE IÑUPIAT AND ARCTIC ALASKA

An Ethnography of Development

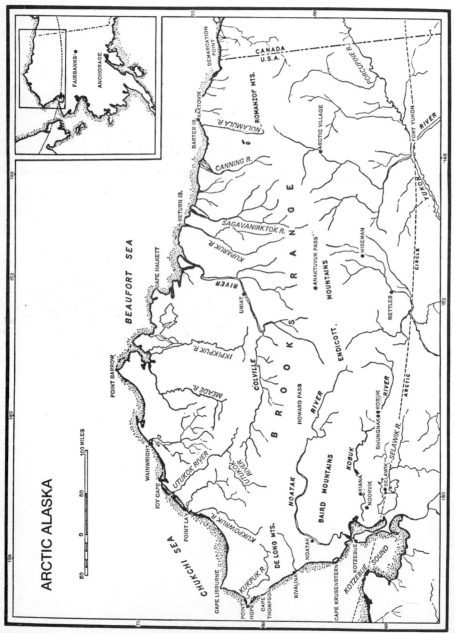

Map 1. Arctic Alaska in 1958

THE IÑUPIAT AND ARCTIC ALASKA

An Ethnography of Development

NORMAN A. CHANCE

The University of Connecticut

HOLT, RINEHART AND WINSTON

FORT WORTH CHICAGO SAN FRANCISCO PHILADELPHIA
MONTREAL TORONTO LONDON SYDNEY TOKYO

Publisher: Ted Buchholz
Acquisitions Editor: Chris Klein
Project Editor: Michael D. Hinshaw
Copy Editor John Dycus
Production Manager: Monty Shaw
Art & Design Supervisor: Vicki McAlindon Horton
Cover Designer: Vicki McAlindon Horton

Library of Congress Cataloging-in-Publication Data
Chance, Norman A. (Norman Allee), 1927–
    The Iñupiet and Arctic Alaska : an ethnography of
development / Norman A. Chance.
        p.   cm. — (Case studies in cultural anthropology)
    Includes bibliographical references.
    ISBN 0-03-032419-X
    1. Eskimos—Alaska—Social conditions.   2. Rural development—
Alaska.   3. Eskimos—Alaska—Economic conditions.   4. Eskimos—
Alaska—Government relations.   I. Title.   II. Series.
E99.E7C52   1990
305.8′9710798—dc20   89-24526
                                                                                  CIP

Requests for permission to make copies of any part of the work should be mailed to:
Copyrights and Permissions Department, Holt, Rinehart and Winston, Inc., Orlando,
FL 32887

Address editorial correspondence to: 301 Commerce Street, Suite 3700,
                                                          Fort Worth, TX 76102
                        Address orders to: 6277 Sea Harbor Drive, Orlando, FL 32887
                                                          1-800-782-4479, or 1-800-433-0001 (in Florida)

Printed in the United States of America

0 1 2 3   039   9 8 7 6 5 4 3 2 1

Holt, Rinehart and Winston, Inc.
The Dryden Press
Saunders College Publishing

Foreword

ABOUT THE SERIES

These case studies in cultural anthropology are designed to bring to students, in beginning and intermediate courses in the social sciences, insights into the richness and complexity of human life as it is lived in different ways and in different places. They are written by men and women who have lived in the societies they write about and who are professionally trained as observers and interpreters of human behavior. The authors also are teachers, and in writing their books they have kept the students who will read them foremost in their minds. It is our belief that when an understanding of ways of life very different from one's own is gained, abstractions and generalizations about social structure, cultural values, subsistence techniques, and the other universal categories of human social behavior become meaningful.

ABOUT THE AUTHOR

Norman A. Chance is a Professor of Anthropology at the University of Connecticut. Born in Lynn, Massachusetts, he received his initial training in anthropology at the University of Pennsylvania prior to receiving his Ph.D. from Cornell University in 1957. After spending five years at the University of Oklahoma he accepted a teaching appointment at McGill University in Montreal, Canada, eventually becoming the founder and first director of its Programme in the Anthropology of Development. In 1968, he returned to the United States to establish a Department of Anthropology at the University of Connecticut where he continues teaching today.

Among his academic activities, he has held postdoctoral research fellowships from Harvard University, the Russell Sage Foundation, and the Arctic Institute of North America. His field work has been undertaken in the American Southwest, northern Canada, China, and Arctic Alaska. He has served on numerous national and international committees, panels and boards including those of the National Academy of Sciences, National Research Council, American Association for the Advancement of Science, American Anthropological Association, and the Arctic Institute of North America. In addition to his other publications, Chance has written two previous case studies in this series: *The Eskimo of North Alaska* (1966) and *China's Urban Villagers* (1984).

Before becoming an anthropologist, Chance had two decidedly non-

Photo 1. The author preparing for a flight to Alaska in 1985.

academic interests, music and flying. Early musical studies at Eastman School of Music and Oberlin Conservatory led to a decade-long involvement as jazz drummer and band leader, while washing planes for flying lessons culminated in a forty-year commitment to the joys and adventure of flight. He is presently an instrument-rated pilot with more than 1,000 hours of airtime, including those undertaken with his anthropologist-pilot wife exploring the mountains, river valleys, and wilderness areas of Canada and Alaska. In summers when not engaged in anthropological endeavors, he can likely be found flying a faded antique Piper Cub in the skies surrounding his farm near North Hatley, Quebec.

ABOUT THIS BOOK

In the tightly drawn compass of this case study Norman Chance has augmented his earier fieldwork with his most recent. The result is an ethnography of traditional Iñupiat culture, with a bonus: an analysis of recent and current development in the arctic, and a prospectus for the future.

What this case study says about oil development and the North—and oil development and the Alaskan native population—is made especially significant by the catastrophic oil spill near Valdez, where an Exxon tanker struck a reef well outside the regular sea traffic lane. Eleven million gallons of crude oil were spilled. The life-rich sea and beaches of this area, one of the richest maritime resource areas of the world, have been irretrievably damaged. Alaska's natives and others who depend upon such resources for a significant part of their subsistence are seriously affected, but the disaster affects all of us. This was an anticipatable accident but one that no governmental, corporate, or private agency appeared ready to cope with. The costs of "development" are high.

The Alaskan native population has good reason to be suspicious of plans, promises, and contracts issuing from mainstream individuals, organizations and bureaucracies.

The significance of this case study is not limited to Alaska, or to the Arctic. It extends to all the regions of the world where development is taking place, and this includes virtually every place on the globe. Though we tend to think of Third World countries as most dramatically caught up in "development", the technologically advanced western nations are undergoing late phase development that involves many of the same processes of dislocation of human populations and other animal life, reallocation of resources and opportunities, and environmental degradation.

In our field research in Western Germany since 1959, we have observed the far-reaching effects of agricultural, educational, industrial, technological, and administrative "rationalization"—an advanced form of "development". The results are by no means all positive, even in a situation where administrative and technical control would appear to be sophisticated and able to anticipate consequences. And yet we see in Western Germany apparently unanticipated negative consequences in the form of environmental degradation and a redistribution of resources such that the rich become richer while the lot of others is not improved, a process that continually alienates both industrial and agricultural workers. The "Green" movement in Germany, like "Greenpeace" in this country, elects relatively radical means to ameliorate these consequences, but with few outstanding successes. Apparently an attitude of conservation—of human, animal, and environmental resources—has not yet become a part of the ethic of "development" anywhere. We are being forced to reevaluate the balance of costs and benefits of "development" worldwide. This case study is a significant contribution to this reevaluation.

This text is intended for undergraduate readers, students in the social sciences—not anthropology alone. Norman Chance is an experienced author and teacher. He has written two other outstanding case studies for this series— *THE ESKIMO OF NORTH ALASKA* (1966), and *CHINA'S URBAN VILLAGERS* (1984). His experience is demonstrated in the clarity and balance of this case study.

George and Louise Spindler
Series Editors
Ethnographics
Calistoga, California

For Iñupiat elders of earlier years

and

Iñupiat youth who tread new paths today

Preface

In the sixteenth century during the Spanish Conquest of the Americas, Bartolomé de las Casas, the Bishop of Chiapas, posed a question that few government and religious leaders wanted to hear. This occurred in 1550—fifty-eight years after Columbus and his crew set sail for India, twenty-eight years after Cortez had conquered Mexico, and eighteen years after Pizarro's conquest of Peru. Addressing the Council of the Indies, a government agency designed to deal with problems concerning Indian affairs in the New World, Las Casas asked: By what right did Spain subdue these "Indians," take control of their land, and forceably use their labor?

Arguing before the Council, he stated that indigenous people are endowed with natural rights, including the right of liberty, and therefore, they should not be enslaved. The Council, sufficiently challenged by Las Casas' legal, religious, and moral arguments, temporarily ceased expeditions to the New World without the express permission of King Ferdinand. The King concurred and on April 15, 1550, he formed a commission of fourteen jurists and other learned individuals to meet in Valladolid and consider the issue. As the Latin American scholar Lewis Hanke (1959:ix) notes in his description of the event: "Then, for the first and doubtless for the last time, a colonizing nation organized a formal inquiry into the justice of the methods used to extend its empire."

Juan Ginés de Sepúlveda, leading the opposition to Las Casas, proposed to the newly formed commission that since the Native people had no science, no written laws, no private property and other accoutrements of civilized society, it was the responsibility of the Spanish expeditions to bring these and similar advantages to the Indian people. Furthermore, stated Sepúlveda, by depriving them of such ideas and products, they would be "greatly retarded in their development."

The great debate at Valladolid ended in 1551.[1] While Las Casas was able to draw attention to the appalling injustices being perpetrated on the Native people of the Americas, neither he nor his associates could stop them. Refusing to make a formal recommendation to the King, the commission disbanded shortly thereafter and the Conquest was renewed. Was testimony ever elicited from the Native people? No Spanish record exists of such activity. Were any Native leaders involved in the debate? Perhaps, but again, no

---

[1] I am indebted to Justice Thomas Berger for bringing this historic debate to my attention.

written record is available. Nevertheless, the issues addressed then continue to be raised today. Such controversies have also received the attention of anthropologists—which is hardly surprising, given the discipline's efforts in studying human societies and attempting to understand the various ways in which we have lived. But what of the answers? Does anthropology have a significant contribution to offer those seeking deeper understanding of the kinds of questions once posed to the Council of the Indies? And if it does, what is it?

Early anthropologists, educated in the universities of western Europe and North America from the late-1800s through the initial decades of the twentieth century, were among the first to try their hand at responding. At the time European and American governments and industries were actively competing for control over much of the undeveloped world and exporting capital and new technology to those areas in which they had achieved dominance. Social and cultural anthropologists, more experienced than most regarding the nomadic, pastoral, and agricultural peoples of these regions, soon found that their knowledge assured them of an audience by the colonizing governments. And with that recognition came financial support for further research.

Eventually, numerous reports highlighting the customs, laws, and beliefs of culturally distinct peoples in Africa, Asia, and the Americas began appearing in government documents, books, journals, and magazines. Some are now classics in the field. But whether by circumstance or design, much of this early ethnographic reporting supported the popular ideology of the time, which placed the economic and cultural development of white Anglo-Saxon society at the pinnacle of civilization, followed by the "others," the subjects of investigation, most of whom were black, yellow, or brown. As George Stocking (1968:113) writes in his book *Race, Culture, and Evolution: Essays in the History of Anthropology*, "By the middle of the nineteenth century, a rough sort of hierarchy of human races had become an accepted conventional anthropological wisdom."

Nor has the ghost of this intellectual past been completely laid to rest. Michael Asch (1983:203) succinctly states in his critique of development theory that once hunting and gathering peoples (such as those found in northern North America) come in contact with complex societies, they tend to be perceived as evolving ". . . slowly but inexorably toward that more complex form." Furthermore, in keeping with western liberal tradition, this transformation process is commonly seen as being voluntary. Thus, for example, the Iñupiat of North Alaska are supposedly free to choose whether they wish to adopt newly available technology and Euro-American lifestyles.[2] However,

---

[2] Thirty years ago, the term *Eskimo* was regularly utilized to distinguish the Arctic peoples of the circumpolar north. Today, the more common usage in Canada and Greeland is *Inuit*. In Alaska, Eskimo is still used to distinguish this population from the other two Native peoples, Indian and Aleut. However, precise English usage now designates *Iñupiat* (*Iñupiaq*, singular) for Native Alaskans from north and northwest Alaska, and *Yup'ik* and Siberian *Yup'ik* (or *Yuit*) for those living in the southwest and St. Lawrence Island (see Woodbury 1984).

once such choices are embraced—and it is almost always assumed that they will be—this will eventually culminate in the abandonment of their existing way of life. By implication, if traditional culture is doomed, these people must further choose whether to become integrated into the dominant capitalist society with its wage-based, commodity-oriented economy, or find themselves relegated to a marginalized form of dependency. Correspondingly, for development experts and applied social scientists holding this view, the task becomes one of determining what factors are most likely to assist in furthering this adjustment in as harmonious a manner as possible.

Such a perception has a long history in Arctic Alaska—one, I must add, that my early research helped to sustain.[3] When I first set out for Alaska's North Slope in 1958, I too wanted to learn how the Iñupiat were adapting to the changes stemming from their increased economic, social, and political involvement with the outside world. My methodology followed that of many Arctic-oriented, micro-level, ethnographic studies of the time. Utilizing a community-focused approach, I analyzed such topics as economic livelihood, socialization, relations among kin, village-level leadership, and community politics.[4]

I concluded that the people of Kaktovik, the North Slope village that served as the focal point of much of my research, had not only become deeply involved in the wage economy, but they had done so without the usual social and personal disruptions frequently accompanying rapid change. That is to say, their "integration" was a positive one (Chance 1960). Suggested reasons for this positive adjustment included: continued viability of part-time subsistence hunting: stable kin ties; successful realization of newly defined material goals; the congruence of Iñupiat leadership traits and those required of whites; and the ability of the Kaktovik villagers to maintain their local political autonomy within the context of the new wage economy.

On the negative side, continuing research suggested that although the increased use of western technology such as outboard motors and snowmobiles was a key factor enhancing the efficiency of male subsistence hunters, this technology carried considerably fewer benefits for Iñupiat women, whose definition of worth within the community was diminished as the making of skin clothing and similar traditional skills were replaced by items of com-

---

[3] A clear illustration of this perspective is found in the 1968 Statement of Purpose of the Arctic Institute of North America, a well-known northern research center: "The Northern Indians and Eskimos are faced already with adaptation to a strange way of living which eventually will absorb them and extinguish their own cultures. Research is needed on how best to ease their problems in becoming adapted to conditions that require them to work in a time-controlled, wage-earning economy, and to accept life in a developed community. Historical, linguistic and ethnological research is needed also to record for posterity their historical cultures." It should be noted that in sharp contrast to this earlier position, present-day Institute policy actively supports the cultural enhancement and political self government of northern Native peoples.

[4] In Alaska, such studies include those of Foote (1959), Gubser (1965), Hippler (1969), Hughes (1960), Ingstad (1954), Milan (1964), Nelson (1969), Oswalt (1963), Sonnenfeld (1957), and Van Stone (1962). Spencer's major work (1959) encompassed all of the North Slope but focused on Barrow.

mercial manufacture. This, in turn, adversely affected the psychological health of Iñupiat women and, by implication, gender relations within and between families (Chance 1965).

Most Iñupiat, on the other hand, looked at the situation quite differently. While quickly acknowledging their interest in and appreciation of western technology, goods, services, schooling, and religion, they strongly disagreed with the notion that such an acceptance would result in the loss of their cultural way of life. Nor did many want to fully relinquish their subsistence activities for the supposed security of wage employment. In fact, men who were offered full-time wage contracts usually turned them down unless they could have some regular time off to pursue their hunting and fishing interests. Thus, the Iñupiat disavowed a premise commonly held among many non-Natives that wage labor was the ideal form of economic enterprise to be sought whenever possible. They were, to be precise, quite *selective* in what they wanted to adopt and what they didn't. This is an especially important point, one to which we will return.

Reflecting on this research, I would like to think that much of the cultural description offered at the time remains valid in light of present knowledge— an evaluation of some importance, as the book I wrote in 1966, *The Eskimo of North Alaska*, is today being used as a history text in Iñupiat classrooms (Will 1984). But to reach such a conclusion requires that I assume the data on which I based my analysis exists quite independently from my investigation. While such an empirical approach is appealing, it nevertheless contains a hidden pitfall: that what are often considered ethnographic facts are not true pictures of social reality, but rather representations by the investigator *about* that social reality (Ennew 1976). Furthermore, such representations are likely to be influenced by the theoretical orientation of the investigator. Bronislaw Malinowski (1915:599), one of anthropology's important historical figures, acknowledged part of the difficulty when he wrote following the conclusion of his first field work in the early 1900s:

> A field ethnographer has to describe facts in their essential aspects; and that means to select. And selection implies the possession of theoretical principles of classi- fication—defined criteria as to what is essential and what is not.

But it took Thomas Kuhn's (1962) *The Structure of Scientific Revolutions* to pinpoint the crux of the problem. In this highly respected work, Kuhn demonstrated that once scientists accept the same paradigm (a theoretical model for research), they tend to share common assumptions about the world, think in similar ways, and undertake similar kinds of research. Trained to see what they see, they may systematically ignore other aspects of the problem that fail to conform to their expectations.

Thus, facts not only inform theories but theories also inform facts in the sense that they influence which are selected for attention and which are left out. Given this selection process, it behooves a reader to look closely at the particular theoretical principles guiding the work of an investigator and weigh any "facts" offered in support of a conclusion in light of these propositions.

Several brief examples drawn from my early Arctic research highlight the nature of the problem.

First, the leading theoretical orientation dominating my anthropological upbringing was called "functionalism." This approach emphasized the homogeneous autonomy of culture and the cohesive elements of society, ". . . stressing the harmonious adjustment of (its) parts, social solidarity, and the like" (Barrett 1984:49). I have since come to appreciate how easy it is to confuse theoretical perspectives—in this case, the homogeneity and autonomy of culture—with concrete reality. In such instances, the built-in premises of the theory can easily lure the investigator into seeking a functional symmetry that simply isn't there. More specifically, on arriving in the Arctic in 1958, I found diverse groups of Natives and non-Natives with differing economic and political agendas actively contending with one another for control over available resources. But the conceptual approach I was using stressed the importance of cultural autonomy, homogeneity, and harmonious adjustment with correspondingly lessened regard for issues of economic conflict, cultural discord, and emerging class differences. As a result, although I was able to capture the "integrative" features of Iñupiat life quite well, my understanding of conflicts—especially those occurring between Iñupiat and Euro-Americans—was more limited.

A second example is intimately connected to the first. In undertaking a study of Iñupiat acculturation during the late 1950s and early 1960s, I drew on the concept of "westernization," a popular term of the day. However, this concept has since come under attack for being less a scientific concept as an ideological one which frequently hides, consciously or unconsciously, the injustice of colonialism and the accompanying exploitation of colonized peoples. As will be seen later, the present volume attempts to correct this earlier omission.

Finally, my earlier writing also largely disregarded a particular feature of the colonial experience that has now become an important area of anthropological investigation—changes in gender relations linked to the rise of industrial capitalism. The rapidly growing literature on women and Third World development is helping us understand how this expanding system replaced indigenous forms of economic cooperation and social support with a patriarchal structure in which men were considered the major providers and women (and children) dependent possessions.[5] But when I first entered the Arctic, the male-dominated profession of anthropology had done little to promote the exploration of this subject among its mostly male graduate students. As a result, existing sterotypes regarding women remained largely unchallenged. Fortunately, due in large part to the substantial research efforts of many women who entered the discipline in the 1970s and 1980s (and greater

[5] Needless to say, perceiving women as (men's) "possessions" was not limited to early periods of capitalist development. In the 1950s, for example, American marriage ceremonies were regularly concluded with the statement by a religious or secular official: "Now I pronounce you man and *wife*."

recognition given to their important forerunners), today's young anthropologists are less likely to carry these ideological biases into their field work.[6]

Theories, of course are not the only factors influencing an investigator's
choice of topic. Pragmatic questions also intervene. Just as governments in
an earlier colonial era once sought ethnographic information from anthropologists, enabling them to more effectively control their regions of dominance, so, too, anthropologists of a more contemporary period have been
asked to undertake investigations of a similar ethnographic nature. In the
1950s and 1960s, many sociocultural studies of Arctic Alaska were given
substantial logistic and financial assistance by the U.S. Office of Naval Research and its affiliated Arctic Research Laboratory at Barrow; the U.S. Air
Force-supported Arctic Aeromedical Laboratory; and the U.S. Atomic Energy Commission (including its weapons branch), which incorporated as part
of its research a human ecological study of the impact of setting off an atomic
blast along the coast of Northwest Alaska. The basic task of the military
assigned to the Arctic was defense. And that defense included the need to
determine the status of Alaska Native populations living within the military's
defined perimeter of interest—including the Natives' economic, social, and
political relations with one another and the outside world. Those anthropologists interested in undertaking such acculturation studies were welcome to
apply for support. Those wishing to explore other topics pertaining to art,
mythology, religion, or similar ethnographic subject usually had to find their
funding elsewhere.

Did such logistic and financial support offered by the military influence
the selection of topic for study? Charles Hughes (1984:24), in a summary
article analyzing Arctic ethnography undertaken since 1945, has written:

> For a variety of reasons best illustrated by a sociology of knowledge perspective
> on the ways World War II affected the academic community, much research by
> anthropologists . . . began to take on a form that had implications for the prob-
> lems of contemporary life. A great deal of the research . . . was designed ex-
> plicitly to be of use to the administrator, the policy maker, and the economic
> developer.

A key lesson to be drawn from these reflections is that learning is a
continuing process. It is never static. Thus, in striving to understand the ways
of the Iñupiat and other Arctic peoples, I have become increasingly mindful
of the importance of their historical interconnections with the larger world
system. As will be seen in the pages that follow, gaining this knowledge
required considerable attention be given to an analysis of the workings of this
larger system and how its history has intertwined with that of the Arctic's
original inhabitants. Furthermore, as anthropologists are wont to emphasize,
it was also necessary to conduct comparative investigation of similar peoples

---

[6] I, too, have benefited from these studies of gender relations. Of particular significance for this
volume is the research undertaken by Nancy F. Chance (1988) on changing gender relations of
Iñupiat women on Alaska's North Slope and in urban Anchorage.

elsewhere—for only by seeing how given events are intimately linked to comparable forces present in other settings can we come to appreciate the common themes of historical process along with the uniqueness of cultural difference. Though differentiated by culture, we are all united by history.

N.A.C.
North Hatley, Quebec

Acknowledgments

This study is based on research that spans over thirty years, from 1958 to 1989. The initial field work, begun in the summer of 1958, continued during part of the winter of 1960 and the summers of 1961 and 1962. The isolated Alaskan village of Kaktovik, located along the Arctic coast near the Canadian border, was the focal point of much of the early research, although Barrow and Wainwright were included as well. Anthropologist Jean Briggs joined the project in 1961, spending most of that summer at Kaktovik and the next at Wainwright. We supplemented the field work at Barrow during short periods en route to and from the other villages. *The Eskimo of North Alaska*, published in 1966, was based on this early field work.

During the latter half of the 1960s, several short trips to central and north Alaska enabled me to keep abreast of important events. Then in the spring of 1970 I again returned to Barrow and Kaktovik. Together with Nancy F. Chance, also an anthropologist, I focused on changing patterns of Iñupiat education as part of a larger evaluative study undertaken at the request of the Ford Foundation. This trip provided significant insights into the dramatic changes beginning to occur as a result of the 1968 oil discovery at Prudhoe Bay on Alaska's North Slope.

Many researchers have since studied the impact of that momentous event and the Alaska Native Claims Settlement Act, which followed shortly thereafter. But it was not until much later that Nancy Chance and I returned to Alaska to undertake ethnographic field work. During July and early August of 1985 we assisted Rosita Worl and Charles Smythe of Chilkat Institute in their study of changing social and economic life in Barrow. That same summer, we were able to make a short trip to Kaktovik as well, re-establishing old ties and making new ones with Iñupiat residents in that village.

The final phase of the research culminating in the present volume was conducted from January to May of 1986 and May of 1989—again, in conjunction with Nancy Chance who was then undertaking her own study of urban Iñupiat women and development. Most of my time was spent in Anchorage, obtaining both archival and contemporary data from numerous government and private agencies and corporations having interests in North Alaska, as well as coming to know those Iñupiat who had moved there from the North Slope.

I am most grateful to the many individuals, agencies, and foundations that provided extensive assistance, encouragement, and financial support for this research undertaken during the past three decades. In the early years, financial aid came from the American Philosophical Society, a Lincoln Ellsworth Memorial Fellowship of the Arctic Institute of North America, the U.S. Office of Naval Research, and the National Institute of Mental Health. Invaluable aid was also provided by the Naval Arctic Research Laboratory, Barrow, Alaska; the Arctic Health Research Center of the U.S. Public Health Service; the Russell Sage Foundation; and McGill University's Centre for Northern Studies.

In the final phase of the research, financial support was again generously provided by the American Philosophical Society and the University of Connecticut Research Foundation. Other individuals and agencies contributing recent assistance include staff members of the North Slope Borough: John W. Carnahan, Director, Special Projects; Dave Fauske, Director of Telecommunications; Earl Finkler, Director of the Planning Department; Kathy Itta and Leona Okakok, Liaison Officers of the Commission on Iñupiat History, Language, and Culture; Fenton Rexford, Project Director of the Borough's Kuparuk Industrial Center; and Chris Wooley, Oral History coordinator. In addition, Jim Sykes, Judith Brogan, and Susan Burrus of Western Media Concepts, Inc.; Dave Hickok of the Arctic Environmental Information and Data Center; Dorik Mechau of the Alaska Humanities Forum; and Bob Anderson and Lare Aschenbrenner of the Native American Rights Fund were also helpful.

To Ernest "Tiger" Burch Jr., Nancy F. Chance, and Nick Flanders, whose detailed constructive criticisms of earlier drafts of this book deftly steered me away from shallow shoals, a very special debt of gratitude is acknowledged. Others helped by commenting on specific sections, including Robert Bee (U.S. government policy), Harold Kaveolook (Kaktovik village life), Steve Langdon (Parts I and II) and Dalee Sambo (Part III).

Dalee Sambo, Special Assistant to the President of the Inuit Circumpolar Conference, also was especially generous in sharing transcripts and documents of the Alaska Native Review Commission—a historical and contemporary resource of immense value that will be cherished by Native and non-Native peoples alike.

Appreciation is expressed, as well, to Rosita Worl and Charles Smythe of Chilkat Institute, who not only provided me with the opportunity to work with them on their study of Barrow in 1985, but who shared so much of their knowledge during that brief summer period.

Any book written with students in mind will benefit from a critical review by students, especially those having a strong interest in the north. Thus, I want to express my appreciation to those enrolled at the Center for Northern Studies, Wolcott, Vermont, who in 1988–89 carefully reviewed earlier draft chapters of this book; in particular, Catherine Adler, Amy "Supy" Bullard, Bobby Downs, Ken Ferris, Michael Johnson, John Tuxill, and Mary Yunak.

Of other researchers who have offered guidance on various occasions over the years, I would like to especially acknowledge the assistance of Gary Anders, Asen Balikci, Fred Bigjim, Max Brewer, Jean Briggs (particularly for her research on child-rearing practices in Kaktovik and Wainwright in the early 1960s), John Collier, Jr., Dave Damas, Nancy Yaw Davis, Dennis Demmert, Don and Berit Foote, Lou Giddings, Charles Hughes, Irma and John Honigmann, Bill Irving, Diamond Jenness, Dorothy Knee Jones, Judy Kleinfeld, Helge Kleivan, Steve Langdon, Margaret Lantis (who first introduced me to the north), Helge Larsen, Edna Ahgeak MacLean, Steve McNabb, Fred Milan, Tom Morehouse, Gail Osherenko, Bob Rausch, George Rogers, Marianne Stenbaek, Frank Vallee, Jim VanStone, and Oran Young. All demonstrated that wonderful colleagiality so characteristic of northern scholars.

A special thanks also to Daniel Akootckook for several of his hunting photographs he passed on to me many years ago. I wish I had more! Other photographs were generously provided by John Schwoerke of the Stefansson Collection Dartmouth College Library; the archival staff of the Anchorage Museum of History and Art; and the staff of the North Slope Borough Planning Department.

As always, the Spindlers, George and Louise, editors of the Case Studies in Cultural Anthropology series, have offered their creative blend of constructive criticism and continuing encouragement in a most fruitful manner, making the book a truly collective endeavor.

The professionalism of the editorial staff at Holt, Rinehart and Winston has made our working relations a highly enjoyable experience. To Mike Hinshaw, especially, a note of appreciation for his skillful editing and sheperding of the book through the production maze.

In conclusion, I want to comment briefly on my relations with those Iñupiat residents of Kaktovik and Barrow who have shared their life with me—in particular the Akootchooks: Daniel, George, Isaac and Mary, Thomas and Myrtle; Archie Brower; Fred and Dorothy Gordon; Al Hopson, Harold and Mae Kavelook; Vincent Nageak; Herman and Mildred Rexford; Mary Ann Rexford Warden; Pete Sovalik, Simon Tagarook, and many others. Without the offering of their extensive knowledge, this research could not have been undertaken. They were, in a very special sense, my teachers, and for that I am grateful.

Figure 1. Pages from Norman Chance's field journal—June 1958.

Contents

Illustrations

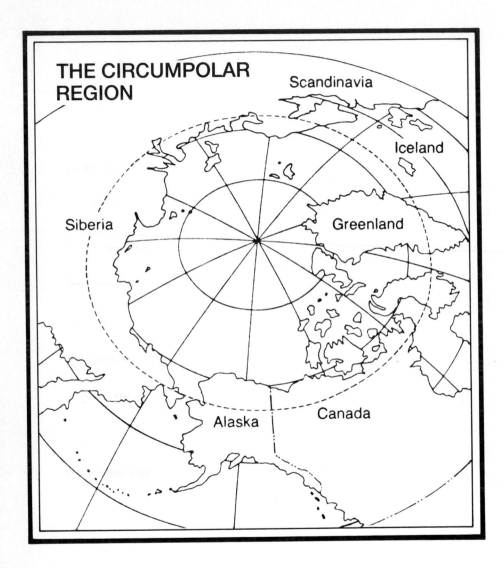

Map 2. The Circumpolar Region

Introduction

PEOPLE AND THE LAND

Land has always been the centerpiece of Arctic Alaska. Economic developers, aware of the area's immense natural wealth, call for maximum accessibility of petroleum, gas, zinc, lead, silver, coal, and similar nonrenewable resources contained within its borders. From their perspective, a major problem limiting the state's growth is land withdrawal, millions of acres having been placed into restrictive categories associated with military reserves and federal or state parks, forests, wildlife refuges, and wilderness areas.

The land and surrounding sea also play an increasingly important role in America's defense strategy. This change is associated with two factors: significant improvements in military technology and greater concern over the protection of Alaska's mineral resource development such as the large industrial petroleum complex located along the coast of the Beaufort Sea at Prudhoe Bay. Both superpowers are well aware that eastern Siberia and western Alaska are only fifty-seven miles apart and that the shortest route between their industrial heartlands is over the North Pole. Today, American submarines carrying the latest missiles with the newest nuclear warheads ply the same Arctic waters as the latest Russian missile-carrying submarines with their newest warheads; each is capable of breaking through the ice at numerous points to deliver its payload to industrial targets in the U.S. and Europe. Other military activities include the modernizing of radar stations, assigning airborne warning and control system aircraft to the area, and expanding military ground forces designed to protect industrial and defense installations throughout the region.

These recent industrial and military developments have not gone unchallenged. Major environment-oriented organizations (such as the National Wildlife Federation, the Sierra Club, and the Wilderness Society), with a combined membership of millions, support powerful lobbying staffs based in Washington. Sometimes in joint actions and sometimes individually, these groups regularly challenge any congressional legislation or military appropriation that is perceived as threatening the preservation of Alaskan wildlife refuges and wilderness areas. From their perspective, the fate of Alaska's Arctic wildlands can be assured only if the forces advocating oil, gas, and other nonrenewable resource development in these areas are soundly defeated.

As the region's predominant residents, the Iñupiat have equally strong views on how the land should be used. While desiring the economic advantages

1

Photo 2. Iñupiat hunters near the Brooks Range.

that stem from local mineral extraction, they nevertheless fear the possible outcome. To what extent will increased petroleum and gas development increase the likelihood of a major oil spill? Such an accident could easily bring about a change in the annual migration route of the bowhead whale, driving it farther north away from coastal villages. The loss of this animal to a sea mammal-oriented society would be highly significant, not only in reducing an important source of nutritional sustenance, but in weakening their cultural identity as well.

The Iñupiat and neighboring Kutchin Athabascan Indians see a similar danger from prospective oil exploration in the northeast corner of Alaska where the Porcupine Caribou Herd, one of the largest in the world with more than 165,000 animals, pastures on the tundra of the Arctic National Wildlife Refuge. As stockholders of Native corporations with land rights in the refuge, these Alaskans want to benefit from the leasing of this potentially rich land to oil companies. But as subsistence hunters, they are very much concerned over the future of their traditional economic livelihood. Such concerns sometimes drive a wedge between those northern Natives deriving much of their livelihood from subsistence hunting and fishing and those who look to wage employment as their major means of economic sustenance.

Attempting to arbitrate conflicts between these rival groups are the various branches and agencies of the federal, state, and local governments. Yet here, too, conflicting interests are the norm. One agency within the government such as the U.S. Corps of Engineers may actively help develop mineral resources, while another, for example, the U.S. Fish and Wildlife Service, tries to protect the environment. Similar competing priorities and interests characterize relations between governments. Although the federal government is the primary owner of petroleum-producing property in Alaska, its general revenue needs are only minimally tied to these lands. Thus, its perspective on oil extraction is more likely to address national energy levels, international trade, and foreign policy issues.

The revenue base of the state of Alaska, on the other hand, is intimately related to oil. The Prudhoe Bay field, the largest single accumulation of crude oil ever discovered in North America, is located on lands owned by the state. In the fifteen years following that discovery in 1968, the proportion of the state budget utilizing petroleum revenues rose from an annual average of about 12 percent to more than 90 percent (Morehouse 1984:3). Still, whether the focus is political or economic, national or regional, both the federal and state governments have important vested interests in developing Alaska's mineral resources and assisting those corporations extracting them, for revenues from companies such as these are central to their financial welfare.

ALASKA'S NATIVE NORTHERNERS

Alaska's Arctic population also faces many new challenges. As a result of the oil discovery at Prudhoe Bay, the U.S. Congress was forced to address a long-standing conflict over the legal ownership of Alaska's land, a dispute that was at least partially concluded with the passage of the 1971 Alaska Native Claims Settlement Act (ANCSA). Under the act, Alaska Natives retained forty-four million acres of land and $962.5 million in compensation for the extinguishment of all other aboriginal claims totaling 330 million acres. Importantly, the act also obligated the Native population to establish twelve in-state and one out-of-state regional profit-making corporations and more than 200 village corporations to serve as vehicles for the ownership and management of the land and money which then became corporate assets. For the first twenty years, between 1971 and 1991, Native Alaskans were to be the only voting shareholders in these corporations, after which they were expected to operate under the same legal arrangements as corporate entities elsewhere. By enacting ANCSA in this manner, Congress strongly rejected the concept of tribal government where land could be held "in trust" by the U.S. Department of the Interior. Such an arrangement was considered a serious impediment to Native assimilation.[1]

Prior to passage, the act received almost unanimous approval by the state-wide Alaska Federation of Natives.[2] Yet many Natives had little understanding of its broader implications. In particular, most village residents did not realize that the conveyed land would belong to the corporations rather than to them; nor that as a corporate asset, the land could be lost through corporate failures,

[1] As described by William Van Ness, staff assistant to Senator Henry Jackson, the principal designer of ANCSA: "The act was . . . a very radical effort at social engineering and it was done on a very, very calculated basis." (Van Ness 1984:375)

[2] Notably, the one Native group voting against the bill was the Arctic Slope Native Association.

hostile takeovers, and taxation. As a result, by the late 1980s, there was a growing feeling among Alaska Natives that they had been cheated; several amendments were made in the original legislation to reduce the possibility of their losing their lands.

On Alaska's North Slope, where a borough form of city government has been functioning since 1972, a different picture emerged than in other areas of the state. Due to the borough's ability to tax oil revenues from Prudhoe Bay (which lies within its borders), as well as to draw on state funds for city services, millions of revenue dollars became available to build modern high schools, provide housing with heating systems and running water, and offer similar accoutrements of a modern lifestyle once limited to communities far to the south. Such a dramatic change occurring over a few short years seems almost unbelievable to those who once hauled ice for water and used dog sleds for travel. Yet children growing up on the North Slope today have little understanding of these traditions; recent advantages are quickly taken for granted.

Will these new forces—economic, social, political, legal—so overwhelm the Iñupiat that they will be unable to find new ways to assist in their self-determination? Even if protective legal entities are developed, will the next generation of Native Alaskans actively support them? Today, Iñupiat elders express considerable concern over such matters.

By contrast, younger Iñupiat, while encouraged to respect their elders' views, often have different agendas. Is an Iñupiaq youth who speaks English with friends, has little interest in traditional dances, and prefers Big Macs to seal meat no longer an Iñupiaq? Can the same be asked of Iñupiat university graduates whose knowledge of finance and management enable them to take responsible positions in village and regional corporations? The questions are rhetorical. Of course the people are still Iñupiat. Although such activities may not characterize the Iñupiat of the past, neither do they necessarily lessen their cultural participation in the future. Culture is never static, composed only of isolated activities. The systems of meaning that we call culture contain an immense range of flexibility while at the same time offering a blueprint for shared behavior.

Such a perspective is clearly reflected in the statement of an Iñupiat woman given at an Alaska Native Women's Statewide Organization (1982:37) conference held in Barrow in 1982:

> Just what is being an Iñupiaq? Are we Iñupiat because we live in this land with a cold climate? If this is so, why then am I still an Iñupiaq when I travel to other faraway places which are cold, too? Then I do not think that my living here makes me an Iñupiaq.
>
> Or am I an Iñupiaq because of my diet, the food I eat? Am I an Iñupiaq just because I eat Iñupiat food? And if this is so, should I eat more and more Iñupiat food so that I can become a good Iñupiaq? This is probably not so because earlier today I saw a white man eating dried Eskimo meat and seal oil although he is not an Iñupiaq. So I do not think my food makes me an Iñupiaq. . . . But I want you all to think this over. What is an Iñupiaq? If I am an Iñupiaq, how am I so?

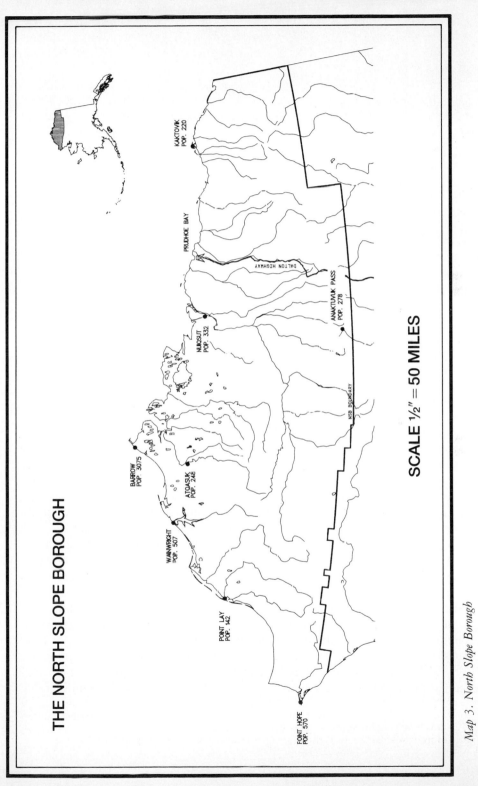

THE NORTH SLOPE BOROUGH

SCALE ½" = 50 MILES

KAKTOVIK
POP. 220

PRUDHOE BAY

DALTON HIGHWAY

ANAKTUVUK PASS
POP. 278

NUIQSUT
POP. 332

NSB BOUNDARY

BARROW
POP. 3075

ATQASUK
POP. 246

WAINWRIGHT
POP. 507

POINT LAY
POP. 142

POINT HOPE
POP. 570

Map 3. North Slope Borough

Photo 3. Iñupiat sharing maktak *(whale skin with blubber) following a successful whale hunt.*

Along with questions of cultural identity, the Iñupiat of Alaska's North Slope are having to address additional problems common to circumpolar and similar isolated hunting and gathering peoples who have become actively involved in the economic, social, and political life of industrial society. Of these problems, one that often produces the greatest apprehension is the people's fear of losing their land. Every culture needs a material foundation for its continuity. For the Iñupiat, it is the tundra and sea of Arctic Alaska. The issue is not simply one of subsistence, as crucial as that economic endeavor is. Use of the land and sea also entails special responsibilities including the *sharing* of resources with others. Nor is the environment viewed only in natural terms. It is also endowed with cultural attributes that enrich nature.

By contrast, under a capitalist economic and political system, alienable property ownership is considered an inalienable right. Land can be bought and sold like any other commodity. Furthermore, the American marketplace has little interest in sharing, cultural beliefs, or communal stewardship in which land is to be treated like a gift to be held in trust for future generations.[3]

So, too, mainstream America has its cultural beliefs that support these economic relations. As the anthropologist Joseph Jorgensen (1984:184) has stated in his analysis of the impact of energy development on rural populations: American values associated with economic development include beliefs that most problems can be solved by technology; that "progress" is intimately

---

[3] Nor is the commodity principle limited to land and the natural resources it contains. Labor is another commodity that can be purchased and sold, as increasing numbers of urban-based Alaskan Natives seeking jobs in industry and service centers are coming to learn.

associated with capitalism's need for continual growth; that restrictions placed on the competitive free enterprise system should be minimal; and that individual initiative to excel (even at the expense of others) is to be admired and emulated.

Still, it would be inaccurate to conclude this introduction on such a note. For just as Iñupiat economic life contains within it opposing forces for change, so does capitalism contain within it forces for change. In the chapters that follow, we will examine these opposing forces to see how they have influenced Alaska's political economy both historically and at present. The emphasis on history reflects a belief that the causes of present human action must be sought in the past, whereas the comparative approach enables us to trace the intertwining of different societies with different cultures holding different agendas. Combining the two immediately focuses our attention on the unfolding of *connections*—connections between ecological, economic, social, cultural, and political forces that have laid the basis for interaction between the people, land, and sea of what has become the American Arctic. That, in essence, is what this book is about.

It takes as its fundamental premise that for more than one and one-half centuries, the residents of Arctic Alaska, Native and non-native alike, have been joint participants in a much larger worldwide process of change initiated by European expansion in conjunction with the Industrial Revolution. This is not, therefore, a simple portrayal of how Alaska's original northern inhabitants have lived off the land and sea, although attention will be given to that impressive achievement. Nor is the focus simply one of "adaptation" or "dependency" in which a small, once isolated population seeks to accommodate itself to the growing dominance of Euro-American society. In fact, Native northerners have been active participants in the dramatic transformation taking place in Alaska. In other contexts, they have been its casualties.

This endeavor, then, is in many respects quite different from my earlier book on the subject, *The Eskimo of North Alaska* (1966). There I devoted considerable attention to the acculturation of North Alaskan Iñupiat in the 1950s and early 1960s. Although material from that work is used here (especially in Part Two), the overall emphasis shifts to the historical and contemporary political economic-cultural process *itself*. This involves not only an examination of those institutional forces referred to earlier, but also competing discourses—an ethnography of ideas and agendas—offered *by* those contending forces. Included are the perspectives of teachers, missionaries, the military, federal and state governments, the mining industry, oil corporations, environmentalists, and, of course, the Iñupiat; each expressed in terms of their particular interests, opportunities, and constraints.

In Part One, *Connections*, we turn our attention to the first Americans who came to this continent and to what happened following their arrival. Through archeological studies, we learn of connections established between these small bands of Arctic hunters and gatherers and their trading partners, including those still living on the Asian mainland. We follow the descendants of these earlier Americans as they traveled across the Canadian Arctic to

Labrador, Newfoundland, and Greenland where they met Norse explorers from northern Europe. We then trace the arrival and interests of European colonists in the western Arctic, the Russian, British, and American explorers, whalers, traders, trappers, teachers, missionaries, and government agents, and we learn what Iñupiat responses were to these incursions. With increased military involvement in Alaska during and after World War II, community life changed even more.

Part Two, *Village Legacy*, deals with the results of that period, describing in detail the impact of colonialization and militarization on Iñupiat culture in the 1950s and early 1960s; how changing technology and wage labor influenced the way they made their living; and how outside governmental, religious, and educational institutions helped to reshape gender, family, and other social relations within North Slope villages.

In Part Three, *Politics, Petroleum, and Profit*, more recent changes in Arctic Alaska are explored, particularly those stemming from statehood in 1959 and the discovery of oil in 1968. It is here that polarizing issues and policies pertaining to competition and cooperation, economic growth and conservation, wage labor and subsistence, dependence and self-reliance, assimilation and self-determination, are viewed in depth.

HISTORY, MODERNIZATION, AND DEVELOPMENT

Throughout this endeavor, we will see how history is made by the active involvement and struggles of human beings. Although no universal laws of social development emerge, certain patterns do appear that are worthy of careful review. Most obvious are those linked to the historical unfolding of economic, social, and political relations in the nineteenth and early twentieth centuries between a rapidly industrializing America and the Alaskan Iñupiat.

Two distinct interpretations of these changing relations should be kept in mind. One, commonly associated with what has come to be called "modernization theory" (Rostow 1960), assumes that industrialization is itself a liberating force. Hence, societies already industrialized serve as models for those who have not yet achieved this status; and by implication, "undeveloped" ones now entering this arena must tread a similar path as those that came before, thereby reproducing the achievements of the former. Such a view is recognized far beyond the boundaries of the circumpolar north, since it has been utilized often by international development agencies such as the World Bank in their relations with Third World governments and by various national development agencies in their contacts with "tribal" and other minority peoples at home.[4]

---

[4] Socialist countries also see industrialization as a liberating "productive force," although in contrast to capitalist-oriented perspectives, such development is placed within the larger context of class differentiation and conflict.

However, in recent years this theory of modernization has been criticized by those who claim that its fundamental premise is false. Specifically, they reject the view that industrial capitalism developed *separately* from the rest of the world, emphasizing instead that it grew in conjunction *with* it. Continuing the analysis, they propose that beginning with industrial expansion, these "undeveloped" nations became "underdeveloped" in the sense that their increasing involvement with capitalist countries led to systematic relations of exploitation, organized by the latter for their own advantage. Thus, according to this perspective, in most if not all instances, the growth of capitalism actually promoted the very underdevelopment that now characterizes so many Third World countries.[5] Although the lack of national boundaries separating culturally distinct, disadvantaged peoples from the state *within* a capitalist country make the circumstances quite different, a historical analysis of their changing economic situation suggests that similar patterns may be at work here, too. The economic and cultural decimation of indigenous Native North Americans in the 1800s brought on by disease, dislocation, and slaughter, along with the wholesale importation of western cultures, are often cited as an example.

Of course, these economic, social, and political relations between advantaged and disadvantaged groups are not static. Indeed, they have varied greatly over the past several centuries. In Alaska, one contemporary illustration is the greatly expanded role of multinational petroleum corporations in shaping the state's economy following the discovery of Arctic oil. Some of these corporations are so immense that they have revenues larger than the gross national product of a number of Third World countries.

Conservationist critics concerned with environmental degradation frequently target the Alaskan operation of these conglomerates, accusing them of pursuing construction and maintenance practices on wildlife lands and seas that are highly detrimental. The 1989 *Exxon Valdez* tanker oil spill in Prince William Sound—the worst in America's history—is a well-known case in point. Emphasizing that simple energy conservation measures such as improved auto fuel efficiency are a far better way to develop a sound energy policy, they conclude that the "cost" in environmental damage is simply not worth the additional benefit in oil production. Petroleum companies respond that new technologies enable oil to be extracted without incurring the type of environmental damage that happened earlier. Others less concerned with environmental issues offer a more positive evaluation of recent multinational corporate endeavors, pointing to the large capital expenditures these firms have committed in the area, thereby providing an opportunity for many Alaskans (including some Iñupiat) to develop an economic base from which they can achieve a significantly increased long-term prosperity.

Clearly, such a debate falls within the mainstream of discussion regarding

---

[5] For a portrayal of recent world history by an anthropologist taking this view, see: Wolf (1982). The most well-known exponents of this theory of underdevelopment are Frank (1971) and Wallerstein (1974).

Photo 4. The beauty of the Arctic wilderness—summer, 1958.

the best strategy for Alaska's northern development. It is grounded in the view that nature is a commodity among other commodities, to be protected as much as possible as long as it doesn't impede the achievement of material fulfillment or national defense. Underlying this message is the belief that once nature is subjugated, it becomes an object for human satisfaction. Furthermore, whatever problems emerge in the process of achieving this subjugation can be solved through the utilization of advanced science and technology. Science thus becomes the means of dominating nature for the material benefit of humankind.

Is there an alternative discourse to the one just presented? There is, but it is so well concealed by the cultural and economic values associated with the professed ability of science and technology to solve our energy and environmental problems, *and* by the perceived separation of nature and society into two distinct realms, that one must search diligently to find it.[6] This is ironic, for the essence of this alternative view has been around since the beginning of human history. Its fundamental edict is that human beings are not *distinct* from nature but are a vital part *of* nature. Indeed, one need go no further than the Iñupiat and other Arctic peoples to find such a perspective expressed today, although the ideology of science as cure-all and the conquest over nature as the means to achieving a materialistic life-style has gained sufficient ground that its cultural expression is considerably more muted than in years past.

It is perhaps easy to disregard a perspective on the human condition that

[6] A noteworthy historical study of this topic has been undertaken by William Leiss (1974) from which several of the ideas discussed above are drawn.

has the audacity to challenge a core assumption of industrial society. Yet the implications of such a step are highly significant. Industrial nations are already consuming a disproportionate share of the world's natural resources. Even more resources will be depleted in an effort to clean up existing pollution. It is little wonder that questions increasingly are being raised concerning the ecological limit of the utilization of nature by industry.

In summary, we can see that humankind faces two immense problems, one pertaining to the unequal distribution of productive wealth among the world's peoples and the other to the deterioration of the environment. In fact, as we will learn later on, an inextricable bond exists between these two problems, suggesting that efforts at resolution will eventually require joint attention.

Addressing major questions such as these, involving as they do the whole of humanity and its future, are far beyond the scope of this book. But that does not mean they should be set aside, for the initial step in solving large problems is to break them into more manageable units in the context of particular historical circumstances. Once these elements are grasped more clearly, then the various parts can be rejoined and the whole issue seen with greater understanding.

There is, of course, a potential danger in carrying out such an effort. One may focus so minutely on the parts that the larger picture gets put aside and lost. Social scientists, for example, would be poorly advised to try to understand the relations of political power in a given society without taking into account the economic resources of the area, how labor is organized to tap those resources, and the rights and obligations involved in their distribution and consumption. Thus, a key component in undertaking any ethnography is the study of connections. Indeed, as Eric Wolf (1974:x) states in his classic book on the subject, "In contrast to the anthropological traditions of other countries, . . . American anthropology put a premium upon intellectual synthesis, upon the tracing out of connections where others saw only divergence. Thus, (it) grew up as a discipline between disciplines, and not merely as a discipline in its own right."

In the chapters that follow, we will see how this holistic emphasis, so vital to anthropological inquiry, is an essential tool helping us to understand how human beings have made their own history in the Arctic from their arrival thousands of years ago to the present.

PART ONE | Connections

One day an avingaq *decided to venture outside of his hole and assess the rest of the world. When he stood up on his hind legs, lo and behold, to his surprise, he was able to reach the heavens! When he reached down, he felt the ground. When he reached in all directions, he was able to touch the limits of the world! He concluded that he was the largest person on the face of the earth. In reality, the poor mouse had surfaced from his hole in the ground into an old Iñupiaq boot sole turned ouside down! The top of his heaven was the sole of the* atungak *and the outer limits of his world were the sides of the* atungak.

When I think of this story, I am mindful that I should consider all facets of a situation before I make any conclusions. I should not limit myself to what is around me, but I should explore and search for other information, lest I be like the poor mouse.

Edna Ahgeak MacLean, Iñupiaq (1988)

This is what we have to do. We have to look beyond the horizon because when you look into the horizon, you think that is the end—but it is not. You walk to that horizon again and there is another horizon. You can go all the way around the world in this manner. If we can look at it that way, we will be better off. Otherwise, we will get too caught up in one simple thing, or one matter, or one problem. We have got to look at it from all angles.

Robert Mulluk, Iñupiaq (1984)

1/The Long Journey

PURSUING THE PAST

The history of human beings is short by geologic standards, yet it covers millions of years. In trying to understand this development, we can call upon ten thousand years of quite satisfactory records, which then trail off into the silence of the hunter's and gatherer's Stone Age world. The rest of this time has left no legend on human tongues and an extremely sparse record in the soil. Of the momentous transformations occurring then, all that remain are a few broken skulls, teeth, bones, and a scattering of simple tools—not much help in our search to comprehend this long journey of the past. Furthermore, unless we listen carefully, even these simple clues tell us false stories, for they are but scraps of a larger collection, the other items of which have not been preserved. Beyond recall are tote bags nursing mothers invented to carry their infants while foraging for food, tinder designed for starting fires, or thoughts of ancient parents leaning over a fevered child.

Still, archeologists have much to offer in interpreting these fragments of the human adventure. And we can utilize, as well, one of their guiding principles, cultural ecology, and its corollary, *adaptation*. Without such an approach, these prehistoric detectives would be presenting us with a conglomeration of unrelated facts. But given such a clarifying paradigm, we gain contextual meaning—an essential feature of any anthropological inquiry. This approach is especially germane to studies of the circumpolar north, for as every North American school-age child knows, the Arctic has always served as a natural laboratory, testing the northerner's ability to survive in a severe environment.[1]

Given these environmental limitations, the Iñupiat have met the challenge with ingenuity and skill. Yet they followed long after the first inhabitants of the region. Humans entered the New World by way of Beringia, an intercontinental land bridge half the width of the United States, connecting the region of Bering Strait with Siberia. We know little of human antiquity in this northern sector of the Old World, although archeological remains from

---

[1] Archeologists and cultural ecologists devote substantial attention to issues of human adaptation (and ultimately survival) in the natural world. Much has been learned from such studies. However, the concept of adaptation needs to be used with care, for people not only adapt to a given environment, they also alter it.

the Lake Baikal region of the Trans-Baikal date as far back as 13,000 to 25,000 years ago. These residents of the Russian steppe-tundra were not northern remnants of Ice Age Neanderthals but fully human *homo sapiens* Mal'ta, one of the most well-known archeological sites located on the Angara River near the modern city of Irkutsk, contains numerous winter semi-subterranean houses constructed of large animal bones and reindeer antlers, covered by skin or sod exteriors. Based on artifact distribution, Soviet archeologists were able to distinguish between the activities of women and men, the former staying close to the settlements and the latter ranging widely, searching over the surrounding steppes for mammoth, woolly rhinoceros, and reindeer. Other northeast Siberian sites such as Dyukhtai Cave, excavated in 1967, turned up mammoth and musk-ox remains in association with distinct bifacial (flaked on both surfaces) spear points, arrow points, and scrappers, the latter probably used in butchering. Reliable radiocarbon dates for this latter site range between 14,000 and 12,000 years. Recent research, both archeological and genetic, has led to numerous speculations about the geographical origin and time of arrival of these Asian ancestors to the New World. Almost certainly there were Stone Age peoples at the outer frontiers of northeast Asia along the shores of the Bering Sea by 18,000 years ago, and perhaps much earlier than that.[2]

How they crossed is not difficult to imagine. Even in historic times, the Yup'ik Eskimo have gone back and forth between the two sides of the Bering Strait by skin boat, so it is easy to envision earlier water crossings. Yet boats were probably not needed (or available) to these land-based Upper Paleolithic Siberians, for between 25,000 and 14,000 years ago the Strait was mostly dry, part of a huge northern land mass linking the two continents. As the intense cold of the last glaciation turned water into ice, the sea level dropped and Beringia emerged.

Whenever the first Paleo-Arctic peoples arrived in Alaska, they had no destination in mind. Rather, as described by Louis Giddings, an early leader in Alaskan archeology, they were simply "existing and adjusting at random to the environment, the sons sometimes hunting beyond the range of their fathers but never really leaving home." To the first Americans, then, the momentous crossing between Siberia and Alaska, occurring gradually over many generations, was simply an exploration of a new hunting territory, nothing more.[3]

---

[2] A brief summary of the peopling of America can be found in Fagan (1987). The following draws in part on his review.

[3] It is more accurate to think of Beringia as a homeland for these Paleo-Arctic peoples than as a bridge or corridor to the New World. Indeed, given the huge glacial ice sheets isolating Beringia from the rest of the North American continent, Alaska, both biologically and geographically, can be viewed as part of Siberia.

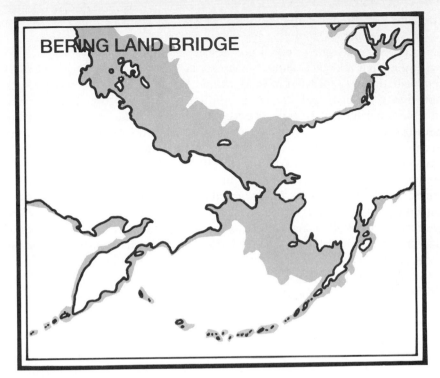

Map 4. Beringia: the Bering land bridge.

THE FIRST AMERICANS

Once in the new continent 12,000 or more years ago, these isolated Paleo-Arctic peoples continued hunting the rapidly disappearing Pleistocene fauna that had been their major source of food and clothing. However, with the major climatic changes of the late Wisconsin glaciation and early postglacial times, Beringia was flooded and the mammal population either moved east and south, or dwindled and died. In what must have been a time of great stress, the first Americans did the same. Though a few Paleo-Arctic archeological sites have been found in the Canadian Yukon near the Alaskan border, the Brooks Range, and to the west and south, little is known about their technology and way of life.

Those who followed these people out of Asia appear to have arrived at different time periods. While numerous theories have been proposed, extensive studies in archeology, physical anthropology, and linguistics suggest that the ancestors of present-day Alaska Natives can be traced to two migrations occurring 10,000 to 5,000 years ago. The first group spoke *Na-Dene*, a language family that includes Athabascan-speaking peoples of Alaska, northern Canada, British Columbia, and California as well as the Apache and Navajo of the southwestern United States. Basically an inland population, they moved widely through the interior and northwest coast of British Columbia early in the postglacial period.

A second, maritime-oriented group arrived later, perhaps 7000 to 6000 years ago. This "Aleut-Eskimo" group spoke what is called *Eska-Aleutian*, a linguistic family separated into Aleut and Eskimo. Eskimo is further subdivided into *Iñupiaq* and *Yup'ik*, a difference similar to that found in the romance languages of Europe. The geographic boundary separating these two subdivisions occurs at Unalakleet, just north of the mouth of the Yukon River. Mutually comprehensible dialects of Iñupiaq are spoken from Point Barrow all the way east to Greenland (although from Barrow south to Unalakleet a number of dialects exist, making it difficult for local Iñupiat to understand the Greenlandic *Kalaallit* dialect). Skeletal and genetic studies of Aleuts and Iñupiaq- and Yup'ik-speaking Eskimo also suggest that they are the most Asian of all Native Americans—and thus the last representatives of this area to come to the New World. Eska-Aleutian languages, too, show strong Asian roots, particularly among the Chukchi-speaking peoples of far northeast Siberia.

ESKIMO SUCCESSORS

Sometime prior to 4000 years ago, the Aleut and Eskimo diverged, the latter eventually establishing their own adaptable culture largely based on sea and land mammal hunting and saltwater and freshwater fishing. From this time onward, archeologists have been able to trace fairly accurately the technological development of North American and Greenlandic Arctic peoples. In Alaska, this tracing began with the *Northern Archaic* period, represented by a diversity of side-notched projectile points, notched pebbles, end scrappers, and other tool types. This was followed by people who developed what is called the *Arctic Small Tool Tradition*, typified by a technologically sophisticated microblade industry and finely made lithic weapon inserts.

Another major tradition, the *Norton* culture, came into being 2,000 years ago. Named after Norton Bay in Alaska where the earliest sites were found, this sea mammal-oriented population arose along the shores of the Bering and Chukchi seas, eventually spreading to the Firth River in the Yukon Territory of Canada. Though not commonly associated with the far north, a highly developed variant of the Norton tradition is found in the famous Ipiutak site at Point Hope on Alaska's North Slope. The inhabitants of this large village of more than 600 houses have provided a wealth of information concerning early North Alaskan Iñupiat life (see: Larson and Rainey 1948).

At the same time people were inhabiting Ipiutak, members of the *Old Bering Sea* culture occupied other coastal villages on Cape Prince of Wales, Saint Lawrence Island, and the adjacent Siberian shore. They lived permanently on the coast, hunting land and sea mammals. Cultural similarities with modern residents of the area leave little doubt that continuous development

Photo 5. The umiaq *of the past is still in common use today.*

from one to the other has taken place. The earlier people associated with the Old Bering Sea culture traveled by *qayaq* (kayak) and large *umiaq* skin boats in summer and hand-drawn sled in winter. Their houses were small semisubterranean dwellings with an efficient cold-trap entrance to hold the heat inside. The long residence of these Old Bering Sea people in this region is intimately related to the abundance of walrus that inhabit the area. Having resolved many problems of subsistence, they were able to devote increasing amounts of time to developing the technical and artistic skills for which they became known.

The *Birnirk* people, first coexisting with the nearby Ipiutak, eventually replaced them and went on to become the dominant culture in North Alaska from which today's North Slope Iñupiat derive. It may be that a decline in the availability of caribou and fish forced the people to improve their sea mammal hunting. But whatever the reason, they—and the *Thule* people who grew out of the Birnirk—became pre-eminent hunters of the sea. Skilled boatmen, they applied their ingenuity to designing devices to improve the hunting of walrus and whale. The large *umiaq* boat, its covering skin carefully sewn together by women, was refined to boost its efficiency in hunting the whale.

The captains of these whaling boats and their wives were individuals of high prestige, respected for their leadership and ritual knowledge as well as hunting prowess. As their technical skills increased, they modified their clothing, allowing them to remain out-of-doors for longer periods. Their houses, too, with the cold-trap entrances, improved heating efficiency in winter tem-

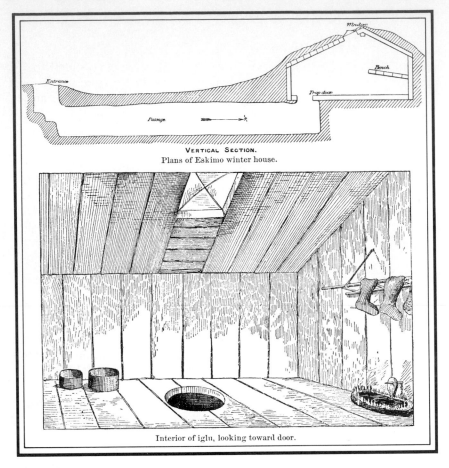

Plans of Eskimo winter house.

Interior of iglu, looking toward door.

Figure 2. Plan of a winter house at Point Barrow in the late 1800s, as described by Murdoch (1892).

peratures, which could drop to minus-60 degrees. Soon the Arctic coastal villages of Point Barrow, Point Hope, and Wainwright became major whaling communities, which have continued in importance to the present.

By the thirteenth century, the Thule people had traveled thousands of miles, building settlements throughout central and eastern Canada into Labrador and Greenland. Eventually, they met strange men with beards who came from the east in large wooden boats. They were the Norse who had crossed the north Atlantic to Greenland, Labrador, and Newfoundland around 1000 A.D. Calling the Thule people *skraelings* ("barbarians"), the first European immigrants to North America regularly traded iron implements for locally made products of seal and ivory. Two hundred years later, these early Norse settlements died out. It took another five centuries before explorers, this time from Russia and England, renewed contact with the Arctic's Native North Americans.

IÑUPIAT: THE REAL PEOPLE

Prior to the arrival of European explorers in the late eighteenth and early nineteenth centuries, Arctic Alaska, stretching from Norton Sound to the Canadian border, was the location of numerous *Iñupiaq*-speaking groups, each associated with a particular territory. As described by Burch, an anthropologist with extensive knowledge of northwest Alaskan Iñupiat, some of these people remained close to their home districts while others were more mobile.[4] All, however, tended to be endogamous. That is, along with spatial differentiation, marriages commonly occurred within rather than between groups. Along with clothing styles, personal adornment, and other features, subdialect differences also served to distinguish the groups. Though each group spoke Iñupiaq, regional variation was sufficiently distinctive to enable listeners to link accent with locality, thereby allowing individuals to immediately determine the other's home district.

The major social entities comprising these differing districts or localities were networks of large, bilateral, extended families tending toward patrilocality, each composed of three to four generations and each containing numerous married siblings and often cousins. Burch uses the term "local family" to describe these social units. Since the family was usually too large for a single dwelling, adjacent houses were utilized by "domestic families" (Burch 1975:237). In ecologically less favorable districts, local families might include a dozen or so members, whereas in highly productive areas local family size could reach fifty or more. Major population centers such as Point Hope and Point Barrow, located along sea mammal migration routes, contained several large local families clustered in distinct locations or neighborhoods, each set linked by affinal and consanguineal kinship ties.

Politically, these families were autonomous, segmental groupings, roughly equal in status, with no external "chief," council, or other recognized form of government capable of exerting control. Internally, a well-defined hierarchy did prevail based largely on relative age, sex, and a sufficient number of younger siblings and cousins to make the elder statuses meaningful. In most instances, these elders served as advisers rather than day-to-day decision-makers.

The male family head was an *umialik*, often translated as "boss" or "rich man."[5] All umialiks and their wives were considered "bosses" within their own local families. But to become a "rich" umialik required a large local family composed of many active male and female hunters and skin sewers. As holders of considerable wealth and high social position, these successful

---

[4] What follows draws on several of Burch's writings concerning traditional Iñupiat life (see: 1975; 1980; 1981).

[5] When Europeans first came in contact with Iñupiat living in small settlements, they often assumed that the umialik was the local "village" chief maintaining political power over the whole group, and that since this individual regularly conferred with other informed members of the community, the latter group must be some kind of village council. This was an erroneous assumption.

umialiks were powerful leaders, a trait shared only with the religious shaman (*angatquq*). Indeed, many umialiks were shamans as well. Though not accorded formally defined authority, they regularly won the right to lead through their personal attributes of hunting, trading, and human relations skills, energy and wisdom. These qualities were what gained them their following, and their following was what provided them their wealth. Such qualities were requisite to keeping such a group intact since membership was voluntary and could change at any time. Among members of a given family, mutual aid was the norm.[6]

In larger families, the food obtained from hunting, fishing, and gathering was turned over to the umialik and his wife. She, particularly, kept track of what was available, what was needed, and what could be redistributed to others. Hence, the larger the family, the greater the redistribution process, and the more extensive the power of the umialik and his primary wife (*nuliaqpak*).

Highly successful umialiks could further expand their families, and therefore wealth, by obtaining additional spouses. Thus, the only factor limiting family size other than the capability of its members was the availability of local resources. Over several generations, some families were able to command far more goods and resources, while others, smaller in size, had less. Small families resulted from factors such as accidental death, poor health, weak management, and limited hunting skills. But whatever the cause, fewer relatives meant less people to count on in time of need. In the larger settlements, such as the whaling communities of Point Hope and Barrow, this differentiation culminated in a recognizable system of stratification whereby a small number of families were able to attain more wealth and power than those less endowed. Such power was not hereditary, however. As climatic or other natural events significantly reduced the food supply, or as less competent umialiks assumed leadership, the mantle would pass to more fortunate or more capable families.

It is often thought that prior to the arrival of Europeans with their guns and whale bombs, the available land and sea mammal population could easily support small aboriginal groups living more or less permanently in the area. In a few localities this was so, but for most, not only was seasonal mobility the norm, but the threat of disaster—climatic alteration, tidal wave, disease— was ever present. Climatic changes, especially, could seriously reduce the availability of fish and game such as salmon, caribou, and ptarmigan. Regardless of the locality, the result was famine. Indeed, there are recognizable periods in Arctic Alaska prior to the arrival of Europeans (for example, between 1838 and 1848) when several territories were completely depopulated through famine or disease. Eventually, a few ex-residents returned, or if they

---

[6] Ernest Burch (personal communication) provides an excellent contemporary illustration of how the system worked. A friend asked a young Barrow man why he gave all the game he killed to his parents. His response was that when he did that, it "somehow grew," and any time he needed anything, he could go to them and get it. Such a reciprocal relationship is typical of that occurring in the past between an effective umialik, his wife, and younger kin.

had died out other marginal members of adjacent areas moved in to fill the vacuum, and life continued.

One important aboriginal Iñupiat institution uniting family members was the *qargi*, a kind of family gathering place. Although an overturned boat placed downwind on the beach could serve as a simple qargi, the structure was usually a building of some permanence. Prior to the arrival of Christian missionaries in the 1890s, every Iñupiat settlement had one or more of these ceremonial houses. Children joined the house of their father, and on marriage a woman transferred to that of her spouse. During the day, it was a common meeting place for boys and men, while girls and women commonly spent their working hours in family houses. In the evening, the qargi became the family social center where members and friends regularly played games, told stories, danced, and participated in various rituals. With the opening of the ceremonial season in the fall, men spent much of the day there in work and recreation. Wives brought them food and sometimes remained to join in games and dancing. Occasionally men and older boys slept in the qargi. Recreational activities reached their peak in mid-winter. Games of physical strength, gambling, storytelling, and string-figures were common. Friendly competition between qargi groups was formalized in wrestling matches and contests in weight lifting, jumping, chinning a bar, miniature bow and arrow shoots, and kickball.

The qargi dances took several forms. Some dances, limited to men, portrayed a particular event such as the search for polar bear or a joke played on a friend. Women's dances were usually more static, consisting of rhythmical movements of hands and body performed in a given location. Sometimes couples danced in unison or as part of a larger group. Mimicry in a dance also was common, the target being anyone the dancer wished to make fun of. Accompaniment was provided by drummers, beating tambourine-type drums and chanting. The blend of the beat and rhythmical rise and fall of voices, punctuated with shouts of *auu yah iah*, quickly drew qargi members to the dance floor. In the larger villages, two or more local families occasionally joined in an arranged feast, dance, or athletic contest. In these communities, poorer Iñupiat households might be allowed to observe or participate in qargi events of more well-to-do families in return for their maintaining the building, running errands, or otherwise assisting the owners (Burch 1980:296).

The self-sufficiency characterizing the traditional Iñupiat family should not be taken to mean that economic relations between local families in a given locality were nonexistent. In times of plenty when ice cellars were full, the need for interfamily cooperation was minimal. But one never knew whether a full cellar this year would be followed by an empty one the next. When a local family had little food and a neighbor had more, a request for assistance would carry more weight if the one without had been generous in the past. Thus, in times of need, sharing across family lines was common, each local family knowing it could count on another's offer of surplus food when the occasion arose. Only during periods of famine or plenty would the arrange-

Photo 6. Traditional drumming and dancing are still popular on Alaska's North Slope—Barrow 1958.

ment be likely to break down. In the former instance, families split up anyway, seeking relatives in other localities where food was more plentiful. In the latter, the need was simply not there.

Cooperative hunting also linked families. Notably in such endeavors, the individual recognized as the most skilled hunter assumed leadership, regardless of family membership. Given the importance of a successful hunt, choosing the most knowledgeable individual to lead the effort was far more effective than limiting the selection to a member of one's family. Once harvested, the game was divided among the individual participants according to a set of rules overseen by the group leader (*ataniq*). When returned to the hunter's family, the game would then enter the family redistribution system.

Along with sharing and cooperative hunting, interfamily ties in a locality were strengthened by other linkages, such as those established through intermarriage. Since there were a limited number of potential partners within a local family (in addition to rules against incest), exogamy was frequently practiced. Hence, affinal ties became widespread, further strengthening interfamily bonds. Relations between cousins of the same sex and approximate age were close, as were friendship groupings among those holding common interests. Larger villages with several local families had a shared playground where friends could play a form of soccer or other games. In such villages an annual or semiannual gathering of all the village members (*qatizut*) brought the whole community together for a week of feasting, entertaining, sporting events, and demonstrations of magic put on by a local shaman.

It should be noted, however, that since there was no political structure

overseeing these various relations, parties involved in conflicts had no su-
perordinate body to whom they could turn. The only real security lay with
one's kin and, secondarily, in the hope that an adversary's kin would act to
keep the situation from getting out of hand—a gamble at best. In larger
coastal settlements especially, conflicts often festered, leading eventually to
blood feuds between families. Under these circumstances, one family member
would be unlikely to stray into the other family's neighborhood for fear of
being attacked, or even killed. While the circumstances of Arctic living may
well have encouraged cooperation among differing kin groups, strong ties
with one's own kin comprised the essence of Iñupiat social relations.

If interfamily cooperation was limited within given localities at this time,
it was practically nonexistent in relations between localities. More precisely,
it was frequently violent. In the western part of Arctic Alaska, early explorers
such as Beechey (1831), Kashevarov (VanStone 1977), and Simpson (1875)
reported that open warfare between members of differing localities was a
normal occurrence.[7] The Iñupiat, it appears, were far more aggressive than
might be surmised from reading a grade school text.

Small warring parties of equal size might meet, recognize the difficulty of
achieving a satisfactory outcome, and go their separate ways. But if the two
parties were unequal in strength, members of the weaker had reason to fear
for their lives. Strangers had the most difficult time of all. Burch (1975:24–
25) describes the classic case of a seal hunter cast adrift on the ice as a result
of shifting wind and current. Depending on the weather, the hunter might
drift for weeks before going ashore. Once observed by local residents, he
immediately had to identify himself—meaning, indicate whether he had kin
in the locality. If the answer was no, he might be beaten to death. In most
instances, therefore, a stranded hunter would hide from people until he could
determine the location of his nearest relatives. There are even reports of
hunters returning to the ice when discovered in hostile territory, survival
being more likely there than in a region without kinsmen![8]

Nevertheless, just as blood feuds within settlements were moderated by
kin-based and cooperative economic linkages, so, too, were hostilities between settlements tempered by similar alliances. Two were of particular importance: trading partners (*niuviriik*) and co-marriage or "spouse-exchange"
(*nuliaqatigiit*). By means of a trading partnership, an Iñupiaq could extend
the process of cooperation to non-kin, thereby ensuring additional assistance

---

[7] A. F. Kashevarov's journal of his exploration in a skin boat from Cape Lisbourne to just
west of Barrow in 1838 provides a dramatic account of these interterritorial conflicts. Landing
at a settlement of 300 people, he reported: "The Kayakishgvigmuits were friendly; they warned
us of the next people, the Kakligmuits (i.e., Barrow Iñupiat), describing them as evil." Traveling
farther up the coast, he stoped at a ravine and found "human bones strewn everywhere. . . . In
other graves there lay human bodies that had not yet decomposed and beneath each was a bow
and arrows" (VanStone 1977:54). His journal contains several other references to ongoing hostilities between members of different Iñupiat settlements. It is interesting as well to contrast the
disregard for slain bodies in warfare with the ritual treatment of bodies killed in blood feuds or
murder within given settlements (see: Burch 1974).

[8] Further discussion of traditional Iñupiat relations with strangers can be found in: Correll
(1972), Heinrich (1955 and 1963), Pospisil (1964), Ray (1967), and Spencer (1959).

Photo 7. Traveling by dog team on the spring sea ice.

in the form of protection, food, goods, and other services. Co-marriage was a nonresidential arrangement between two conjugal husband-wife couples united by shared sexual access.[9] In each instance, the alliance served to connect single individuals across territorial boundaries. These were highly institutionalized arrangements expected to last throughout the lifetime of the participants. In periods of war, such ties tempered the amount of killing. In periods of peace, partners and co-spouses were key linkages in the conduct of interterritorial trade.

Interterritorial hostilities closely followed the seasonal round of subsistence activities. By common agreement, from late spring through the fall a truce was observed. This coincided with the period of greatest productivity and most extensive interterritorial trading. Then in late fall when darkness began setting in, hostilities commenced. Any stranger observed in a given territory at this time was assumed to be either a spy or a member of an opposing group of warriors unless proven otherwise. Exceptions included journeys to or from a Messenger Feast, a ceremonial gathering of local families from different localities whose leaders were either trading partners or linked by co-marriage; and visits to relatives in other territories brought on by problems of famine in the individual's home district. Strangers who could not provide such justification were beaten or killed.

[9] This arrangement occurred within as well as between villages and territories. In describing the former, Heinrich (1955:135) has written: "The transfer of marital partners usually lasts for a week or several weeks, but one night would be sufficient to set up the relationship. The usual procedure is for the males to exchange homes at night and return to their respective homes for the day." For fuller elaboration, see Heinrich (1955), Burch (1975), and Correll (Burch and Correll 1972).

With spring came a general truce. Iñupiat men living in the Kotzebue area north of the Seward Peninsula put away their weapons and moved onto the ice for sea hunting and, later, to pursue schools of sheefish. Women took responsibility for processing these harvests. Farther north at Point Hope, Wainwright, and Barrow, coastal Iñupiat hunters spent most of April and May searching for the bowhead whale, which was en route to summer feeding grounds in the Beaufort Sea. At this same time, hunters would occasionally stalk caribou along the upper Utukok and Colville rivers.

From June and early July when the ice left, some North Slope coastal people spent their time at seal and duck hunting camps while others headed east for the trade fairs at the mouth of the Colville River and at Barter Island. Most inlanders also moved down to the coast just after breakup in late June or later. July called for another move to the fish camps although men spent most of their time hunting caribou. Later in the season, women turned to harvesting large quantities of berries and vegetable products. Farther south, the residents of Kotzebue Sound had been spending their late spring hunting the *beluga*, a white whale of twelve to fourteen feet long that frequented the area in large numbers. With the end of the beluga hunting season, and after the women had finished drying the whale skin and blubber (*maktak*) and storing it in pokes, the people could turn to less strenuous activities, including participation in the large trade fair at Sheshalik on the north shore of Kotzebue Sound.

This fair, involving two thousand or more participants, regularly included boatloads of people from Siberia as well as inland and coastal Iñupiat. Local trade goods such as pokes of oil, seal, whale, and walrus meat and maktak, ugruk skins and rope were exchanged for Russian tobacco, regional specialties such as jade, pottery, and Siberian reindeer skins, beads, caribou skins, and furs. Social activities included dances, athletic contests, feasts, and more serious negotiations between members of different localities concerning disputes of the recent past.

Farther north, the North Slope Iñupiat held their major trade fair in June at Nigliq on the Colville River delta. An Iñupiaq elder from Barrow, who as a child participated in one of the last trading fairs at Nigliq in the 1880s, remembered it fondly (Hoffman, Libbey, and Spearman 1988:40):

Right after the nalukataq festival, people from Nuvuk (Barrow) start getting ready to go to Nigliq for the trade fair. I traveled with my parents, Akuvaaq and Qin-aluqana, along with my brother . . . and his wife. We always travel together with other families and stick together no matter what the problem may be. We never leave anybody behind when they have a mishap. Before leaving, each traveler makes sure they have enough food to travel with, like sugar, flour, tea, shells for the rifles, tobacco, and whatever else is necessary to carry. I don't remember exactly what year or how old I was due to the fact that we did not have any calendars to go by. The other thing, or rather the main thing the people traded with, was seal pokes filled with maktak blubber, and whale meat, all put in separate pokes. They also had fox skins of different varieties to trade with the dried caribou skins that are used for bedding. . . . Before reaching Nigliq you can start hearing

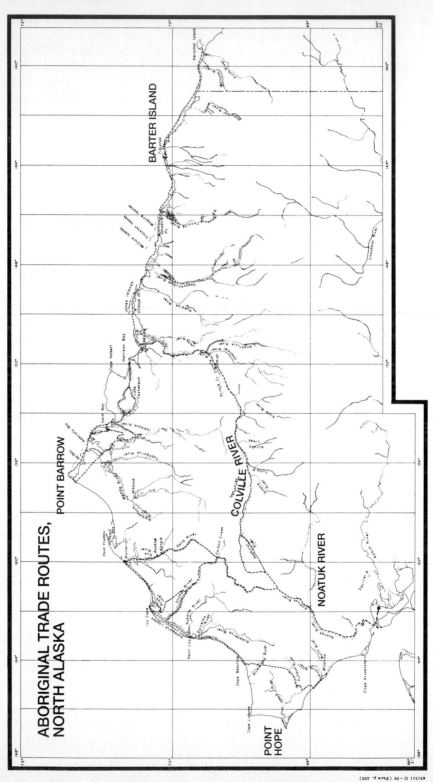

Map 5. *Traditional Trading Routes, North Alaska (from Spencer 1959)*

Eskimo drums beating and it is such a joy to hear their beat knowing that you are expected and are welcomed by the people. Whenever the visitors are entering the mouth of the river they put up a flag to let them know that they are visitors. It was a custom for visitors to put up a flag so that they could become a part of that village. After the big Eskimo dance, they start the trading . . .

We can see that for many hundreds of years, the Iñupiat of Arctic Alaska lived in distinct, territorially based populations. Highly competent, they had an intimate knowledge of their environment. Their economic and social life was organized around interlocking bilateral kin ties, extending to other localities through co-marriage. Although rights and responsibilities of relatives differed according to the closeness of the relationship, the collective labor of the group was nevertheless seen as being mobilized by linkages between kin. Largely self-sufficient and politically autonomous, these kinship groups maintained active trading relations with other Iñupiat, Siberian and Alaskan Yup'ik, and Athabascan Indians. Given the scope of what was available to them, material wants were largely met; if the technological means for development were minimal, they were nevertheless adequate. Everyone had access to the principal means of production—the land—and could make or obtain the tools with which to tap its treasures. Natural disasters of one sort or another, usually due to changing climatic conditions, caused occasional demographic fluctuations. Slowly increasing population along with improved technology influenced the nature and productivity of these territorial units as well. But such changes, falling within the realm of experience, were for the most part predictable. And since the growth of knowledge from one generation to the next was minimal, the concept of time was cyclical rather than chronological and linked to the structure of recurring seasons. For the Iñupiat prior to their encounter with the West, people rather than things were the crucial resource.

2/Colonial Encounter

IN SEARCH OF WEALTH

In many respects, the history of colonialism is a history of the accumulation of capital. With the rise of capitalism in England, the demand for raw materials, land, and labor increased dramatically. Quickly outstripping England's ability to obtain such resources within its own borders, the country's new entrepreneurial leaders had to look elsewhere. In an effort to compete with Britain for world resources and markets, other European countries followed suit. Extensive natural resources contained within United States territory initially slowed the thrust of its colonial expansion, but only briefly.

During the mercantile phase of capitalist development from the sixteenth to the nineteenth centuries, England and Europe expanded their overseas trade, in the process establishing many outposts in Africa, Asia, and the Americas. Then, following a host of technological discoveries in the early 1800s combined with cheap labor drawn from a dislocated rural peasantry, an explosion occurred in economic growth. This, in turn, created a new class of industrial entrepreneurs. While these early capitalists maintained a high standard of living, their reverse counterparts—the peasants deprived of their land, overseas peoples sold into slavery, conscripted to armies, mines, or plantations, and driven into cities to find work—faced great hardship. The expropriation of natural and human resources served the needs of England's and Europe's new industrial class far more than it did the indigenous population for it was in this context that major profits were extracted and capital accumulated.

In the Alaskan Arctic, capital accumulation largely followed this classic historic pattern. Russian penetration effectively began in 1741 when Vitus Bering, a Dane on a mission for the Russian government to determine where Asia ended and America began, sailed from Siberia across what would be named the Bering Strait. Significantly, the survivors of this expedition returned with valuable fur seal and sea otter skins along with information regarding the habits of animal life among Alaska's newly discovered Aleutian islands and offshore waters. With this discovery, the pelts of which brought high prices in world markets, the czarist regime recognized that it could expand its revenue considerably. In a few years, large numbers of Russian traders began cruising these waters, conscripting Native Aleut labor and demanding from them annual tributes of fur.

Decimated both by the importation of new diseases and their subjugation, the Aleuts underwent a precipitous 30-year decline from an estimated 12,000 to less than 2000. This diminished labor force, combined with a severe reduction in the sea otter population, forced the private Russian traders to seek profits farther east. At this time an active intercontinental trade in furs was already moving from Alaska to the Chukchi and then to the Russians at Anadyr. In 1799, attempting to exert greater control over this trade, the government granted the Russian-American Company a royal charter giving it exclusive hunting and trading privileges in Alaska south to California and north to the Yukon River. Soon, permanent posts were set up at Norton Sound and on the lower Yukon. Still, Russian colonization of Alaska was relatively insignificant. Settlers in the southeast never numbered more than 850. Deprived of material comforts and regularly threatened by hostile Tlingit Indian clans fighting to retain their land, the rewards of becoming a permanent resident of Russian America were few indeed. In the Arctic, contacts with the Yup'ik and Iñupiat were even more limited. Only one expedition, led by Kashevarov in 1838, came to within a few miles of Point Barrow. Although valuable ethnographic notes were taken, there was little indication that fur trading could be profitable this far north.

While the Russians were pushing east into Alaska, the British were expanding west. Almost a century earlier, England, not unlike the government of Russia, had turned over vast territories of central Canada to the Governor and Company of Adventurers trading into Hudson's Bay, better known as the Hudson's Bay Company. Protected and supported by the constabulary, this early corporate-like entity was able to extract exchange conditions that generally resulted in a significant transfer of wealth from northern Canada to the "mother country." Further exploration of Canada and Alaska's Arctic waters was encouraged by Britain's offer of a 20,000-pound prize for the discovery of a Northwest Passage to the major trading centers of Asia. As part of this endeavor, two Englishmen, Sir John Franklin and Captain F. W. Beechey, were asked by the British Admiralty to map the coast west of the Mackenzie River in 1826. Beechey sailed through the Bering Strait toward Point Barrow, while Franklin pressed west along the north coast from Canada hoping to meet Beechey coming from the opposite direction. Franklin only reached Return Reef, halfway to his destination, but several of Beechey's men did arrive at Point Barrow in August of that year.

Although Franklin and Beechey had relatively little contact with the North Alaskan Iñupiat, they both noted the extensive trade carried on by these people with other Native groups. In his journal Beechey remarked: "The inhabitants of Point Barrow had copper kettles, and were in several respects better supplied with European articles than the people who resided to the southward. . . . The copper kettle in all probability came from the Russians." (Beechey 1831:572) Several years later, following the disappearance of the 1845–48 Franklin Arctic expedition, a massive search was undertaken to find

Figure 3. First western illustration of the Iñupiat of Point Barrow, Alaska (from Beechey 1831).

the lost explorers. John Simpson, a ship's doctor for the *Plover*, one of the search vessels, wintered at Point Barrow in 1852–53 and 1853–54. The report of his experiences provided the outside world with the first detailed knowledge of these most northern Iñupiat. Explanations for the copper kettles also became clear when Simpson began inquiring about the Iñupiat's involvement in intercontinental trade.[1]

For the Russian leaders of this era, maintaining direct sovereignty over the land was secondary to expanding commercial endeavors. However, by the 1860s, even these ventures had become more difficult. Faced with a decline in fur-bearing mammals, the Russian-American Company was in financial trouble. A recent war with the British in the Crimea had drained the national treasury, and defense of newly obtained eastern possessions appeared less and less viable. To increase their liquidity and reduce their colonial responsibility, Russia offered to sell Alaska to the United States government for $7,200,000. In the spring of 1867, without consulting the original occupants of the region or obtaining title through purchase or treaty, the sale was completed. The one reference in the treaty to Alaska's Native people did not address the issue of status, rights, or land ownership. It simply stated: "The uncivilized tribes will be subject to such laws and regulations as the United States may, from time to time, adopt in regard to aboriginal tribes in that

---

[1] Actually, tobacco provided a more dramatic illustration of this trade than copper kettles. Tobacco originated with Native Americans far to the south. It was introduced to Europe by the Portuguese in 1558. Grown there, it was carried across Europe to Siberia by the Russians. The Chukchi and Siberian Yup'ik used it as a trade item in their exchanges with the Iñupiat (see: Oswalt 1979:205).

country." From that moment on, the future of Alaska Natives was linked politically to that of other Native Americans living far to the south.

WHALING AND TRADING

Prior to the discovery of the northwest whaling grounds, this activity had been limited to the Atlantic and southern Pacific oceans. But with the discovery in 1835, large numbers of American vessels began cruising north of 50 degrees north latitude in the area between the Asiatic and American coasts. Most animals taken were "right whales." But in 1843 as the fleet continued to push farther north to the Kamchatka Coast and the Okhotsk Sea, it found the larger bowhead. Then in July 1848, when the bark *Superior* out of Sag Harbor, New York, passed through the Bering Strait into the Chukchi Sea, a major turning point occurred in the industry. Poised at the gates of the Arctic with the headlands of East Cape, Siberia, 25 miles to his left, Cape Prince of Wales equidistant to his right, and the complaints of a nervous crew ringing in his ears, Captain Thomas Roy entered the largely unexplored waters of the Chukchi Sea. Soon he spotted a walrus skin-covered umiaq and then six more, all together carrying more than 100 Iñupiat, paddling toward his ship from the American shore. A thousand miles from the nearest whaleship and greatly outnumbered by the possibly hostile Natives, the captain and crew were relieved to find a southwesterly breeze carrying the bark beyond the reach of the Iñupiat. The next day, as the *Superior* moved out from under a thick chilling fog, the crew was again startled to find the ship being approached. But this time, it was surrounded by a vast number of bowhead whales. That moment defined the whaling discovery of the century.[2]

Shortly thereafter, ships began frequenting the Chukchi Sea north of the Bering Strait. Based in New England and California, these vessels spent December to March in the waters surrounding the Hawaiian Islands in search of the sperm whale. In spring they sailed for the Bering Strait and beyond, looking for the bowhead or "polar whale." The bowhead, far larger than the sperm whale, regularly yielded a hundred or more barrels of oil along with highly profitable whalebone. These creatures migrate north toward Point Barrow during May and June and then veer east, finally arriving at their summer feeding grounds in the Beaufort Sea. During the fall, whaling ships followed the whales as they retraced their path along the north Alaskan coast and across the ocean to the western Chukchi Sea.

The period following this discovery represented the highpoint of American whaling in Arctic Alaska. Between 1846 and 1851 an average of 638 ships a year, with a value of close to 20 million dollars, sailed from thirty-nine ports on the East Coast. With seventy million dollars invested, the whaling industry supported 70,000 employees (Bockstoce 1986:94). For the first few years, the

[2] For an in-depth historical analysis of the whaling industry in the western Arctic, see Bockstoce (1986). Some of the material that follows is drawn from his excellent account.

Figure 4. Kotzebue Iñupiat seeking to trade (from Beechey 1831).

financial successes of the whaling fleet were phenomenal. Several years of
sharp decline followed and then came another rise, a pattern that continued
for decades, due in part to the concentrated local harvesting of whales, their
defensive responses, and changing ice and wind conditions. A few whalers
expressed concern that if the massive harvest continued, it would eventually
result in the bowhead's extinction. But the drive for profit far outweighed
concern investors might have had for the bowhead's future. No national or
international legal constraints restricted this depletion; thus, investors or
ships' captains practicing voluntary restraint simply profited less than their
more active colleagues.

While the whalers sought pure whale oil for the tanning of leather, preparation of woolen cloth, illuminants, lubricants, and other industrial uses, it
was baleen that brought the highest profit. Baleen are long, thin, flexible
strips of keratinous plates (similar in composition to human fingernails) found
inside the mouth of the bowhead enabling it to strain tiny shrimp, plankton,
and other food from the water. Baleen was commonly used in Europe and
the United States for such manufactured products as buttons and corset stays.
In 1840, with a change in women's fashions calling for whalebone hoops to
buoy out full skirts, their worth doubled.

By the mid-1860s, however, the value of whale oil on the petroleum market had dropped, due largely to technological developments. One of these was camphene, an oil substitute. While cheaper to produce and offering a brighter flame, its major limitation was the smell. A more significant development was the rise of the American petroleum industry following the 1859 discovery of crude oil in Titusville, Pennsylvania. Soon, substitute products became available for almost every known use of whale oil. To assure continued profits for its commercial backers, whalemen had to find larger numbers of whales in a shrinking resource base as well as seek other alternatives. The first option took the whalers steadily northward into even more dangerous waters with a proportionate loss of ships. The second forced them to consider the arduous task of walrus hunting. Thus, by 1867, when Alaska was purchased by the United States, whalers had become a common sight along the North Alaskan coast, their crews occasionally mingling with the local population. More significant exchanges with the Iñupiat came from independent traders who followed the whalers in part to provide them with goods and services. Iñupiat trade included the sale of ammunition, flour, black tobacco, matches, lead and molasses for whalebone, caribou meat, and fur clothing.

Although outlawed by the U.S. government, whiskey also was a much-used trade item. Laden with liquor, schooners from Hawaii, San Francisco and other West Coast ports made huge profits frequenting Alaska's Bering Strait and more northern coastal villages. As much as $200 worth of furs and other goods might be exchanged for one bottle of whiskey. In 1859, one captain found he could "buy a hundred dollars' worth of bone or fur for a gallon of rum which cost 40 cents at home" (Bockstoce 1986:184). United States Customs Revenue Service ships such as the *Bear* and *Corwin* regularly patrolled these coastal areas to discourage such practices, but their success was minimal.

Heavy commercial harvests substantially reduced the bowhead population at the same time that the American Civil War further stimulated the market. To maintain their profit level, whalers turned to walrus hunting. Walrus oil brought slightly more than whale oil, due in part to its ease of refining. But the work was harder. The season began in June in waters between St. Lawrence Island and the Bering Strait, continued in early July on the north shore of the Chukchi Peninsula, and then moved into the northeast Chukchi Sea. Most walrus, frequently hundreds at a time, were shot on ice floes. It is estimated that whalers captured approximately 150,000 walruses, 85 percent of which were obtained between 1869–78. Given the number of animals wounded without being taken, the total kill was probably twice that amount (Bockstoce 1986:135). The result of this slaughter for Alaska's northern Natives in general, and for the Bering Strait people in particular, was devastating. One whaling captain, Frederick A. Barker, shipwrecked in 1870, wrote in a New Bedford, Massachusetts, newspaper of his stay with the Eskimo:

> Should I ever come to the Arctic Ocean again, I will never catch another walrus, for these poor people along the coast have nothing else to live upon. . . . I felt

like a guilty culprit while eating their food with them, that I have been taking food out of their mouths, yet although they knew that the whaleships are doing this, they still were ready to share all they had with us. (Barker 1870–71)

Over the next ten years, starvation and death were increasingly reported in the press. Some observers blamed the effects of alcohol brought to the villages by traders, but a more realistic explanation focused on the loss of sea mammals by a Native population with limited other resources on which to draw.[3] Overhunting by Natives supplied with rifles by Americans and the British was similarly responsible for a severe decline in the Western Arctic caribou herd, which had a comparably devastating effect on the inland Native population.

Also in the 1870s the steam vessel was introduced into the whaling fleet. Contact between whites, who were now better equipped to winter in Arctic waters, and the Iñupiat increased proportionately. Iñupiat men were hired to work as seamen, boatsteerers, and caribou hunters, while women were sought as stevedores and seamstresses above deck and as "seasonal wives" below. As shore-based whaling and trading stations were introduced at coastal villages, contact became even more pronounced. Eventually, steam-driven whaling ships began sailing east of Barrow toward the Mackenzie River delta near Hershel Island just across the Alaskan border in Canada. By 1886, they had reached Barter Island, and two years later they crossed the U.S.-Canadian border. That year, a boatsteerer working for Charlie Brower, a shore-based whaler at Barrow, reported seeing at Hershel Island whales "as thick as bees" (Bockstoce 1986:256). Shortly thereafter, the area was filled with ships wanting to tap the new whaling grounds. This was also the time in which the few Iñupiat families living in northeast Alaska, including the area of Barter Island and Kaktovik, offered to supply overwintering whalers with food in exchange for ammunition, flour, tobacco, and other western goods.

Occasionally, vessels were caught in new winter ice of the Beaufort Sea and destroyed. In 1897 six whaling ships were trapped off Point Barrow, following which 275 marooned men spent a year living with the Iñupiat. Concerned for the men's safety, U.S. government agents sent 362 reindeer overland to Barrow from herds already located at Teller, Alaska, far to the south. However, since the Barrow Iñupiat were already caring for the marooned men, some of the herd was turned over to the villagers.

Whaling continued to be sufficiently profitable through the first few years of the twentieth century that a number of Iñupiat entered into business for themselves. In 1908 the explorer-anthropologist Stefansson found several Iñupiat at Point Barrow maintaining as many as six boat crews and paying equal

---

[3] In 1890, a one-time whaler and Alaska census-taker, Henry Woolfe, summarized the seriousness of the situation in a government report: "Now the natives along the coast from Point Hope to Point Barrow consider it a very lucky catch to shoot 10 walrus during the season, where formerly 500–600 were obtained." (Woolfe 1983) Needless to say, by this time, commercial walrus hunting had been abandoned.

wages with whites. A crew member's earnings of $200 for the six-week whaling season could provide a family with sufficient purchasable commodities to last a year.

Eventually, women's fashions changed and the price of baleen collapsed, and with that came the slow demise of commercial whaling in the Arctic. From 1848 to 1908, the industry had dramatically changed Iñupiat economic, social and cultural life. With newly obtained repeating rifles, Iñupiat and whites together had so reduced the number of land and sea mammals that the old subsistence economy was severely jeopardized. The introduction of whiskey as a trade item disrupted and demoralized village life. The spread of new diseases such as measles, smallpox, and influenza, to which the Iñupiat had no immunity, took a devastating toll. Small settlements disappeared, and larger ones like Point Hope lost as much as 12 percent of their population in one year. In 1900, more than 200 inland Iñupiat trading at Point Barrow died of influenza following the visit of a whaling ship. Two years later more than 100 Barrow Iñupiat perished in a measles epidemic. A decade and a half later, another major influenza epidemic reached Wales at the western tip of Seward Peninsula. Known as the "big sickness," more than one-third of the town's 600 Native residents died within a week. For these Iñupiat it was a disaster of major proportions.[4]

THE "BIG SICKNESS"

On Christmas eve of 1918, a young Iñupiaq from Nome arrived in Wales. Ill with fever, he had lain sick in his sled while his dogs brought him to the door of his home. Two days later he died of "Spanish Influenza." Although a virulent virus that had caused millions of deaths in other parts of the world, doctors in Nome and nearby Teller were unfamiliar with the disease and how to treat it. Within a week, 197 people from Wales had died, with hundreds more sick and dying. Of Teller's Iñupiat adult population, 199 died in the same period.

Overwhelmed by the disease, the resident government nurse in Wales was helpless. Having neither food nor medicine to deal with an epidemic, she could only comfort as best she could those who flocked to the schoolhouse, many of whom remained, too sick to crawl back to their homes. Young boys were asked to kill reindeer from nearby herds, the meat from which was turned into broth to feed the motherless babies and sick adults. As more and more died, their bodies were removed to vacant school rooms and eventually to the Presbyterian Church where they were placed side by side, awaiting burial. Family sled dogs, uncared for by dying adults, broke their tethers and

---

[4] Although the story that follows concerns the Iñupiat of Seward Peninsula, considerably to the south of Alaska's North Slope, the portrayal is important for its illustration of the influence and power exerted by white colonizers three-quarters of a century ago.

roamed the streets seeking food where they could find it, including frozen human remains in abandoned Iñupiat houses.[5]

Similar events repeated over and over again brought an overwhelming pall to the village. Through fear, many homes had been abandoned, the residents crowding into the school, church, and other nonresidential buildings. Rumors were rampant that a terrible spirit had come from some unknown area, perhaps across the strait in Siberia. It was not until several months later that a relief party arrived in Wales with flour, tinned milk, sugar and coffee for the survivors, and shovels with which to bury the dead. Digging a common grave, all the remaining bodies were placed in it and a large white cross raised that could be seen for miles out to sea.

Knowing that most families had been wiped out by the disease, a man assigned to replace the deceased local district superintendent brought with him a sheaf of marriage licenses, signed by proper Nome authorities, but minus the names of the contracting parties. On arriving, he called the remaining adult survivors to the schoolhouse and made a speech. He told the widowers, widows, and others of marriageable age that because the disaster had left so many children without parents, he, representing the government, would have to place the homeless children in an orphanage far away, where they would be irretrievably lost not only to the village but to the surviving loved ones as well.

He offered one alternative, which if accepted, he said, had to be implemented immediately. All widowers "here and now" were to choose from among the widows new wives, and marriageable youths were to select spouses as well. The acting superintendent, utilizing the authority of his office, would then marry all at the same time.

Without further discussion, widowers and young unmarried men were told to take a position on one side of the large room, with the widows and young unmarried girls on the other. Each man was asked to select a wife from the facing line; the couple then stood aside and gave their names to the secretary who wrote them on the marriage certificate. If any man hesitated, a spouse was selected for him. After the licenses were filled out, a mass ceremony was held in which the substitute district superintendent formally pronounced each couple "man and wife." With the bodies of loved ones still lying in the chapel or in the process of being buried by the relief party, the Iñupiat men were basically coerced into selecting mates.[6] Once the ceremony was completed, the couples were told to gather up their respective children and return to their homes.

Some, of course, were unwilling or unable to participate. In writing about

[5] The portrayal that follows is largely drawn from a typewritten manuscript, Seventeen Years with the Eskimo, written by Henry W. Greist, a medical missionary of Quaker persuasion. Part I of the manuscript is available in the Alaska Resources Library of the U.S. Department of the Interior, Anchorage. Unfortunately, Part II, dealing mostly with Dr. Greist's years at Barrow, is lost.

[6] Since the Greist manuscript gives no indication that women were asked to be involved in the selection process, it seems most likely they were not.

this episode from knowledge gained through interviewing villagers, the missionary Henry Greist described one such instance:

> One wealthy Eskimo, a man of some fifty years of age or more, stood silently with downcast eyes in that line, for like all good natives, he regarded "government" as sacred, to be obeyed without question. His late wife was a woman of rare character, capable, educated, refined. Their home, an exceptionally good one, was a happy center. When asked to choose a wife, he remained silent, with bowed head. Then, the superintendent chose for him a young girl not one-third his age. But it so happened that she, little more than a child, had a sweetheart who could not be present that day. She was greatly distressed and crying as he led her to the table and accepted their marriage license, only to be later told that she was wedded to this man nearly old enough to be her grandfather.
>
> That afternoon he, being the gentleman that he was, took her to her newly wedded mother and there left her, securing a divorce later; and in the end she was able to marry the man of her choice. Nor did this grief-stricken man ever marry again, holding the memory of his dear wife as sacred.
>
> The Eskimo are human and many are Christian men and women; and may not be mated as are horses and cattle. Unhappiness hung over Wales village for years, and it was rare that I heard singing in any home when the man was absent. Few divorces were had, for divorce now in Alaska costs a large sum, thanks to the new constitution and a few unscrupulous attorneys. Divorce also demands a trip to Nome, Fairbanks, or other legal center, which often would prove a very great hardship to the native. And, too, wedding vows are very generally considered by the Eskimo as binding, to actually hold "until death doth separate."

The villagers also took in all the orphans, distributing them as best they could among remaining relatives and friends. That few children were turned over to an orphanage was very much in keeping with the Iñupiat pattern of adoption; how the Iñupiat might have handled the crisis in earlier years is open to conjecture. While the action taken by the acting superintendent in trying to resolve the tragedy may have reflected concern, it also demonstrated the arrogance of power in a colonial setting.

HERDING AND TRAPPING

As the precarious health of the Iñupiat became known in the East, U.S. governmental and private agencies began taking more concerted action. Lack of education in hygiene and health care, along with the perceived need for greater "industrial and moral training," also was seen as cause for federal concern. Thus, schools were erected in the 1890s at several points along the northwest coast, in most instances to be run initially by religious institutions. To reduce the competition for converts, major churches in Alaska divided their missionary activity into specific territories with the region north of the Brooks Range allocated to the Presbyterians and Episcopalians. Medical missionaries also arrived at Point Barrow and Point Hope at that time. When the school was constructed at Wainwright, this village was assigned to the

Barrow Presbyterian mission. Farther west in the Kotzebue region, the Friends (Quaker) Church became the dominant missionary influence, and southwest of that in Unalakleet, it was the Swedish Evangelical Mission Church. The Seward Peninsula was assigned to the Congregationalists, Norwegian Lutheran, and Methodists.

In an attempt to resolve both the problem of depleted game resources and instill a new entrepreneurial spirit, the U.S. Bureau of Education (which had been given the responsibility for the welfare of the Iñupiat) actively introduced reindeer herding to the Alaskan North. In a brief statement seeking a budget line from Congress, Dr. Sheldon Jackson (1890–91), the General Agent of Education for Alaska, provided the rationale for the proposal:

> A moderate computation, based upon the statistics of Lapland, where similar climatic and other conditions exist, shows northern and central Alaska capable of supporting over 9,000,000 head of reindeer. To reclaim and make valuable land, otherwise worthless; to introduce large, permanent, and wealth-producing industries, when none previously existed; to take a barbarian people on the verge of starvation and lift them up to a comfortable self-support and civilization, is certainly work of national importance.

Eventually approved by the government, reindeer were purchased from the Siberian Chukchi and shipped across the Bering Strait by American revenue cutters in the 1890s. Herds were supervised by church missions (and later schools) throughout Northwest Alaska and by Chukchi and Lapp herders brought over to instruct Yup'ik and Iñupiat men in handling the animals. After serving an apprenticeship, an individual received the loan of a small herd. Since reindeer multiply rapidly, herdsmen were assured of being able to repay their loan easily. Eventually, these herds grew to substantial size. The Iñupiat herd at Barrow, which began with 125 deer, expanded to 30,000 by 1935 (Sonnenfeld 1959:331). Between 1918 and 1934 the Wainwright herd increased from 2300 to 22,000. The 1250 deer imported to Alaska from Siberia between 1892 and 1902 had increased to more than 600,000 by 1932.

One reason for this spectacular growth was that the reindeer were introduced into an environment that had been largely cleared of their only possible range competitor, the caribou. Reindeer simply took over a vacant ecological niche. Yet the success of this venture proved temporary.

At Barrow, initial interest in reindeer herding was stimulated by a decline in the whaling industry. But by 1940, there were less than 5000 domestic reindeer, and by 1952, there were none. A similar pattern emerged throughout Alaska. Of the 600,000 head present in 1932, only 200,000 remained by 1940. A decade later there were only 25,000.

At the time, explanations for the decline focused on overgrazing, along with disease and predation. But of equal if not greater importance were changes in government administration and policies, new opportunities for Natives to gain a cash income, and changing attitudes of the Iñupiat toward subsistence hunting and wage labor.

Reindeer arrived in Barrow to relieve the crews of six whaling ships stranded in the area in 1897–98. Since the Iñupiat had been able to support the whalers with caribou meat, of the 362 reindeer driven north by the government only 180 were killed for food. One hundred of the remaining deer were turned over to the local Presbyterian mission and twenty-five to an Iñupiat apprentice who had helped drive the herd north. Except for a few left at Point Hope, the rest were returned to the large deer encampment at Cape Prince of Wales.

At the heart of the reindeer program was the apprentice system designed to provide the Iñupiat (and Yup'ik) Eskimo with a new, commercially viable economy. Initially, in 1894, apprentices were to be given two deer at the end of the first year, five after the second, and ten deer in each succeeding year that they remained active herdsmen. In addition, they were to be "fed, clothed, housed, and instructed at the expense of the government." Shortly thereafter, however, the payment in deer was rescinded because: "Experience has shown that the apprentice at the (reindeer) station makes a better living than his associates at home. When he completes his apprenticeship it may be proper to give him some deer for a start, but if this is done, it will be as a gift and not wages" (Jackson 1896:111).

Several years later, the policy shifted again. The apprentice program was reduced to four years, each individual receiving a loan of six to ten deer depending on the length of time spent in the program. At the end of the four years, the participants would be loaned additional deer to assure their having a herd of fifty animals. By this means, Eskimo herders could support their family from the sale of surplus deer. However, on the North Slope, which had no market for reindeer meat, the hoped-for entreprencurial self-reliance was simply not possible. Instead, reindeer herding was viewed by the Barrow and other North Slope Iñupiat largely as an extension of their earlier subsistence hunting practices. Still, given the dramatically increasing number of deer, more and more Iñupiat began buying them, bypassing the period of apprenticeship. By 1913, a teacher at Barrow had described the expanding herds as being like "a savings bank." Owners, leaving their animals in the growing herds, could reap the benefit of the expansion without having to give up their hunting and trapping activities. Iñupiat apprentices, too, could benefit since in addition to receiving "wages" (including ammunition), they were allowed to trap near the herd, an easy process because foxes often frequented herding grounds in the search for food.

But as owners and reindeer increased, so did the problems. One difficulty was how to maintain a proper record of ownership. For small family-owned herds, the problem was minimal, but as the herds grew larger, mismarking of strays and calves became more common.

A different problem emerged following the U.S. Reindeer Service's proposal that individual herds be consolidated into central ones under the control of "corporations" that would assume the responsibilities of management. Proposed in 1911, the policy urged that Natives relinquish their individual ownership, receiving in turn a proportionate number of shares in the corporation. By the mid-teens, it was firmly in place. However, many owners were dissatisfied with the consolidation, saying they had "lost" a great many deer in the actual ownership count.

To this was added another incident that caused great disruption—the burning down of the Barrow schoolhouse in 1928. The schoolhouse contained all the records of reindeer ownership. As reported at hearings sponsored by the U.S. Reindeer Service, Charlie Brower, a white entrepreneur living at Barrow, remarked: "Today, there are probably 20,000 reindeer running loose. . . . No man knows how much he owns. The people who owned the biggest herds have lost their interest. They are practically wild, running in with the caribou." Although the problem was eventually resolved in 1930 when another set of records was found, considerable damage had been done. As herding became more sporadic, wolves, which had increased proportionately with the reindeer population, enlarged their predations. This scattered the animals, making herding more difficult. In addition, the wilder the deer became from lack of herding, the farther they roamed from their home ranges.

As the mixing and breeding of domestic reindeer with caribou became more common, these animals frequently found themselves in the sight of an Iñupiat hunter's rifle. Who was to say whether this four-legged creature was someone's reindeer or simply a stray caribou separated from the larger herd? Anyway, for the Iñupiat as well as other northern hunters, any game was fair game when need was the chief criterion.

By 1939, almost all the Barrow deer had become lost, and wages for apprentices had been canceled. Similar losses were common in other areas of the Arctic. In an effort to revive the industry, the government again supported apprentices and offered improved training in herding practices. At Barrow in 1943, 2700 deer were loaned from the nearby Wainwright village herd and three defunct companies reinstituted. But for the most part, government support seemed insufficient to draw the interest of the North Slope Iñupiat. Government leaders were also concerned that such efforts were promoting dependency rather than economic self-reliance. As stated by a white superintendent of one of the Barrow reindeer companies: "The natives must be brought to the realization that the responsibility for maintaining their herds is theirs, and not the responsibility of the government." He elaborated:

> Getting the local native to do a little work for the company now and then without always expecting pay for same (is difficult). . . . Natives want too much pay in shares when labor is given. . . . Too many deer are used by herders at reindeer camps during the year. . . . Hunters and (Native) trappers killing deer without a permit, claiming deer were almost dead, or had a sore foot and so on. . . ."
> (Annual Report, Northern Frontier Reindeer Company, 1941)

Earlier experience with whalers, trappers, and government officials had, of course, led the Iñupiat to expect a supply of goods or cash in return for their labor. Having adapted to these economic relations, they looked on these proposed changes far less favorably. As long as government subsidies continued, apprentice workers could be found and the herds adequately tended. But by 1944, when the reindeer companies were again perceived as being sufficiently self-sustaining, the government subsidy was withdrawn once more. That summer, a new airfield was constructed at Barrow and Iñupiat were hired as laborers. The Navy also arrived, planning a detailed exploration of petroleum deposits known to be in the area. With these opportunities for a cash income, reindeer herding suffered accordingly. By the end of the summer, a major herd was lost. It was located that winter, only to be lost again, finally being found by several Iñupiat working at a coal mine on Meade River sixty miles to the south.

Ultimately, in an effort to forestall a collapse of the reindeer industry throughout much of the Alaskan Arctic, the U.S. Reindeer Service proposed that herds be removed from "corporate" ownership and board directorship and placed in the hands of individuals. As stated in a Reindeer Service Circular of 1944, "Herders will be encouraged to take good care of reindeer if they own the reindeer, because they will be planning and working for themselves. The better they manage the reindeer, the more money they will make. If they neglect the herd, they will suffer the loss of their reindeer business." Thus, the Service tried to distance itself from a failing industry. But it was too late. By May 1946, more herds had been deserted. Additional loaned deer were lost the following year. By 1952, the last of the remaining Barrow reindeer had disappeared. Similar losses were reported at other reindeer herding villages on the Slope. But in Barrow particularly, lack of herd supervision had suffered from the availability of a cash income that was far more appealing.

New employment opportunities, though significant, were not the only factors causing the final demise of the North Slope reindeer industry. Not to be discounted was the resurgence of the caribou population, which the Iñupiat could again count on in their efforts to maintain an economic lifestyle free of the constraints associated with herding. This distaste for herding was further enhanced by the government's seemingly endless policy changes. Thus, while there might have been some novelty in owning a small group of reindeer, once that novelty wore off, the problems became clearer. Then as government policy forced the consolidation of herds, even greater difficulties emerged. At Barrow, following the burning of the schoolhouse and records of individual ownership, herding hardly seemed worth the effort. Although the collapse of the fur trapping industry during the Depression of the 1930s provided an incentive for reindeer herding, it was short-lived. By World War II, furs again had increased in value, thereby drawing the attention of those Iñupiat who, under other circumstances, might have retained their interest in herding.

Farther to the south in the Seward Peninsula, where opportunities for marketing reindeer meat were greater, the Iñupiat faced a different set of problems, many of them precipitated by the unethical practices of incoming white entrepreneurs. In 1915, the Lomen Reindeer Corporation was established by two brothers who soon began invading rangeland controlled by the U.S. Department of the Interior and occupied by Iñupiat herders. When government policy forced the Iñupiat to place their reindeer under the direction of corporations, their animals were placed in the same herds as those of the Lomen brothers. Through various forms of manipulation, such as marking all maverick deer under the Lomen name and miscounting the number of newborns, the Iñupiat soon realized that they were being cheated. But given the lack of government intervention on their behalf, all they could do was complain to their reindeer district representative.[7]

Throughout much of this period, the Iñupiat were presented with the problem of how to obtain cash to buy flour, tea, cloth tents, iron tools, and tobacco, now defined as essential. One likely prospect was participation in the expanding fur trade. Given the declining price of baleen in the late 1800s, the whaling industry had been forced to expand its fur-trading efforts. By the early 1900s, more than a few whaling ships had been converted into trading vessels outfitted as general stores (Bockstoce 1986:202). Meanwhile, the Iñupiat were expanding their on-shore trading activities as local "big men" became powerful traders. By the 1920s, fox fur had become a particularly important item of trade. Although the Iñupiat had previously supplemented their hunting with trapping, the latter now became a major livelihood. Pelts sold for as much as $50 and the rarer blue pelts brought more than $100. An annual income of $3000 to $4000 was not unusual; in rare instances, a trapper's income could exceed $7000.

This new commitment to trapping brought about a number of unforeseen consequences. Traditional hunting patterns had been based on strong cooperative ties linking several related hunting partner families. Trapping, in contrast, was a more individualistic enterprise involving, at most, two related families. Furthermore, unlike whaling, trapping required that the Iñupiat give up a portion of their subsistence activity, mainly early and mid-winter sealing and late winter-early spring caribou hunting.[8]

Finally, for those Iñupiat living in larger villages, trapping cut deeply into the winter period previously devoted to community activity such as informal visiting between friends and relatives, storytelling, and a continual round of entertainment in the qargi. Once committed to a cash economy based on trapping, considerably more of the long dark winter was spent living in lonely driftwood cabins along the coast far removed from friends and relatives. For these Iñupiat, the consequent isolation soon affected long-standing patterns of family and village cohesion.

It would be difficult to estimate the extent of change that might have occurred if trapping had continued for several additional generations. Instead, following the worldwide Depression beginning in 1929, it abruptly became uneconomical. Fox pelts brought such a low price that the Iñupiat were forced to return to a more self-sufficient subsistence mode of life. Fortunately, seal, walrus, whale, and caribou had again become plentiful and could be hunted

---

[7] Twelve Iñupiat stated in a 1930 letter: "The strife between the Lomen's and the Eskimos will never end until the Eskimos have been given their rights back again. . . . We cannot stand (that) our reindeer are decreasing instead of increasing. In a few years we Eskimos will have nothing to live on. We are looking to the government to uphold our rights." (Nash 1934:73)

[8] In this special sense, trapping had a greater impact than commercial whaling (Sonnenfeld 1957:308).

regularly. Family and community sharing was strengthened, although the local qargi houses (viewed with a highly critical eye by missionaries) had all but disappeared. At this time, the Alaskan Native Service division of the Bureau of Indian Affairs encouraged the production and sale of Native handicrafts such as ivory carvings and baleen baskets (Lee 1983:15).

Native co-operatives, originally organized as reindeer stores, were restructured to aid in developing economic independence and increasing the capital of local shareholders. Although control of these stores soon fell into the hands of a small number of powerful Iñupiat families (usually those who had been successful in whaling and reindeer herding), they did have the effect of tempering the prices asked by local white traders. They also provided a local outlet for Iñupiat hunters to sell fresh meat, which was then purchased by those families engaged in non-hunting activities.

Other sources of cash income became available in the middle to late 1930s with the introduction of old-age pensions, general relief, Aid for Dependent Children allotments, and similar government subsidies. Post offices, located in each community with a school, provided salary for an Iñupiaq postmaster or postmistress, and wages were paid to school janitors, Native store employees, and mission helpers. Nevertheless, until the end of World War II, the economy of Arctic Alaska was both unstable and unpredictable. General health was so poor that half the young Iñupiaq men volunteering for military duty were turned down as physically unfit. Ninety percent of Alaska's deaths from tuberculosis occurred among the Iñupiat and Yup'ik Native peoples (Alaska Health Survey Team 1954:32; Flanders 1987).

Following the war, additional economic opportunities emerged. In 1946, the U.S. Navy began exploring for petroleum in the region north of the Brooks Range and set up a large construction camp a few miles from Barrow village as the base of operations. Iñupiat were encouraged to seek employment at the camp, and those who passed the physical could earn $6000 per year. So many jobs became available that some Iñupiat moved to Barrow from villages as far away as Point Hope and Aklavik in Canada. At the same time, the U.S. Coast and Geodetic Survey undertook extensive mapping of the northern coast, and positions as surveying assistants and guides provided still more short-term employment. These opportunities were followed by the construction and maintenance of Distant Early Warning radar stations, including one at Kaktovik on the northeast coast. Still, while some Iñupiat were becoming relatively affluent, most continued to rely on hunting and fishing to supply their basic dietary needs.

MISSIONS AND SCHOOLS

For Arctic missionaries in the colonial era, the primary goal was to replace Iñupiat religion with a more humane Christian one and to restore a moral basis for a society that they saw as defiled and demoralized by whalers and traders. However, shortly after their arrival on the North Slope in 1890, the missionaries began carrying other responsibilities, too. For the first four years, the Presbyterian Mission Board contracted with the federal government to operate a school at Barrow for Native children. Medical care was provided through the services of Dr. Richmond Marsh, a surgeon and Presbyterian missionary who spent much of his time in Barrow from 1895 to 1912. Eight years later, the mission board opened and staffed a small hospital until it was taken over by the U.S. Indian Public Health Service in 1936. Prior to reindeer herds being transferred to government teachers in 1904, missionaries in several northern villages assumed responsibility for supervising that activity as well.

There is no question that the offering of such educational, medical, and economic services helped considerably in converting the Iñupiat to Christianity. Those few northern missionaries who took the time to learn Iñupiaq and translate large numbers of hymns into the Native language also gained stature in the eyes of their new parishioners.

Most significant was the fact that traditional Iñupiat religious beliefs were built on fatalism. Although an individual could try to exert influence over supernatural spirits by means of magic or ritual or by following designated taboos, the Iñupiat considered himself largely at the mercy of hostile forces. The assumed power contained in songs, charms, and names might help, especially when tapped by shamans. But even this effort frequently proved ineffective.

Missionaries, on the other hand, guided in their discussions with the Iñupiat by having learned at least something of their language and culture, often acknowledged that such traditional religious beliefs were true—only that the spirits described by the shamans were actually devils in the Christian lexicon. They also pointed out that not only were shamans unable to cure measles, tuberculosis and other diseases then sweeping the Arctic, but the shamans themselves seemed prone to the same diseases.[9] White Caucasians, on the other hand (most of whom were presented by the missionaries as being at least nominal Christians), appeared to have little difficulty with such illnesses. And finally, the parishioners were reminded, if death did come from such a disease, believers at least had an afterlife to anticipate.

Thus, Christianity offered both a "civilized" world of education and medical care and a supernatural world of hope in place of the constant threat of hostile spirits. It wasn't long before shamanism began losing its appeal.[10] However, once committing themselves to Christianity, the Iñupiat faced new challenges pertaining to such matters as housing, morality, subsistence, and maintaining "proper" relations between gender and kin.

---

[9] The shamans' lack of interest in seeking medical help from their missionary competitors might well have been a factor in their succumbing to such illnesses.

[10] This should not be taken to mean that spirit possession, trips to consult spiritual forces, the use of objects to diagnose and cure illness, and similar traditional religious activities were not continued. They were (and still are today), but under a different guise. Speaking in tongues, for example, is recognized by several fundamentalist churches as an event involving direct contact with the supernatural.

Viewing traditional Native sod houses as dirty and confining, missionaries urged the Iñupiat to build wooden structures whose ease in cleaning would reduce sickness and disease. But with this change in house construction came other problems. Particularly severe was the difficulty of finding scarce drift-wood along the shoreline to heat the frequently cold and drafty rooms. Nor were these small dwellings any less crowded, the new occupants squeezing into them in the same manner as they had their previously warmer, draft-free, sod homes.

Similarly, the Native custom of removing most clothing when entering a warm home from the cold out-of-doors was challenged by the missionaries who saw such behavior as less a matter of comfort than of morality. Yet when the Iñupiat accepted this action as immodest and began wearing more un-derclothes inside their homes, their comfort suffered and quite possibly their health as well. So, too, the qargi was viewed negatively by missionaries who feared that any center where unsupervised young people congregated freely at night and where Native dancing was regularly held would not bode well for the civilizing process. Far better that evening activities be confined to the mission building where church meetings, held almost nightly, could assure a proper atmosphere for the socializing of young and old alike.

In matters pertaining to subsistence, the Iñupiat were soon faced with a dilemma. A number of evangelical missionaries, some of them living in villages to the south of the North Slope, began preaching that hunting and fishing were forbidden on the Sabbath. Other missionaries put forward a less literal view, but the large majority of Native converts treated the edict as an incon-trovertable statement of religious commitment, even if it meant spending less time in the search for food. In so doing, the Sabbath became equated with older traditional Inupiat taboos. As suggested by Stefansson (1913:89) in writing of his experiences along the Arctic coast during the early 1900s:

> Under the old religion it used to be believed that sickness, famine, and death were caused by such trivial things as the breaking of a marrow bone with the wrong kind of hammer, or the sewing of deerskin clothing before enough days had elapsed from the killing of the last whale or walrus. To avoid breaking these taboos meant prosperity and good health, and the gaining of all the rewards (or rather the escape from all the penalties) provided for by that system of religion. Similarly, now that they know about salvation and damnation it seems but logical to them that one may be gained and the other be avoided by the mere observance of such simple prohibitions as that against working on Sunday.

Thus, instead of simply rejecting older shamanist rites, newer Christian symbols were *substituted* for the old. Charms were replaced by miracles, songs with prayers. But each new effort was still expected to produce an immediate effect similar to that sought in the past.[11] By 1908, when Stefansson returned

---

[11] For further elaboration, see Sonnenfeld (1957). As will be seen in a later chapter, these two interpretations of proper Christian practice continue to provoke controversy among members of differing church groups today.

to the Arctic after a short time away, he found that almost every Iñupiat he met along the northern coast had become converted to this "nativized" Christianity.

While this religious response to the Sabbath became common throughout Arctic Alaska, it caused greater difficulty in whaling communities such as Point Hope, Wainwright, and Barrow, for in these localities, whales were only captured during the six-week spring hunting season. The meat was then collectively distributed throughout the village and stored in ice cellars for later use. But when Sunday was designated as the Sabbath, one-seventh of the time used in hunting this important animal was no longer available. The result was a loss of traditional food and a weakened pattern of community-wide collective sharing.[12]

The Presbyterian surgeon-missionary Dr. Marsh, who perceived the literal interpretation of the Sabbath observance as presenting a serious obstacle to obtaining subsistence food, tried to dissuade the Barrow Iñupiat from applying this belief too precisely. But he found that even when food was in short supply, most Iñupiat still considered it inappropriate to hunt on Sunday, the point being that one should not offend the supernatural. Drawing on the local value that waste was inefficient and therefore inappropriate, Marsh proposed that not to hunt on the Sabbath represented a "wasted" opportunity. He suggested also that since the animal world did not abide by such prescriptions, neither need the Iñupiat. But it appears from the written accounts of the time that both arguments failed to convince.

Nevertheless, one enterprising missionary from Cape Smythe with a keen appreciation for the pragmatic power of syncretism recommended that a "wise" Eskimo could indeed preserve the semblance of the Sabbath and still obtain needed food on that day. As reported to Stefansson (1914:340–341) by an Iñupiaq living in the Colville River area who was following the advice of this missionary, if one kills a caribou on Sunday, the procedure should be as follows: "The hind legs must be dismembered at the hock joint and then the saddle in one piece removed from the trunk of the kidneys. The skin must then be hurled as far as one can from the skinning place. This is food for God. The next day the saddle may be picked up and used for food, but must on no condition be removed the day the animal was killed (Sunday)."

Finally, it should be noted that acceptance of the Sabbath as a day of rest didn't just reduce the time available for hunting, fishing, and gathering of wild plants. It also encouraged the purchase of food at the local store or trading post, a process that drew the local people ever more deeply into the cash-based economy of the outside world.

Christianity brought with it other changes as well. For example, becoming a Christian carried with it acceptance of monogamous marriage—preferably

---

[12] It should not be forgotten, of course, that prior to the arrival of missionaries in the Arctic, traditional Iñupiat taboos also restricted whaling, caribou hunting and similar subsistence activities.

one that would last a lifetime. In earlier years, Iñupiat marriages were not only more flexible, they could also be easily broken by either party without undue difficulty or criticism. But with the joint introduction of Christian practices and civil laws, marriages were sanctified by the church and legalized by the government. As a result, divorces were far more difficult to obtain. No longer could either partner declare a mismatch and walk out the door. So, too, the parents of children born out of wedlock were criticized by missionaries as morally weak. Monogamy was the rule, and pregnancy out of marriage was actively condemned.

While a failed marriage presented a dilemma to both spouses, the problem was considerably more severe for the woman who, as a newly initiated member of the patriarchally oriented church and society, was expected to carry the responsibility for keeping the household together. In the eyes of the Euro-American world as seen through the teachings of the missionaries, a woman's major task was to maintain a sound Christian home, "carrying for the needs of husband and children with happiness and joy."

Efforts to educate the Iñupiat in such an ideology took many forms. In Sunday sermons, sewing circles, and church schools, women were regularly informed that as wives and mothers, they should assume greater responsibilities in the "private" sphere of the home and leave the more important "public" economic and political activities to the men.[13] Thus, in weekly church-sponsored Mother's Meetings, Iñupiat women were taught how to properly bathe and weigh babies and learn other aspects of their care and feeding while their husbands were out hunting food. Husbands and fathers, seen as providers, needed dedicated wives and mothers who were good supporters.

Eva Richards (1949:116), a Presbyterian missionary who wrote a book detailing her experiences in the North Slope village of Wainwright in the 1920s, reflects this attitude in describing the qualities of one of the village's leading families:

> I was highly entertained this evening when Segavan, one of Wainwright's more enterprising and progressive citizens, came in. Segavan, you know, of the nice clean igloo, whose wife carefully wipes the cups before pouring tea. And a high pride he takes in his well-ordered home, as any man would who can boast of such a household; meals well-cooked and served when men are hungry, his woman clean, with a heart in her tasks, busy with affairs of comfort and warmth and serenity, bearing his children with joy and inner gladness. A living palpable pride is Segavan's and he delights in telling it.

[13] As early as 1879, the Woman's Board of Home Missions of the Presbyterian Church had laid out the ideology of gender reflecting this view that was to guide missionaries in bringing Christian religion to Native Americans west of the Rocky Mountain territories. Summed up in a church report of the time, these boards labored "to lighten the burdens and brighten the homes of these devoted ones battling for the Lord on the rugged frontier. . . . They were the nurseries for the idea that woman's work was needed to supplement men's work in the outward, aggressive activities of the Church"; (Scovel 1879). For a fuller treatment of changing gender relations among the North Slope Iñupiat at this time, see Chance (1988).

Photo 8. The Barrow Presbyterian Church and manse.

Once an active co-partner in subsistence, sharing, and socialization, Iñ-upiat women found that under the banner of being good wives and mothers, they carried considerably more household responsibilities and had far fewer freedoms than previously.[14]

While northern Christian missions took on the task of converting Iñupiat souls, the federal government committed itself to changing the minds of Iñupiat youth. Before the arrival of school teachers and missionaries, Iñupiat socialization was largely focused on learning how to survive. A child's education entailed continual observation mixed with regular instruction tempered by practical experience. During his observations of Barrow in 1881, the explorer Murdoch (1892:417) wrote that young children picked up most of what they learned from watching their elders. By 6 or 7 they looked for bird eggs and searched for small animals. At the age of 12 or 14, boys "were entrusted with a gun and seal spear and accompany(ed) their fathers to the hunt." Those slightly older joined a whaling crew. In similar fashion, Murdoch reported how young girls frequently imitated their mothers in learning how to sew; and by the time they reached adolescence they were taking an active share of responsibility in preparing food and making clothes.

Actually, the learning process of young Iñupiat included an even wider range of activities associated with subsistence. The report of a Barrow teacher

[14] Included among these household responsibilities was a significant increase in the number of children to be cared for. The shift from a seminomadic to a more sedentary lifestyle (strongly encouraged by the missionaries) was an important factor in this increase as was the improving health care services that helped to reduce infant mortality.

in the early 1900s captures this broader set of educational experiences quite well:

> The Eskimo child differs from the average white child in that at an early age he is thrown upon his own resources as far as trading and bartering are concerned. For instance, there came into the harbor last fall, just before the close of navigation, a whaling schooner. That evening after school, about a dozen boys between the ages of 9 and 14 got into a native boat and went over to the ship. The crew of the ship was composed mostly of Eskimo from Siberia. These school boys in some cases traded the very clothes they had on their backs—custom-made goods shipped from Seattle in the summertime; hats, caps, coats, suspenders, shirts, undershirts; not to mention pocket knives, mouth organs, and various other artifacts —for things the Siberians had to trade. After it was all over, they came back to the school house and during the evening hour entertained us with a recital of their experiences, laughing and joking at the deals they had made. And I could see they had driven some shrewd bargains with the Siberians. (U.S. Bureau of Education 1910:11:31)

As can be seen from this teacher's report, the trading skills learned as a boy provided an important enhancement to the more traditional pursuits of hunting and fishing. In fact, the latter skill was almost as essential to Arctic survival then as had been the completely self-sufficient hunting and fishing skills of earlier centuries.

But such a process of socialization was hardly what the federal educational authorities had in mind for Alaska's Native population. Their educational agenda was of quite a different kind. The first formal expression of governmental thinking about Alaskan Native education came with Congress' passing of the Organic Act of 1884 following the territory's purchase from the Russians in 1867. This act, in addition to establishing a government in Sitka, directed the Secretary of the Interior to provide proper education for all Alaska children, regardless of race. The policy implemented by the U.S. Bureau of Education (1898:xlix) was "to provide such education as to prepare the natives to take up the industries and the modes of life established in the States by our white population, and by all means not try to continue the tribal life after the manner of the Indians in the western states and territories."

As was the case with British colonial views of Native Americans in the seventeenth and eighteenth centuries, the U.S. government's perception of the Iñupiat was based on a set of moral beliefs and myths that together provided the rationale to maintain the earlier tradition. The most predominant myth characterizing this segment of the colonial period was associated with "Social Darwinism." Simply stated, Social Darwinian theory explained the dominance of Euro-Americans in technological, social, and cultural spheres as a result of their "natural" superiority. That is, human beings invariably arrange themselves according to their innate abilities. Since Euro-Americans were obviously more "advanced" than Alaska Natives, this must represent a unilinear law of nature. Additional support for this moral belief was derived from the assumption that mental abilities were superior to physical ones,

Perceiving Native people to be more concerned with developing their physical prowess and hunting and fishing skills than their mental development, further evidence of their inferior status was seemingly provided.[15]

Failure of many Native Alaskans to assimilate into the economic and social mainstream was often explained by reference to these assumptions of natural inferiority characteristic of the time. To speed the assimilation of all Native Americans, including Alaskans, the federal government introduced compulsory schooling. As put forward by the Commissioner of Indian Affairs in his 1899 annual report: "Indians must be absorbed into our national life, not as Indians but as American citizens. The Indian must be 'individualized' and treated as an individual by the Government. . . . The Indian must be prepared for the new order through a system of compulsory education, and the traditional society of Indian groups must be broken up." By this time, schools had become established in northwest Alaskan coastal villages from the Seward Peninsula all the way to Point Barrow.

For several decades, utilization of the educational system as an instrument of assimilation was far less pronounced among the Iñupiat of Alaska's North Slope than it was farther to the south. Separated from the rest of Alaska by the Brooks Range, few opportunities were envisioned for any sustained economic enterprises other than whaling and trapping. Thus, it seemed sensible at the time to limit the educational process to more practical matters. In the 'teens and early 1920s, North Slope schools were conducted as much for adults as for children, emphasizing as they did the development of "domestic industries, household arts, personal hygiene, village sanitation, morality, and elementary English." (U.S. Office of Education 1910–11:8).

Then in 1924, following legislation making all Native Americans U.S. citizens, a significant shift occurred in Alaskan educational policy. The legislation's importance in shaping the future of the Iñupiat makes it worthy of an extended excerpt. As offered by the Superintendent of Schools in Alaska (Ostermann 1952:17–18):

> We do not consider it a good thing to keep any people in the world down artificially. In a country where civilization has penetrated there is no longer a primitive phase. The one problem to be tackled is to make the transition from a primitive life to a more enlightened phase of culture as painless as possible. We consider that we owe the Eskimo within Alaska the same privileges as any other American citizen, and one of the greatest privileges to which all have the right is access to good schools. At school is laid the foundation of life; at school is formed the basis on which the young people must afterwards do their work. Between the natural life of an Eskimo and the life of an American there is such a gulf in all fundamental principles that we have to begin our education and instruction on an entirely new foundation. We therefore consider that the only foundation capable of leading to anything is the English language, which gives the Eskimo direct access to our culture.

[15] Such myths continue to be expressed in the Arctic today, most commonly phrased in the form of "compliments" about "these technologically oriented peoples" and "their particular fitness for technological occupations." For an illustration, see Slater (1970:4).

On arriving at a Native village, new teachers were encouraged to change cultural practices, denigrate what remained of Native religion, speak out against lax sexual practices and other customs defined as inappropriate, and promote in their place new forms of behavior and thought more conducive to life in a civilized society. Arctic teachers were also informed that children were to be taught in the English language rather than in Iñupiaq. Although not all teachers abided by this edict, the intent of the policy was clear.[16]

Why reject so strongly the Native tongue? Because language embodies cultural ideas, beliefs, and ideals whereby one defines the world. A given language is a kind of cultural vocabulary in which experience is transformed into symbol and then communicated to others. Since the government wanted to superimpose a Euro-American definition of the world on the Iñupiat and other Native Alaskans, their cultural vocabulary had to be replaced with one prescribed from without.

Bitter views of this colonial policy of education have long been expressed by the Iñupiat. Eben Hopson, a highly regarded leader who eventually became the first mayor of the North Slope Borough, once spoke of his early education in such a school. "There were many of us (who) were physically punished if we spoke one Iñupiat word. Many of us can still recall the sting of the wooden ruler across the palms of our hands and the shame of being forced to stand in the corner of the room, facing the wall, for half an hour if we were caught uttering one word of our Native language." (Hopson 1977:3)

Passage of the Indian Reorganization Act (IRA) of 1934 rescinded some of the most prominent features of the federal government's assimilation policy relating to education. The legislation also provided an opportunity to establish new Native-run tribal institutions and Native-owned business enterprises, in the hope that these would promote greater political and economic self-reliance. But yet another shift in government policy followed in the early 1950s that brought back many of the assimilationist strategies of earlier years, plus a new one, a Relocation Program encouraging Native Americans to move away from their reservations to urban areas where employment was more likely to be found. In Alaska, educational boarding institutions such as the industrial training school at Mount Edgecumbe in southeastern Alaska were set up to train Native primary school graduates in practical arts and sciences. But the fundamental question facing administrators, teachers, and students alike continued to remain largely unanswered: What kind of education would best prepare the Iñupiat and other Native Alaskans for the future? Should it be one enabling them to make a productive and creative life in their own villages? Should the curriculum be geared to a life far removed from that earlier environment? Or was there some way to provide for either alternative without incurring expenses far beyond the reach of the agencies concerned?

---

[16] Actually, this policy dated to a much earlier time. In 1890, Alaskan Native teachers were informed that "the children shall be taught in the English language. . . . No textbooks printed in a foreign language shall be allowed. Special efforts shall be put forth to train the pupils in the use of English." (U.S. Department of the Interior 1893:1254)

CHANGING SOCIAL RELATIONS

From this brief historical portrayal, we can see that America initiated its colonialization of northern Alaska (as did Britain in Canada's western Arctic) during a time of rapid industrialization accompanied by significant advances in maritime technology. Rather than having to demand tribute from a subjugated Native population, as had been the case during the Russian colonial period, America's search for wealth in the Arctic was based on a set of economic principles firmly rooted in improving technology, expanding industry, exchanging commodities, and accumulating capital. Also, numerous transient and shore-based whalers, traders, gold seekers, missionaries, teachers, and government agents eventually came north, thereby constituting a much larger segment of the overall population than had been characteristic of the Russian penetration. Furthermore, although the Iñupiat were useful in providing labor, food, and supplies to these white entrepreneurs, they were not as essential in extracting the particular resource as had been the case with the Aleut. Thus, Iñupiat relations with American whalers, traders, and gold seekers differed significantly from those between more southern Alaska Natives and Russian traders where murder and enslavement were commonly practiced. Still, a major lesson to be learned from this comparison is not so much that America's links with Native Alaskans were less devastating than those of Russia, although that is certainly true, but that *different economic activities encourage different economic and social relations*. As for life in the Arctic prior to European penetration, it has already been noted that a high value was placed on cooperative labor among Iñupiat kin, thereby enhancing the likelihood of adequate sustenance. Although rights and responsibilities differed according to the closeness of the relationship, the collective labor of the group was nevertheless seen as being mobilized by linkages between kin. Only following the colonial encounter with Euro-Americans did fundamental changes begin taking place that deeply affected these social relations.

This process can be seen by analyzing the introduction of reindeer to Arctic Alaska in the 1890s. Prior to that time, Iñupiat hunting, fishing, and gathering activities basically used nature's renewable resources. But herding reindeer transformed the people's relationship with their environment in that Iñupiat herders began utilizing it for the production of livestock. In the first instance, the resource was available to those with the skills to obtain it. In the second, it was restricted to those producing it. That is, through ownership and inheritance Iñupiat herders (along with non-Native ones) gained exclusive rights over its disposition—quite a different relationship indeed.[17]

As long as Alaska's Native northerners were able to channel their economic efforts through kin-based relations, any part-time involvement in the

---

[17] This is not to suggest that prior to the introduction of reindeer herding, caribou grazing lands, duck stations, or fishing camps were simply common property available to all. As already noted, territorial boundaries were recognized and enforced throughout Arctic Alaska by distinct kin groups, a process that effectively limited access to such resources by "outsiders" unless appropriate social clearance was obtained (see Burch 1975).

larger economic system supplemented, rather than replaced, their own means of livelihood. However, as commerce and industry expanded and western commodities became more plentiful, the earlier barter-oriented relations once characterizing Native trappers and Euro-American traders increasingly gave way to cash-based relations. Eventually, full-time subsistence production became dependent on western technology, at which point so-called Iñupiat "partners" in the fur trade became part-time subordinate producers in an entirely different form of production—industrial capitalism. Under this economic system, the tie between the producers and the means to produce is largely broken, the results of which not infrequently force large numbers of people into wage work from which profit can be extracted. George Rogers (1972:195), one of Alaska's most respected economists, succinctly described the changed relations stemming from this colonial encounter:

> During the colonial period the Native was treated as part of the environment in which the exploitation was to be undertaken. If they could be turned to a use in serving the purpose of getting the resource out as easily and cheaply as possible, they might be enslaved as with the Aleut, or recruited . . . as a local work force in the harvest and processing of marine resources. If not, they were ruthlessly pushed aside while their traditional resources were exploited to the point of extinction by seasonally imported work forces as was the case with the coastal Eskimo. The impact was on the whole destructive to traditional ways and to the Native people themselves, and their economic participation was marginal at best.

But the impact of Alaska's colonial encounter on the Iñupiat and other Native residents can only be partly understood through the eyes of an academic social scientist. From the perspective of an articulate Iñupiat leader like Willie Hensley, the portrayal becomes more vivid. In a keynote speech given before the Alaska Federation of Natives Convention at Anchorage in 1980, Hensley, a bank president and community leader from Kotzebue, offered his assessment of the colonial experience:

> I think that many people don't understand the massive changes that our people have been through. . . . I think many people forget about the Aleuts and how they barely survived the Russian invasion. People forget about the changes brought about by the whalers and all their liquor, and by the gold rush, the two World Wars, and by the vast populations that came following the highway and the construction of the railroad. Besides the material changes, there was also a great deal of pressure to conform . . . to look the same, to speak the same, and to think the same as others do in America.
>
> The fact is Alaska's Native people, just as the Indian people in the "lower 48," have fought the same tide of assimilation, acculturation, individualization and atomization. This process has taken its toll on our spirit, on our identity, on our language, and on our culture. We have had alcoholism and drugs, drop-outs, family break-up, and crime in our communities because of the pressures we've had on us. We had almost lost the will power to reassert our tribal identity and reconstitute our spirit and of who we are inside.

What problems faced the Iñupiat as they tried to make their living under such circumstances? What was it like to grow up in such a time? How did they attempt to deal with the momentous economic changes impinging on them so dramatically during these early years of Alaska statehood? In Part Two: *Village Legacy*, we will take up each of these issues, especially as they relate to life on Alaska's North Slope in the late 1950s and early 1960s prior to the discovery of oil at Prudhoe Bay.

PART TWO | Village Legacy

We always try to help each other. That is the Eskimo way.
Harold Kaveolook, Iñupiaq (1958)

I'll never forget my first day at school. I had waited for this day for years—
to enter the white frame building where my two older brothers read books and
learned to write their names. I was 6 years old, and didn't know a word of
English. Excited, I jabbered away to all my friends in Iñupiaq.

From the front of the room, the teacher studied us closely. He was a big
man with giant hands, dressed in a white shirt and tie. He walked slowly around
the room and suddenly, out of nowhere, his great big hand grabbed me round
the neck. He shoved a big bar of soap into my mouth, right in front of all my
friends. "No one here will speak Iñupiaq," he ordered. I worked hard to master
English after that. I never again wanted my mouth washed out with Fels Naph-
tha for speaking the language I'd grown up with.
John Tetpon, Iñupiaq (1988)

3/A Place Called Kaktovik

From the window of the small plane I looked down on the flat expanse of tundra one thousand feet below. Small streams and ice-filled lakes added brilliant contrast to the treeless landscape. The surrounding ground was covered with varieties of lichens, sedges, and mosses, giving the region a meadowlike appearance. Through the other window my eye followed the curving shore of the north Alaskan coast over a stretch of open water to the white outline of the pack ice beyond. Just ahead lay a 3.5 mile-long thin strip of land the British explorer Franklin had named Flaxman Island for John Flaxman, an English sculptor and artist.

Beside me, a grey-haired man with bronzed features raised his hand and pointed toward the same spit of land jutting out into the sea.

"Qikiqtaq. Nobody lives there now."

Qikiqtaq—the term the Iñupiat used for the island centuries before the arrival of Franklin. Near a small shoal at the center of the island stood an abandoned house, hedged by a thick growth of tundra grass. Weathered walls still supported the entryway and small food cache above although the sod roof had long since disappeared. A short distance beyond sat a smaller structure, part of a building the geographer Leffingwell used as a campsite during his explorations for the U.S. Coast and Geodetic Survey in the early 1900s. And immediately beyond Qikiqtaq Island, on a small curved point of land, were visible several wooden grave markers bounded by a weather-worn picket fence.

"Did any Kaktovik people ever live here?" I asked the older Iñupiaq sitting beside me. Vincent Nageak once had spent many years in this part of north Alaska before returning to Barrow village, his original home. We both were now heading for the coastal village of Kaktovik, located on Barter Island 310 miles east of Point Barrow and sixty-three miles west of the Canadian border. He planned to visit his sister and other relatives while I was about to begin a study of the community. The time was mid-June 1958.

"A few. Panningona's daughter was born at Qikiqtaq. She married an Akootchook from Kaktovik. Several others lived here, too, but they moved away maybe forty or thirty years ago. Now only one family is left between Barrow and Barter Island. They're over on the Colville River delta. Not very crowded, is it?" He looked at me, a smile wreathing his lined face.

"Not any more." Lapsing into silence, I thought about an associate of

59

Photo 9. Leaving the Colville River for Kaktovik.

Leffingwell, Ejnar Mikkelson (1909:98), who wrote of Qikiqtaq: "On the extreme west end of Flaxman Island there were some houses in ruins, while some tombs showed the last inhabitants had died, caught, as we learned later, in a blizzard and froze to death." Other abandoned camps and villages were scattered along this part of the Arctic coast, the residents drawn to the area for hunting and fishing. Trading, too, had a history here, hundreds of Iñupiat coming together in mid-summer before moving on to Barter Island, the easternmost of four major Iñupiat exchange centers. More recently, in 1923, a white trader, Henry Chamberlain, used part of Leffingwell's house as a trading post, exchanging flour, sugar, tea, coffee, and ammunition for furs trapped by nearby Native residents. Now the area was vacant except for the family on the Colville.

Flying on toward Kaktovik, I continued to observe signs of earlier habitation. From the air, the coast seemed almost like the rough edge of a long detailed map, which when deciphered by Nageak provided insights into the area's history. With the loss of older Iñupiat, who would be left to pass on this knowledge? Could sufficient data be gathered now that would provide a permanent record from which others could benefit? Or would it be up to archeology—the ghost of history—to provide the final summary. Questions without answers. Hopefully, the study I was about to undertake could be of some assistance in this regard. But my major focus lay in contemporary change rather than cultural history.

Eight months previously as a young anthropologist teaching at the University of Oklahoma, I had met Margaret Lantis, a respected Arctic specialist who had recently returned from a trip to north and northwest Alaska for the

U.S. Public Health Service. Fascinated by the account of her experience, I told her of my desire to learn about north Alaska and its people, an interest initially stimulated by Louis Giddings, a University of Pennsylvania Arctic archeologist under whom I had once studied. Did she have any suggestions? Would she help?

Now, having obtained a small research grant, I was following her suggestion that I spend the summer at Kaktovik, a village she had visited briefly and found most interesting. She was especially struck by the fine people she had met there and how well they were adapting to the dramatic changes occurring in the area. Kaktovik (or *Qaaktugvik*, "seining place"), as I soon learned from an Arctic map, was the most geographically isolated of Alaska's Iñupiat villages. For most of its existence, it had not been so much a permanent settlement as a seasonal home for seminomadic hunting families who depended on sea mammals, caribou, and fowl for their sustenance. Before commercial whaling arrived in the Beaufort Sea, the isolation of the region had kept the people from having significant contact with the outside world. Indeed, prior to the arrival of the whalers, most Kaktovik Iñupiat had never seen a *tanik* (white man) in the area.

Then, in the early 1920s, a white trader, Tom Gordon, opened a trading post on the western side of Barter Island. This event provided an opportunity for the people of Kaktovik and the surrounding area to exchange trapped furs for needed items of western manufacture. Aside from Gordon and a few other traders who settled along the coast at that time, the only contacts these Iñupiat had with whites came from occasional visits by explorers, scientists, or Presbyterian missionaries making their way from Barrow to Demarcation Point and Canadian settlements farther to the east. But following the plunge in fur prices caused by the Depression of the early 1930s, Gordon and the few other traders left for Barrow or Hershel Island in Canada, followed in many instances by the still seminomadic Iñupiat.

After World War II and initiation of the Cold War between the United States and the Soviet Union, the American Arctic became increasingly militarized. Although the Kaktovik people had gained some familiarity with the U.S. military during the war as a result of Lt. Col. Marvin "Muktuk" Marston's "Tundra Army" of Alaska Territorial Guard, they were hardly prepared for the events that followed. In July 1947, a construction company arrived at Kaktovik to build an airstrip. This proved to be the first step in what became the North American Strategic Hemispheric Defense Plan to establish a Distant Early Warning (DEW linc) radar network throughout the north from Barrow to Baffin Island in the Canadian Archipelago.

Four years later, the U.S. Department of the Interior authorized the Air Force to assume control over the 4,500 acres of Barter Island, including the site and cemetery of Kaktovik village (Chapman 1951). Shortly thereafter, a secret Defense Department plan to construct an experimental radar line from Barrow to Kaktovik was implemented. By the summer of 1953, large amounts of equipment were stored on the island. Unfortunately for the local residents, the Air Force also decided to expand the airstrip along the sand spit sheltering

Photo 10. Approaching Barter Island by air. The melting sea ice is just off shore.

Kaktovik Lagoon and build its hangar on the very site of the village. Informed by the military that they had to relocate immediately, the local Iñupiat were stunned. Moving equipment and skilled operators were provided by the Air Force, but the labor came mainly from the people. Soon, bulldozers had pushed the remnants of a dozen sod and driftwood houses 1,650 yards up the sand spit to the relocated village site. Loss of their homes and personal possessions, along with the destruction of valuable ice cellars used for food storage, brought an angry response. But given the people's lack of English-speaking skills, confusion over what was happening, and minimum contact with the outside world, little effective protest was mounted.

Eventually houses were rebuilt and ice cellars dug, most of the materials for the former having been offered by the military or obtained from the refuse dump located at the end of the sand spit. Relations between the villagers and the newcomers improved, and by 1957, when the initial radar installation was complete, Iñupiat from Kaktovik as well as from Barrow and other North Slope villages had obtained employment as construction workers and maintenance personnel.

In a little more than a decade, a dramatic transformation had occurred in the lives of these people. What had been the impact of these changes? What was the village like now? More personally, how would the Kaktovik Iñupiat respond to the arrival of an anthropologist they didn't even know was coming? At least I'd have an answer to the latter question soon.

Interrupting my thought, the pilot pointed in the direction of a small island snuggled against the Arctic shoreline.

"Kaktovik, just ahead."

He then reached over toward the panel and turned the radio transmitter to a new frequency. Keying the mike, the pilot made a position report: "Barter Island radar. Cessna 391 over Arey Island. Request permission to land. Have two passengers for the village."

Receiving approval, the man at the controls reduced the plane's throttle and began the long glide toward a gravel sand spit that reached out for several miles along the coast. At the near end of the spit on a high bluff were thirty or more houses of varying shapes and sizes. Some were rough one-room board dwellings with a single window. Others formed long narrow lines. A few had been painted recently, but most were a dull shade of weathered grey. A parka-clad woman was hanging long, thin strips of meat on drying racks constructed of driftwood and rope. Near her, two youths had just finished raising a white canvas tent, no doubt to sleep in during the coming summer. One hundred yards beyond the village on a high knoll, I recognized the H-shaped building and large plastic dome of the new military radar station.

Banking slightly, the plane turned into the easterly wind and began its final approach. As the wheels touched down on the gravel, small rocks slapped against the underside of the plane. Recognizing our startled looks, the bush pilot gave Vincent Nageak and me a reassuring word.

"Here we are. I'll give you a hand with your gear. Then I've got to go up to the radar site for a bite and some gas before I start back. The radio operator says someone from the village needs a ride to the Barrow hospital."

After the plane braked to a halt, Nageak nodded a quick goodbye to the pilot and me, slipped out the door, and with a canvas bag thrown across his shoulder, headed for a large three-room house that stood a hundred yards or so beyond the end of the airstrip. After helping me unload an assortment of bags, boxes, and books, the pilot, too, excused himself and began the trek toward the distant radar site. Did he know where the teacher Harold Kaveolook lived? No. But I might try that partly painted building on the small knoll near the edge of the bluff overlooking the ocean. That's where he held classes before school closed for the summer. I thanked the pilot, stacked my gear against the wall of the nearby empty hangar, and began walking slowly toward the village.

RITE OF PASSAGE

Anthropologists are fond of pointing out that every society defines certain periods in life as times of transition in which socialization processes are greatly accelerated. Some are biological in nature like birth, puberty, or parenthood while others are linked to social changes such as marriage or retirement. In either instance, the passage is clearly recognized and often marked by rituals; hence the term—*rite of passage*.

While this event is usually seen as occurring within a given society, a similar pattern can be observed when anthropologists begin field research in societies other than their own. And as is true with other rites of passage, the

Photo 11-a. Kaktovik Village in summer.

Photo 11-b. Same village in late winter.

event is both important and stressful. To reduce the likelihood of making a serious blunder, the prospective field worker tries to learn as much as possible beforehand about the language and culture of the people concerned, secure permission to enter the area from them, and make practical arrangements for bringing or obtaining adequate food, clothing, and shelter. If the research is located in an isolated region such as the Arctic, these logistic efforts can entail considerable complexity and expense.

Even more important is the need to establish rapport with the people with whom one expects to stay. If they do not wish to have an anthropologist in their midst, the person cannot even begin the investigation. More than a few field workers have been ignored, asked to leave, or even bodily ejected from communities where they hoped to conduct research. Therefore, one of the first tasks facing the anthropologist on arriving at a locale is to give an adequate explanation as to why he or she is there. To those unfamiliar with what such people do, this can be difficult. From the local perspective, a newcomer who appears to have at least some ties with powerful outside government or private agencies, who continually asks questions and who seems not to need to work and yet has little knowledge of how to function in the society—that person is going to invite suspicion. In isolated regions where physical dangers are more pronounced, the community members may also fear that they will have to assume responsibility for this uninvited individual.

In my case, while no one knew I was coming to Kaktovik, several Barrow residents had given me the names of people to contact. One was the local teacher, Harold Kaveolook. An Iñupiaq originally from Barrow, he had been hired seven years earlier by the Bureau of Indian Affairs (BIA) regional superintendent to move to the village and organize a primary school. Arriving in June 1951, Kaveolook obtained enough scrap lumber from the Air Force and local volunteer labor from the community to build a one-room school. By September, when the first class was scheduled to begin, he was ready. Although his own high school education had been interrupted by World War II, Kaveolook soon gained a reputation as a fine teacher. He also took an active role in local Presbyterian Church affairs. Two other Iñupiat leaders had also been recommended to me while I was at Barrow: Herman Rexford and Isaac Akootchook. Both experienced workers as well as skilled subsistence hunters, they were employed by a company under contract to the Air Force. All the Iñupiat I talked with in Barrow had thought the three would support my staying in the village. I was about to find out.

After walking several hundred yards along the airstrip, I finally reached Kaktovik. Looking around, I recognized the rectangular school building to which the pilot had referred. Constructed of large sheets of high-grade plywood, it had four equally spaced glass-paned windows on each side that clearly set it apart from other buildings in the area. Glancing through one of the windows, I was relieved to see someone inside. Moving to the door, I first thought about knocking but decided against it and simply stepped into the room. At a table surrounded by cases of powdered milk and vitamins on one

Photo 12. Kaktovik's first two-story house. Meat on the drying racks includes caribou and seal. Western goods, such as the children's new tricycles, were ordered from a mail order catalog and arrived on the weekly mail plane.

side and stacks of textbooks on the other sat a dark-haired man in his mid-thirties. Looking up as I entered, he nodded noncommittally and said nothing.

"Are you Harold Kaveolook?"

"Yes."

"The teacher at the school?" A foolish question, I thought to myself, since he was sitting in the middle of a classroom surrounded by the artifacts of his profession.

"Yes."

"My name is Norman. Norman Chance. Do you have time to talk?" "Of course," Kaveolook responded, his hand waving me to a tiny metal chair to which an equally small desk was attached. "What about?"

Squeezing into the chair, I explained that I, too, was a teacher from the "states" and that I wished to learn about the Iñupiat.

"Why is that?"

Behind his quiet reserve I detected a slight concern, but certainly not as much as I was feeling.

"Well, actually, I'm an anthropologist."

"Oh."

"I teach anthropology at the University of Oklahoma, in the southwestern part of the U.S." At this point I had no idea whether he was familiar with either anthropology or the University of Oklahoma—only that I was not responding very satisfactorily to his briefly worded questions.

"Arigaah!" (Good!) To my relief, as Kaveolook spoke, he put both hands

on his desk and leaned forward to emphasize his interest. At the same time his sharply chiseled Iñupiat face broke out in a smile.

"So you're an anthropologist. Do you know that the explorer Stefansson once came along this coast back in the early 1900s?"

"Really."

"While here, he asked a young boy if he wanted to join his expedition, but the boy's mother wouldn't let him go."

"What happened then?"

"Nothing. The person still lives here, on the other side of the village. But what about you? Why are you interested in Kaktovik?"

"I want to spend the summer here. Come to know the people. Learn what impact the new jobs are having on the village."

"I see. What are you going to do with this information when you get it?"

"Several things. I want to go back and teach about life in the Arctic, and if I can, write an article or two."[1]

"Are you going to stay up there?" Kaveolook asked, pointing toward the radar site at the top of the knoll.

"No. I brought a tent and food. Just came in on the plane. I hope to find a place somewhere in the village."

"It might be possible. But you'll have to talk with some of the others about that. Maybe the village council. See what they think."

"Like Rexford or Akootchook?"

"Yes. They're working up near the site, but they will be back later. Right now, we're in the middle of our annual clean-up. In the evening everyone is supposed to come together and rake up the village. Those *taniks* up there (pointing again to the radar site), they really push us to clean up. Let us use their trucks, too. We load 'em up and they drive the trash to the big dump at the end of the sand spit."[2]

After further discussion, I thanked Kaveolook for his help and said I would return in the evening. Walking back toward the hangar and my cache of supplies, I noticed a small military-type, canvas-covered quonset hut that had been vacant for some time. A few hours later, with food, clothing, and sleeping bag properly stowed in the hut, and a little canned food in my stomach, I was ready for whatever the evening might bring.

From my *tanik* perspective, the village did need a good cleaning. Trash uncovered by the melting snow was everywhere— boards, boxes, and paper blown here and there; plastic containers lying on the ground; numerous empty oil drums scattered over the tundra. Far out on the sea ice, a row of fifty-

---

[1] In rereading my 1958 notes before writing this description of the interview with Harold Kaveolook, I was struck by my limited appreciation of a fundamental principle of anthropological field work—reciprocity. While I was quick to explain what I wanted from the summer's field work, I disregarded what I could give in return. Certainly on the mind of Harold Kaveolook and other villagers was the question: "What might we gain from having an anthropologist live with us?" The answer will be forthcoming later in the chapter.

[2] The remark contains some potential humor. Tanik (white person) is derived from the Iñupiaq *tanikhlugo* (to wash). In this instance, given the DEW line personnel's desire to see the village cleaned up, the cultural derivation seemed especially applicable.

Photo 13. The author beside his new summer home. The Arctic Ocean is in the background.

gallon drums filled with human excrement stood upright like pawns on a chessboard, waiting for the warmth of the sun's rays to flush them into the ocean depths. Though it was obvious why local DEW line personnel were pushing trash removal—for health reasons if no other—it was equally clear that the idea was almost entirely of external origin. Clean-up may have become an annual event, but it had to be one of recent vintage.

Returning to the village, I found Harold Kaveolook and several other Kaktovik Iñupiat, among them Herman Rexford and Isaac Akootchook, raking trash and loading trucks. Rexford and Akootchook agreed I could stay in Kaktovik; they even seemed pleased I had come. Together, the four of us selected a tent site half way between Kaveolook's one-room school and Akootchook's new two-story house. The location was ideal. Situated on the edge of a bluff overlooking the Arctic Ocean, it also commanded a view of the village. Looking down on the beach, I watched two young boys playing at the water's edge. The pleasure on my face satisfied my three companions. Tomorrow, Harold said, I should let him know if I needed help putting up my tent.

After being introduced to two of Isaac's brothers, Daniel and George, along with several other villagers, I offered to help with the clean-up. Handed a rake, I joined the clean-up crew in the evening venture. An hour or so later, tired from the excitement of the day, I excused myself and headed back toward my temporary home. Though sleep came quickly, it would be several months before darkness descended on Alaska's North Slope.

SETTLING IN

The Kaktovik village that I came to know in 1958 bore little resemblance to that of ten years earlier when a few small driftwood frame and sod buildings lined the long sand spit of Barter Island's lagoon. After being forced off the spit by the Air Force, the Kaktovik residents constructed an assortment of new homes ranging from one-room huts with a single plastic window or skylight to well-built multiroom dwellings. However, houses of close relatives were built close to one another, often next door—just as they had been centuries before. Poorer houses were not unlike those found in poverty-burdened areas of the "lower 48." Assembled with lumber from packing crates, tar paper, and other products scrounged from government and construction company scrap piles, these structures quickly blunted any idealized vision a visitor might have had of an idyllic Arctic village. On the other hand, those Iñupiat who worked for the DEW line radar station or in local construction jobs were able to purchase durable materials with which to put up their homes, including sawed lumber, grade A plywood, glass windows and thick insulation, much of it ordered from urban centers far to the south. Regardless of size, each building had an attached storage shed where rifles, fish nets, dog harnesses, boots, and other outdoor necessities were kept. Fuel oil to heat these homes was often donated by DEW line personnel or summer construction workers. Otherwise, it had to be ordered from outside or purchased at the local Native store—an expensive proposition. A more self-reliant alternative was to use driftwood while keeping an eye out for contaminated oil drums discarded by the military.

Kaktovik houses were constructed by their owners with the help of extended kin. Due to the cost of preservatives and minimal deterioration of wood in this climate, few of the houses were painted. Entering a typical home, a visitor likely would find several benches or chairs, a table, an oil or wood-burning stove, and two or more beds depending on the size of the family. Wood- or cardboard-insulated walls were used to pin up photographs of friends and relatives, religious drawings, and perhaps a calendar received from a mail-order company. Power for radios, clocks, and similar electrical equipment came from gas generators.

A dramatic reminder of the expanding ties between this isolated village and the outside world was a gravel roadway stretching across the tundra from the sand spit at the island's easternmost edge to its highest knoll a mile or so away. At the apex of this small rise stood the large hemispheric dome and modular buildings of the Barter Island military radar site. Several times a week, following the arrival of a cargo flight, a truck, "snowcat," or similar vehicle hauled food, supplies, and other equipment from the sand spit airstrip to the radar station. South of this road facing the distant Alaska mainland, quonset huts were used by private contractors to house white workers temporarily engaged in summer construction projects. On the other side of the gravel road facing the Arctic Ocean was Kaktovik. Here, streets were non-existent. Houses faced each other at all possible angles, seemingly without

Photo 14. Kaktovik children playing along the roadway.

plan. However, as I was soon to learn, this initial impression was deceptive.

In learning about the people, one of my first tasks was to take a village census. Only then could I begin a study of local kin ties: Who was related to whom? In what way were they related? Where did they live? Were residential locations linked to kinship? For the Iñupiat, I knew their kin ties were bilateral in nature; but except for the names of two or three individuals, that was all I knew. Following the suggestion of the teacher, Harold Kaveolook, I decided to enlist the help of two boys who seemed to enjoy spending part of each afternoon exploring in and about my tent, asking me what was in different boxes, looking over my hunting rifles, books, and other supplies brought in from the "outside." A large candy box, though carefully placed out of sight, was continually in mind, and at least once a day in that first week of field work, it was opened and contents shared—much to the delight of Tommy and Jimmy, my two youthful assistants.

The day we were to begin was typical for June—damp and cloudy. Outside my tent, snow and ice that had covered the village for the past nine months was steadily seeping water into minuscule ponds and ditches dotting the landscape. Not far away, eight sled dogs belonging to one of the Akootchook brothers seemed more vocal than usual in letting others know just how bored and uncomfortable they were, staked out in the melting snow with nothing to do. Inside the tent, after satisfying our afternoon sweet-tooth ritual, I broached the subject of the village census to my two young companions. Would they like to help? I made no mention of remuneration nor did they ask. After questioning me briefly about what I wanted to know and how long it would take, they agreed. I then placed a rough map I had drawn of all the houses in Kaktovik on a stool in front of the cot and we got down to work.

"Who lives in that small house over there by the ditch?" I asked Tommy, pointing to the map.

"Oh, the person who lives there is Philip."

"What is his Eskimo name?"[3]

"Tikluk."

"Does anyone else live there?"

"The person who lives there has a brother, Riley."

"And the house next to Tikluk. Who stays there?"

"That belongs to Ologak. She's their aunt."

Several afternoons later, after attaching names and relationships to each house portrayed on the map, we stepped outside to face a surprisingly bright, warm day, the glare of the sun reflecting against the rapidly disappearing snow. Noticing a number of newly visible wires stretching along the ground from a small shed to two houses, I asked what they were for.

"Oh, they are for Riley and Philip's electric generator."

With my eyes, I followed the wires as they led from the Tikluk house over to that of their aunt, Ologak. Looking elsewhere, similar patterns appeared in the retreating snow linking other houses. Suddenly, the investigation we had been making into Kaktovik's kinship affiliations came into focus. The network of ties laboriously listed in my notebook was now graphically illustrated. Extended kin, clustered in houses close to one another, shared electricity from a common generator. Families without kin had separate units. All it took to recognize this arrangement was a village kinship chart, or a good set of eyes and melting snow.

During those first few days of field work, I extended my contacts into the community, buying food at the Native store, helping with the clean-up, visiting people outside their homes, watching recreational activities including the almost endless evening volleyball games, and in other ways learning what I could about Kaktovik. Still, while actively observing village life, I seemed unable to penetrate the reserve with which I was treated by local adults. The inhabitants were friendly in a distant way, but any response on their part to my initial overtures was simply not forthcoming. Though living in Kaktovik, I was clearly not yet a part of it.

Then, one mid-morning on a Saturday, I opened my tent flap to see Harold Kaveolook painting the local school house. I offered my assistance. Handing me a brush, we began covering decaying plywood with fresh white paint. Having a multitude of questions, I nevertheless held off, concentrating on placing an even flow of paint between brush and wood. Eventually, Harold turned toward me.

"How's the study going?" he asked.

[3] Following usage common in the 1950s–60s, the term Eskimo is used rather than Iñupiaq in all direct quotations.

Photo 15. Harold Kaveolook and young helper cutting wooden sticks for later use in staking out ugruk *skins for drying.*

"Fine, I guess." Caught a bit off guard, I realized the tone of my voice and qualifying phrase suggested otherwise.

"People have been asking about you; what you are doing and why."

"Oh."

"I tell them you are a teacher and that you want to learn about our history."

"Do they say anything else?"

"No, not really. Maybe they are just curious."

"I can understand that. I must be the only *tanik* around who isn't working at the site or in construction."

"In this area, it's easy to live off the land if you know how," Harold said. "People don't have to work if they don't want to. Where you come from you have to get a job in order to live. It's much better here."

Though intrigued by his limiting the term "work" to wage labor, I thought it best to keep the discussion on a broader level and therefore asked him to elaborate.

Putting down his brush and turning toward me, Harold spoke slowly and with obvious pride. "Here, you can always count on people helping you out. It's not like that down south. At least not in Fairbanks."

"In Fairbanks? When did you live there?"

"I was born in Barrow. Joined the Army in 1941 and got out in '45. Spent most of my time at Fort Richardson. Drove big trucks for a while, worked as a clerk, and then did some guard duty. After the war, I went back to Barrow, took a bookkeeping job at Arctic Contractors. Then I was asked if I wanted to be a teacher's aide at the local school and I agreed. I came here in 1951. When you get a long-term position, you can afford to take less pay. But if your job is short, you hold out for as much as you can get."

"Is it that way here, too—people working permanently at the site getting less than those in short-term construction?"

"Herman Rexford and Isaac Akootchook were among the first local people to take construction jobs with the Air Force. They learned to drive heavy equipment—bulldozers, spreaders. Became pretty skilled at it, too. Today, they know more about big equipment than many *taniks* who come here."

"Do they get the same pay?"

"Not anymore."

"How come?"

"At first, Herman was a Cat operator making over a thousand dollars a month. Isaac went into carpentry. Joined the union, too. Every carpenter got the same wage. But now, they only receive laborer's wages of six hundred dollars a month."

"Why is that?"

"They were told it's because Eskimos live here anyway while those from the south have to support their families back home."

"But workers are supposed to get paid for what they do, not where they live."

"Yes, that's true."

"What does the station chief say about it?"

"Maybe you will ask him." The slightly higher inflection of the last two words led me to interpret his statement as either question or conjecture. Selecting the latter, I remained silent.

After painting another hour or so, Harold invited me to his house for lunch—my first invitation to a Kaktovik home. Passing through the small outer shed into an equally small living room, he introduced me to Mae, his wife, and their two young girls. A woman in her early thirties, Mae was dressed in a fur-trimmed, long, cloth parka called an *atigi*, under which she had on a sweater and jeans. Following introductions, she brought in a pot of coffee, two metal cups and plates. Stacked high on the latter was a substantial helping of fried chicken, pork chops, and canned asparagus. Placing the plates on a small bench, she quickly retired to the kitchen to join her children in their own meal. Catching me staring at the food, Harold commented without emotion:

"Not exactly an Eskimo meal. With school and all, I haven't done much hunting. But that will change now that classes are over."

"What do most people eat?"

"Right now, boiled caribou mixed with rice and seal oil, crackers or bread, tea, and perhaps a dish of canned fruit. Or instead of fruit, maybe some fish from the ice cellar. Depends a lot on the time of year and whether one has a job. Last night Mae's brother got a caribou only three miles away, so we should have fresh meat soon. Usually, caribou don't come this close to the village, so he was lucky. We even had a polar bear show up a half-mile from here last winter."

"And?"

"A villager got it. All told, Kaktovik people got six last year. Sold the pelts up at the site for twelve dollars a foot."

Finishing the meal, I thanked Harold for his invitation. In response, he smiled and, gesturing toward the village, said, "We always try to help each other here. That's the Eskimo way."

Later, sitting in my tent writing up field notes of the morning discussion, I remembered advice passed on to me by Max Brewer, the senior official at the Arctic Research Laboratory:

"When you get to Kaktovik, remember one thing. Eskimos express themselves differently than you or I. They aren't as direct about what they say. That means you have to listen carefully if you want to understand what they're telling you. Otherwise, you'll miss a lot."

Looking at my notes, I thought back to several of Harold's comments—the pride that comes from being able to live off the land; the freedom this seemingly provides in choosing how much attention to give to subsistence as opposed to wage work; the emphasis placed on helping one another in Eskimo society; the anger felt by villagers over not being paid according to skill level; the ambiguous reference to the possibility of my speaking with the station chief about it. There was quite a bit to mull over in those few short remarks.

Was there a real choice in seeking or rejecting wage work? What implications did such employment have for social relations? What were the areas of convergence in Native and non-Native interests? Where did they conflict? What were the outcomes? In tackling these questions, one point was clear: Understanding the changes taking place in Kaktovik required knowledge of the island's recent white arrivals as well as its Native inhabitants. Still, I was not ready to grab my notebook and head for the radar station on top of the small knoll a half-mile away. It seemed more important to strengthen my ties with the villagers before venturing into that other world.

SOME LESSONS LEARNED

With the coming of summer, the village took on a new sense of liveliness. Hunters, often in groups of two or three, went out after seal, *ugruk* (large bearded seal), and caribou. Women spent much of their time fishing, butchering, and distributing the game. More local residents moved out of their homes into summer tents. Those holding jobs chose locations close to their winter quarters, while those not so employed set up their tents at nearby fish camps. It was obvious from the amount of meat and fish brought back to the village that a significant amount of the daily intake of food was still derived from local sources. Families and relatives with full-time hunters stored significant amounts of caribou, seal, ptarmigan, and duck in ice cellars dug deep

Photo 16. Women in traditional summer dress.

into the permafrost for winter use. The rest relied more on meat, fish, and canned vegetables obtained from the Native store. Caribou was always the preferred food and seal the least preferred. As far as subsistence was concerned, older hunting and fishing skills seemed well-maintained.

Iñupiat clothing, on the other hand, drew more on commercial outlets. Men typically wore leather or rubber-based shoepacks, wool or corduroy pants and jeans, a sweater or western-style jacket, peaked cap, and fur-trimmed parka. Women generally dressed in a long belted cloth *atigi* sufficiently large to accommodate a child on the back. Under this fur-trimmed cloth parka was worn either a fur lining or sweater and jeans. In winter, as I learned later, both men and women switched to highly efficient caribou or sealskin parkas. Sealskin pants and insulated clothing of commercial manufacture were also used for hunting trips, gathering ice blocks, and other outdoor activities. In addition, most Iñupiat had at least one smartly styled suit or dress that they wore to church or similar village gatherings. Lipstick, make-up, and modern hairstyles seemed especially popular among the adolescents.

Several weeks after my arrival, I noticed that a number of Iñupiat men from Barrow and several other villages had been flown in to work at the site. Some were newcomers while others were returning to an area where they had lived previously. The influx of nonrelatives, however, did not appear large enough to disrupt the close kinship and friendship ties characteristic of most of the village residents.

Contacts between Iñupiat and white workers also appeared amiable, both on the job and in evening recreational activities such as volleyball and horseshoes. A summer construction company employee who had been drinking might stroll over to the community, but the village council policy limiting the admittance of outsiders to approved times kept this potentially disruptive force under control. Those who made friends with the local inhabitants and wished to join in their social, religious, and recreational life were welcomed while those viewed as a possible threat were excluded. Any radar station or construction personnel whose drinking or sexual conduct was seen to cause a problem in the village was either reassigned to another location or fired outright, depending on the severity of the offense.

Thus, the dramatic changes occurring in Kaktovik during this first summer of field work did not seem to affect seriously the internal stability of village life. Games, dances, song fests of both a religious and popular nature, and similar recreational activities continually brought people together for periods of fellowship and relaxation. Well-attended Presbyterian Church services involving as many as 80 percent of the population provided the resident Native lay minister with an excellent opportunity to extol the virtues of Christian living; and the enthusiasm of the congregation, expressed in individual prayer offerings, hymn singing, and "public confessionals," reflected the level of community interest and general support of these religious views. In other day-to-day activities such as helping relatives carry water to the home, hauling a whaleboat up on the beach, or caring for a neighbor's children, face-to-face contact was frequent and for the most part positive.

Of course, one had to be careful in making such summations for Iñupiat cultural behavior places a high value on "getting along with others" and "being even-tempered." When an argument broke out between family members or among friends, a maximum effort would be made to keep the conflict under control. If a resolution was not forthcoming, it was far better to leave than express anger over the matter. Correspondingly, those Iñupiat who stayed cool under such tribulations were invariably held up as models, the villagers making remarks such as, "You never see that person getting mad at anybody." Those few who expressed their anger openly usually did so following an episode of serious drinking. But in Kaktovik at this time, such an event was uncommon.

By the middle of the summer, I had become at least peripherally accepted as a member of the community. An important symbolic event assisting in that process was a July hunting trip taken along the Arctic coast with Harold and several others, the results of which included the taking of my first seal. After

Photo 17. Spearing an ugruk *(a large bearded seal).*

beaching the boat on our return, relatives and friends came down to the shoreline to help drag the animals up the steep bank to the homes of the crew members. Eventually, only one seal remained by the water's edge. Surrounding the animal, the villagers seemed unclear what to do. Finally, Harold glanced at me and in his usual quiet manner asked, "Well, Norman. Where shall we take your seal?"

Until that moment I had not considered the seal to be mine. And I certainly had no idea what to do with it. But recognizing the need for action, I suggested that we "take it to Mae." The response was instantaneous. Showing obvious enthusiasm for the way in which I had resolved the problem, intertwined with a few friendly jokes about my hunting prowess, one Iñupiat attached a rope to the head of the seal and we all hauled it up the bank to the village. Already at work butchering others that Harold had caught, Mae acknowledged the addition with the briefest of smiles thrown in my direction. From then on I became more closely associated with the Kaveolook household—needless to say, an identification that gave me great pleasure. Through the sharing of a seal I had become part of a family and, through that effort, part of the village. A fundamental lesson in reciprocity was learned.

That evening, while enjoying my newly defined status as a "great seal hunter," I looked up Vincent Nageak, the man who had come with me to Kaktovik and who had promised to tell me more of the village's past. Having been an important leader at an earlier time, he knew a good deal about the area. Arriving at his house, I found him sharing stories with several, much younger Iñupiat.

"Do you know about the white man who had no use for Eskimos?" he asked his youthful audience. Responding in the negative, they encouraged him to tell them the story. Hunching forward on his bench, Nageak began.[4]

This white man was at his camp on the knoll when a really big storm came up. He went to fetch his cook who was just a ways down the road. He couldn't believe the weather would do him any harm. You see, this big leader, an important head, the one who had acquired the name "general"—just when our weather had become such that nothing could oppose and overcome it— "He didn't want the cook down there to be hungry," he said.

But when he didn't come home quickly they (*taniks*) sounded the alarm which is to be sounded when needed. But we ourselves did not hear it. We who were in the house. We found that Harold Kaveolook, the teacher, had quickly inquired about it when he heard it.

"Our head man has become lost," he said he heard. The head man from that camp out east over there.

We went up there after putting on our whites (clothes) and belts, grabbing hold of some snow knives and saws. As soon as we entered, they all started staring at us.

"Our head man has become lost," they said. The head man of that camp over there on the knoll. "He hasn't gone far off. He's probably just in front of the siren sounding area," they said. "Just a short ways beyond the houses."

When they told us this we left to find him, all walking next to each other in a straight line, calling out to each other; although the southwest wind was fiercely strong; although we could not see each other even this close. We (still) set out to find him, using only our voices. We moved along, we moved along, using our voices. We moved along like that until eventually, a voice began coming from that direction down there (pointing).

"Over here," they said. The middle ones had come upon someone. I quickly started over there. I quickly began following the voices which were making continual sounds. When I reached the place, there was their vehicle, the two people's vehicle. When I peered at my companions there was no way one could make out their faces. Each person was completely white. Looking at the head man, he was just moving his arms, not making a sound. He was already affected by his ordeal.

---

[4] This story was described in greater detail at an Elders Conference held in Barrow in 1978 (Kisautaq–Leona Okakok 1978:440–445). The transcription of that conference, including a literal translation of the story from Iñupiaq into English, offers insight into Iñupiat forms of expression as well as providing valuable information on traditional cultural life and history as seen through the eyes of the older residents.

It was already as if he were crazy, this big, important head man; the one who had already voiced his opinion that if there were no Eskimos in these camps it would be okay.

After staring at him intensively for a few seconds, after telling him, "We are looking for you," calling him by name, he did not respond. I (then) took off my belt quickly and turned my face toward him. He finally said something.

"Oh. I see that you are all Eskimos," he said.

"Yeah, we are all Eskimos," I said as we shook off the snow covering our faces. "We are looking for you, you are lost."

"I am going to freeze," he said.

"Ah, you baby." I quickly went there and grabbed his arm and pulled him. We took hold of the other man, getting him down off of there, and proceeded to hold him by the hand. I was about to hold on to his hand when this Isaac, the one you know, said, "Don't hold on to his hand. Let his disbelieving, daring nature take him along!"

The man began to reel while walking. He was completely wet, all of him. And he was also without one of his boots. We made him walk, shoving him along once in a while. We arrived at the doorway with him. As soon as we arrived, when we had him climb up those steps, he said, "Where are we?"

"Quit making sounds. Keep your mouth shut!" I said to him. I scolded him. "You can talk after a little while. Keep your mouth shut."

He stared intensively at me for a few minutes because I was shoving him along, and when we pushed him in, both of them, we all went in, too. Those next to him took off their coats and taking hold of him, took him off to another room, to a dining table. When we reached that table, they gave him food . . . because you see, he had not eaten. It was sometime around nine o'clock.

After looking intensely for a brief time at these Eskimos who were seated there, he said, "I am not going to eat before these Eskimos here have had something to eat."

"We are going to eat along with you."

"But his clothes," I told the rest of the group there. "Quickly change his clothes, even right there. He might get sick from those clothes." Speaking English, I said this to them. They quickly changed his clothes, toweling him dry, both of them. And then they had him sit down. He was not going to start eating, wanting the Eskimos to eat first. We then began eating.

After we finished he finally said, "I know I would not have been able to last out the night. I realize that I never would have been able to last the night if there were no Eskimos."

As soon as he had said that, the other one said to him, "Remember that you said that Eskimos are of no use whatsoever."

"I have come to realize that only the Eskimos know this, their weather. And I, myself, do not know it all," he said.[5]

And so we told him, "This is the very reason that those who came before you placed two Eskimos at each camp. Because the white man could always get lost, these Eskimos would be of some use to them. Even at this camp, although they might reach their door, they would not know where it is. I think the Eskimos have

---

[5] During the telling of the story at the 1978 Elders Conference, an Iñupiat in the audience shouted, "He may know it (but only) when the sun is shining!"

Photo 18. The Barter Island DEW line radar station.

already helped three people who have become lost like that. Making them stand up, making them go in right there at their door. We see that you are one of those kind," I said to him right there.

"I now realize that every one of those camps should have some Eskimos in them," he said.

Winding up his story, Vincent Nageak looked at the rapt circle of people around him and concluded, "From that point on he constantly told me to keep talking about the weather and the sky—even to those who have no use for Eskimos!"

After hearing Nageak's story and seeing the attention it had received from his youthful audience, I knew it was time to visit the radar site. Tensions lying just below the surface of Iñupiat-white relations now seemed more substantial. The next morning I put on fresh khaki pants and shirt, gave myself a shave, and headed for the building next to the futuristic radar screen standing high on the knoll a half-mile away.

A SENSE OF HISTORY

Though formally designated a military installation, many of the logistic, maintenance, and construction tasks of the radar site were contracted out to private corporations. The sector superintendent in charge of all the sites between Demarcation Point and Barrow was a long-term employee of one of these companies, a person with considerable experience in the Arctic. Having been given his name before leaving Barrow, I at least knew whom to ask for on my arrival. Opening the thick metal door of the modular building, I was met by a civilian clerk who ushered me into a small office at the end of a long, narrow corridor. There, in a small cubicle surrounded by files and other symbols of his status, sat a short, dark-haired man in his late 40s. He offered me a seat.

"Several people have already told me you were living down in the village," he said. "I also got a message from the Arctic Research Laboratory. How is the research progressing?"

The manner in which he asked the question encouraged a pro forma response.

"Fine. But I'm just settling in so I have mostly questions at this point."

"What can I do for you?"

"I'd like to get a better understanding of the kind of work villagers do at the site and what your experience with them has been."

"I see. Well, they do lots of things, maintenance, mostly; although some of the men run heavy equipment and repair machinery, both here and at the smaller stations. It's a six-day work week beginning at 7:30 in the morning. All permanently employed Eskimos work on rotation. They spend six weeks at the main site and then six weeks at a smaller one down the coast a ways. Right now, we badly need eight more Eskimos and will probably have to go to the Barrow village to get them."

"Sounds like there's a quota."

"No, not exactly. But hiring local people keeps the labor costs down. Since there is no union and the Eskimos live here, they don't have to be paid as much. Getting people from outside to come to the Arctic is expensive. You have to offer all kinds of inducements—high wages, bonuses, benefits—and that costs money. The ones who sign on often have families down south to support. Or they want a nest egg, pay off mortgages, something like that."

"But why are local people paid less if they do the same work?"

"Do you know what Eskimos get in Canada for working on the DEW line? Two hundred a month. We give them three times that amount. By comparison, the people here are making out really well. Sometimes I think we do too much for the Eskimos. Eventually, they become unappreciative."

"Why go to Barrow to find them?"

"Some people here don't want to work a six-day week. Others can't because of health problems. Most are in good shape, but anyone with a history of tuberculosis is automatically turned down. Before an Eskimo is hired, he is given a complete medical exam and x-ray at Barrow. Some of these people have spent considerable time in a sanatorium down south. They are not exactly happy when they hear that due to their previous health problems, they are excluded from working here. But that's a firm company policy without exceptions."

"What about women?"

"Women? No women have ever been hired at any DEW line site, Native or otherwise. Strictly a man's world up here. Got enough problems as it is."

"Do any involve local people?"

"Sure. The worst one is that some Eskimos just up and quit whenever they feel like it. From our standpoint, it's difficult to count on them for steady employment over long periods of time. We have, for example, an excellent mechanic, an Eskimo boy who lives down in the village. About two weeks ago, he just took off and went hunting. He didn't say anything to us about it. He just left. I know they look at the world differently than we do, but if they want to work here they are going to have to learn to be responsible."

"Perhaps they have responsibilities at home."

"Could be. But that's no excuse for just taking off. If they want to work, they have to follow the same rules as everyone else. Imagine the kinds of requests I'd get from the other workers if I let Eskimos take off and go hunting whenever they want to. Like I said, sometimes they are unappreciative. Even take advantage of us."

"Really? What's an example?"

"There are lots of them. Take food, water, or fuel oil. Instead of throwing away excess food, our cooks used to pass it on to the villagers. But after a while they just came to expect it. Or water. In the old days, the people here had to take a dog sled out to a fresh-water lake, chop up blocks of ice and bring them back to the village. When the Air Force came, they let them use a weasel tractor to haul ice. But that didn't work out too well so they decided to get the water themselves, put it in fifty-gallon drums, and place them along the road. Each family had its own drum. Now they simply go over to one of the quonsets at the construction camp, turn on a faucet and get their water— hot or cold."

"And oil?"

"It's company policy not to supply heating oil to the village, but we don't care if they use abandoned and dirty oil. The other day, several of the men at the construction camp rounded up fifty-seven barrels of oil and took them down to the village. Some had dirt and water in them. They filled nearly empty drums with oil that had lain around the supply depot for some time. They aren't supposed to do this on company time, but they went ahead anyway. Put the drums on a truck, drove them down to the village, and left them for the Eskimos to use. Other times, I've seen new oil drums sitting next to the houses of men working here. After while, they come to expect these things."

"I expect they see it differently. It is, after all, their land."

"Not really. Of course, they can use any land that is not needed by the military. But they don't control it."

"Who does?"

"The Air Force."

Trying to reduce the growing adversarial nature of the discussion, I shifted my questioning to another topic.

"What about alcohol use here at the site?"

"To my knowledge, there is no problem either here or in the village. Very little hard liquor is brought in although beer flows fairly freely. All the men at the site have a quota of a "six-pack" a week. Occasionally, Eskimos will take advantage of this opportunity, but they can't do much damage on six cans of beer. As for the village itself, the local council determines whether liquor is allowed. But I know of no instance when it has been. I'm sure bottles are flown in on the mail plane once in a while. Some of it comes here and some goes to Kaktovik. But it isn't at all common.

"I did have one problem a while back. A village leader came up to our storekeeper and asked that the beer ration for Eskimos be withheld. Without contacting me, he went ahead and stopped selling them beer. In a very short time, tensions began to rise. One guy in particular, one of our best Eskimo workers, got very angry thinking he was being discriminated against. He was on the verge of quitting and yet he wouldn't tell me or the storekeeper what was bothering him. As soon as I learned what had happened, I called in the local leader and told him under no circumstances were we going to refuse beer rations to any worker at the site, Eskimo or white. He didn't get angry, though. Just accepted the situation and went away."

"How well do the people work together—those in the village and whites from outside?"

"Quite well, really. Life is hard up here, especially in winter. The Eskimos often know more about the weather than we do—what to expect, how to take care of themselves in a snow storm, that kind of thing. You have to respect them for that. We have really bad storms up here with lots of wind. Once, several years ago, a local superintendent got lost in one of those storms. Would have frozen to death if the Eskimos hadn't found him. They are also good workers, especially when they think what they're doing is important. It's just that they always want time off to hunt. That's the big problem."

"I guess they are trying to keep their options open. Hunting has to be their major form of security—that and sharing," I responded, thinking back on the discussion with Harold Kaveolook several weeks previously.

"That may be, but I don't think the emphasis on sharing will last much longer," the sector superintendent said. "A doctor at the Barrow hospital told me recently that Eskimos making high wages over there are plagued by relatives looking for handouts. An uncle or cousin will come around and expect to receive food, clothing, even money, and other things from any family that is bringing in the bucks. Some are even sponging off their relatives right here at Barter Island."

At that point the superintendent indicated he had work to do and would have to excuse himself.

"If you need anything, just let me know. We show movies most week nights. We often loan them to the people in the village, too. So you can watch either place. And feel free to use our camp facilities if you wish. You'll want to shower once in a while living down there in Kaktovik."

Later that morning, sitting in my tent with the comments of the sector superintendent ringing in my ears, I tried to summarize the two pictures of Arctic life that had been presented to me over the summer. One emphasized the intimate relationship with the land and the importance of sharing among its Native inhabitants. In the other, the land and its people were simply a means to the end of winning the Cold War. The former stressed ecological knowledge and cooperation; the latter, political power and competition. I jotted down questions I thought needed further exploration. Some dealt with the impact of technology on Iñupiat culture and identity. Others concerned issues of local political autonomy and economic self-reliance. Still others focused on American Arctic policy and how it related to the Iñupiat. As a world power, the United States was basically interested in developing its natural resources and expanding its military strength.

Still, looking over my questions, I felt dissatisfied. Something was missing. Eventually I realized what it was. In not a single instance had I made any reference to history. If I really wanted to grasp the significance of changes in Arctic Alaska, I had to examine the interlinkages between what was occurring in the present and what had transpired in the past. Only then could I begin to understand what was going on now and perhaps even project a little into the future. I promised myself that on returning to the States, I would dig more deeply into the literature on Iñupiat history and early Euro-American contact.

Several days later, tired from the pressures of field work and knowing I would be leaving shortly, I decided to take the day off. Packing a small lunch, I struck out west with the prevailing wind, following along the shoreline of the Arctic Ocean. The village quickly slipped into the background. After four or five miles, Tom Gordon's old abandoned warehouse came into view. Tilted precariously at the edge of a high bluff a few feet from the sea below, it looked like it could topple at any moment, forever stilling visual reminders of the 1930s when Gordon traded commercial goods and foods for furs along this part of the coast. A few miles farther on, standing at the edge of a long sand spit, I stopped to gaze at the foundations of several ancient Iñupiat sod houses, their base logs almost completely covered by sand. Stepping inside the entryway, I bent down, and after running my hand through the sand several times, turned up a cracked wooden bowl partially held together by sinew, along with the rim of a birch bark basket—all that was left of what no doubt had been a trade item obtained from Athabascan Indians.

Continuing another mile or so out to the end of the sand spit my pace slowed and finally stopped. In front of me was the Arctic Ocean. Behind me lay a tiny thread of sand. Listening carefully, I heard the waves gently lapping against the curving line of beach. Somewhere far to the north a large unbroken mass of ice stretched endlessly out to sea, engaged in a continuing struggle with the sun over the distribution of its frozen cargo. To the south, thirty or so miles away, the snow-capped peaks of the Brooks Range rose sharply toward the pale blue sky. It seemed as though I had stepped through history into another world untouched by human endeavor. The landscape, constant, enduring, permanent, showed no sign of being either friendly or unfriendly. It was simply there, silent and still.

Turning around, I became aware of a slight easterly breeze pulling gently at the hood of my parka. Many millennia ago, peoples out of Asia walked

Photo 19. Land's end along the Arctic coast.

this way on their long journey to Canada and Greenland. They saw the same mountains rising in the sky, watched the same sea carving its imprint on the shore, and felt the same easterly wind brush against their faces. Of their human traces, little remains. Nevertheless, standing quietly along the Arctic shore, I felt a bond with those earlier travelers to this new world.

4/Social Life

It was late summer of 1961, a little more than three years after my first trip to Alaska's North Slope. Vincent Nageak and I were standing on an embankment several hundred yards from Kaktovik village overlooking the Beaufort Sea. The location was a favorite lookout for Iñupiat women whose husbands were out seal hunting. But today we were alone. Cold and foggy, the day was typical for September. As we pulled our parka hoods up over our heads and sat down on a small knoll, it hardly seemed possible that three years had passed since our first meeting. During that time, we had come to know each other quite well. I watched closely as Vincent took careful aim with his boot and kicked a small stone over the edge of the cliff toward the sea below.

"I am leaving soon," I remarked, stating the obvious. My bags and equipment had been packed for two days waiting for a break in the weather so a plane could pick me up. Perhaps today would mark my departure.

"Maybe you won't be back." The slightly higher inflection placed on the last word led me to wonder whether he was asking a question or making a statement of fact.

"I'll be back, but I don't know when."

"Many *taniks* come here. They stay for a little while, and then go home. We get a few letters and a Christmas card or two. Then we don't hear from them anymore. Maybe you are just like the others."

I waited for the reassuring phrase.

"I jokes," he said laughingly and gave me a slight jolt with his shoulder. "But I might not be here when you get back."

"Things will be different, I guess."

"They are different now," he said.

I searched for the right words to ask the obvious question.

"Do you miss the old days, Vincent?"

As usual, he answered by telling a story.

Ten years ago, Apik and I went on a trip to hunt caribou. A day's ride from here a big storm came up. We knew it was going to be a bad one and I pointed my lead dog toward an old abandoned house. Just then, Apik saw a caribou. We stopped and he killed it, but then it was too late to get to the house. The snow came down so thick we couldn't see anything. We had to make a snowhouse in the bank. We had meat, a small stove, and tea, that's all. It was all right for a day or two, but the storm was so bad we could only get a little way toward home before the wind came up and we had to stop again. Pretty soon we run out of fuel. We jump up and down and run around in our little house to keep warm. We think we never get back to our home. But we went on. Next day we made it. Apik, he never liked to hunt after that. He works in Barrow now. But I don't think that old way is so bad. Anyway, people around here, they don't hunt so much anymore. The young ones, they don't even know how.

While listening to Vincent, I glanced down at the beach and saw Isaac Akootchook and Mary, his wife, gather their rifles and gear, put them in their boat, and push off toward the lagoon. Noticing us on the bank, Isaac waved a greeting and then turned back to adjust his outboard motor.

"That Akootchook, he always hunt when he can. His wife's a good shooter, too. He's Iñupiaq, a real Eskimo."

Though having several questions I wanted to ask, I seemed unable to phrase them clearly. I felt Vincent slipping away, the distance between us growing each minute we sat there. He seemed to feel it, too. In keeping with traditional Iñupiat leave-taking, he stood up, smiled briefly, and headed for his sister's house without a word.

Looking out toward the sea, I thought back over the past several years and what I had learned from the Iñupiat. On my return home, I knew I would be writing about life in the North Slope villages that I had come to know. Could I fully describe the changes then taking place in Kaktovik? Not really. Such a portrayal could hardly be undertaken by an outsider. Still, it was important to try for the world that Vincent Nageak, the Akootchooks, Harold Kaveolook, and others knew firsthand was rapidly slipping away and would not appear again. Indeed, for those like Apik, it was already gone. And for their children, it would not even be known.

MAKING A LIVING

In Arctic Alaska, barren land and severe climate have always tested the Iñupiat ingenuity and skill at making a living. Even recent migrants to the far north, whose advanced technology has enabled them to erect an artificial environment in which they can spend most of their time, are only partially insulated from the external world around them. As we learned from Nageak's story about "the white man who had no use for Eskimos," these newcomers often relied so heavily on their artificially constructed surroundings that when their technology failed them, they were unable to cope with changing Arctic conditions.

For most of their history, the Iñupiat had considerably less control over their environment and thus were more dependent on it. Increased opportunities for wage labor in the 1950s and '60s were far from common in most northern villages. Thus, many men and women continued to spend much of their lives engaged in traditional pursuits associated with subsistence hunting and fishing. Since these activities were seasonal, the subsistence cycle of the

Iñupiat was much like that of earlier times. The aboriginal calendar illustrates the significance of the changing seasons for Iñupiat economic and social life:

IÑUPIAT ABORIGINAL CALENDAR[1]

January—*siqinyasaq tatqiq*	"moon of the returning sun"
February—*izrasugruk tatqiq*	"coldest moon"
March—*paniqsiqsiivik tatqiq*	"moon for bleaching skins"
April—*Agaviksiuvik tatqiq*	"moon for beginning whaling"
May—*suvluravik tatqiq*	"moon when rivers flow"
June—*irniivik tatqiq*	"moon when animals give birth"
July—*inyukuksaivik tatqiq*	"moon when birds raise their young"
August—*aqavirvik tatqiq*	"moon when birds molt"
September—*tingiivik tatqiq*	"moon when birds fly south"
October—*nuliavik tatqiq*	"moon when caribou rut"
November—*nippivik tatqiq*	"moon of the setting sun"
December—*siqinrilaq tatqiq*	"moon with no sun"

Spring marked the beginning of the whaling season for the whaling communities of Point Hope, Icy Cape, Wainwright, and Barrow. (Being farther to the east, the Kaktovik season began later.) In April and May, village boat crews encamped on the edge of the sea ice to hunt the migrating bowhead. When a bowhead was caught, all available community members gathered to help with the butchering. The meat was then distributed to relatives, friends of the crew, and other villagers according to certain rules. If the season was unsuccessful, smaller game such as seal, ugruk, duck, and ptarmigan were more actively sought.

In June and July when the ice broke up, attention shifted to walrus and seal, which were pursued in a powerboat or skin-covered umiaq. During the summer, seal, caribou, and fish provided supplemental sources of food. Immediately after freeze-up in the fall, the villagers actively prepared for winter storms and darkness. At Wainwright, Meade River, and several other locations along the Arctic Slope, veins of coal were mined and sacked for winter fuel. If coal was unavailable and lack of cash limited the purchase of fuel oil, driftwood was gathered and stored. This was also the time for repairing houses and storing fresh-water ice in underground cellars for eventual use as cooking and drinking water.

Winter introduced the trapping season which lasted to the middle of March. In the 1950s and early'60s, trapping was of minor importance due to the low price of furs. Polar bear pelts were more valued, bringing as much as $12 or more a foot. During this period, fish were netted in river inlets and seals hunted at their breathing holes. In maximum darkness or during severe storms, stored meat and canned goods were the prime source of food.

In 1961, an older Barrow Iñupiat described this most difficult of seasons:

[1] This calendar is used by the people of Wainwright (see: Milan 1958 and Nelson 1980). Other North Slope villages such as Kaktovik used slightly different ones taking into account seasonal variations in the separate locations. Actually, this modern twelve-month calendar is itself a modification of a traditional one. The latter did not have a twelve-month division but it was considerably more complex.

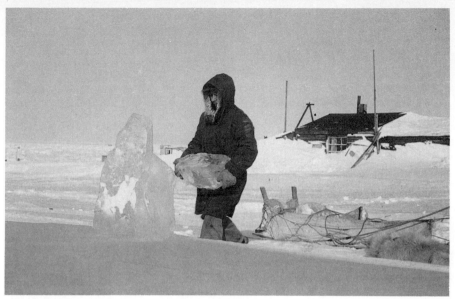

Photo 20. Storing fresh water ice for later consumption.

These are the baddest months, maybe, for the Eskimo. That is when the animals are the hardest to find. These are the coldest days, too. We hunt mostly along the coast, hunt seal. We also hunt polar bear once in a while. We hunt seal when there are leads in the ice at their breathing holes. One way is to sit and wait at a hole for them to come by. It is very hard to do this for long periods. Once I had to wait for four hours.

One of the first times I went out hunting, I saw a really large seal put his head up to the hole in the ice to breathe. And I very much wanted to get that seal, so I wait and I wait and I wait for him to come up again. Smaller seals were coming up but not that large one. They would poke their noses in the hole and I let them breathe. Finally, someone shouted that the ice was breaking at this spot and trying to float me out to sea. So I got up and started to run. I finally reached the shore ice but I never got the seal. When I got home, I talked with my old dad and told him I saw a really big seal at the seal hole, and that I saw smaller ones there, too, and did not take them. I let them breathe. Gee, but my father scolded me. He said, "You went out there to hunt. That's no way to hunt. You are to get all the seals when they are close to you. After that mistake, you won't find any seals in the holes."

Of all the subsistence activities, whaling is certainly the most dramatic. For years, this endeavor has given major support to the Iñupiat's image of themselves as a courageous and daring people—and with good reason. Hunting this largest of mammals in a partially frozen sea is impressive enough with today's efficient technology. Before the innovation of whale bombs and darting guns, it was even more so.

Originally, the harpoon and lance were the essential tools. Attached to the harpoon were two or three inflated sealskin pokes, each with a bouyancy of 200 to 500 pounds. A rawhide line connected the floats to the harpoon head. When a whale was sighted the boat crew launched the umiaq and approached the animal in such a way that the bow of the boat could be placed on its back, or at least close enough for the harpooner to sink one or more of his toggle-headed harpoons into the thick skin. Attached to each harpoon were floats that other crew members quickly cast over the side. The purpose of these floats was not only to indicate the location of the whale, but also to slow it down during its attempts to sound or swim away. Once the whale had become exhausted, the crew could safely approach and the lancer begin his work. The aboriginal lance was ten to twelve feet long and tipped with a razor-sharp flint blade. To prevent the whale from sounding, the lancer severed the tendons controlling the whale's flukes and then probed deeply into its vital organs. As the wounded animal went into its death flurry, the crew retreated to a safe distance. The dead whale was then hauled onto the sea ice and butchered by the local village members.

With the arrival of commercial whalers to the north Alaskan coast, the darting gun soon replaced the harpoon. Its particular advantage was that it carried a small explosive charge which, if well placed, could kill outright or at least do enough damage to make unnecessary the long and dangerous chase. The shoulder gun, introduced at the same time, replaced the lance, for it was highly efficient in ensuring a quick kill. During the height of the commercial whaling activity, the cost of these weapons and ammunition was of little concern since the baleen from a single whale might bring as much as $10,000. After the collapse of the baleen market in the early 1900s, the Iñupiat still relied on the whale for subsistence needs; but the cost of guns, ammunition, and other supplies effectively limited the number of boat crews that could afford to hunt. Since the Iñupiat had little interest in returning to their earlier techniques, the number of boats used in hunting the whale was governed by a potential crew captain's ability to raise the $300 to $400 necessary for outfitting.

In the early 1960s, whale hunting continued to be an essential subsistence activity. Each spring, villages along the coast could count on the participation of several boat crews. In Barrow, there were even more. A usual crew was composed of an *umialik*, the boat captain, a "shoulder-gun man," a harpooner or "striker," and three or more paddlers, although the umialik sometimes fulfilled one of these latter roles as well. Crews were usually composed of extended kin, although in recent years this pattern has become increasingly flexible. During the hunt, crews maintained fairly close contact, and once a whale was sighted and captured, others nearby assisted in towing it to the edge of the ice. Village members then stripped the blubber, following which the meat was divided equally according to custom, with one portion going to the successful crew, another to the assisting crews, and the third to the village "helpers."

In earlier years, an important set of magical practices and taboos were associated with whale hunting. Members of the crew carried amulets; they abstained from cooking in the ice camp; and the shaman performed drumming

Photo 21. A whale's size is truly impressive.

rites. Later, these practices were replaced by Christian prayers that were offered in church at the beginning of the whaling season, and after a whale had been sighted and harpooned.

Other traditional customs associated with whaling have continued. In the 1950s, a preliminary feast for the crew and their families was often held at the umialik's home. At the conclusion of this event, when the crew members were departing for their camps on the edge of the coastal ice, candy was offered to the children. During the six-week whaling season that followed, all the needs of the crew, including food, cigarettes, and ammunition, were supplied by the umialik. Then, as previously, only those men who had a sufficient cash income to purchase the required supplies could claim the status of whaling captain.[2]

Following the whaling season, the Iñupiat turned their attention to hunting walrus and seal. In June and July these sea mammals could be found on ice floes directly in front of coastal villages from Point Hope to Barrow. Walrus herds were hunted in boat crews in much the same way as the whale. However, they rarely were found at Kaktovik due to the village's eastern location far removed from their regular migration path.

Though providing less meat and carrying less prestige than the whale or walrus, seal hunting has always been an important subsistence staple. Fluc-

[2] In the 1970s, easier access to a cash income enabled well-to-do villagers with few skills to sponsor whaling crews. Furthermore, hunting technology had improved so dramatically that even minimally trained crews could on occasion get one of these creatures, a condition often resulting in a whale being wounded without being captured. However, since the early 1980s, quality control in hunting has improved considerably.

Photo 22. Villagers butchering a large whale.

tuations in whale and walrus populations along the northwest Alaskan coast were a continual source of concern. Seals, on the other hand, provided many of the same products as the former and were present throughout much of the year.

This dependence on the seal was reflected in the highly developed aboriginal techniques of hunting it. As described by the old Barrow Iñupiat, during winter when the sea was completely frozen over, seals maintained a series of breathing holes through the ice covering an area of several acres. A hunter stationed himself near one of these holes and with great patience, waited until the seal surfaced. His harpoon was devised so that the head could be detached from the valuable shaft. On sighting a seal, he thrust the harpoon down through the narrow opening at the surface of the ice and into the seal's neck or head. As the animal pulled away, the shaft worked loose from the ivory head. Then, laying the shaft aside, the hunter took hold of the line attached to the harpoon head and pulled the seal to the surface where it was then killed.

During the late spring and summer when seals lay on top of the ice, surface stalking was undertaken. At this time, the Iñupiat ranged over a wide territory, frequently obtaining large numbers of seal in a short period. Prior to the use of the rifle, a throwing (rather than a thrusting) harpoon was used. But since its effective range was seldom more than twenty-five feet, great skill was needed in stalking. A hunter could approach to within 300 yards of the seal without taking special precautions. Still, he might wear light clothing to camouflage himself against the ice and cloud background; or he might wear dark clothing and try to imitate another seal by moving closer at a slower

Photo 23. The results of a successful Dall sheep hunting trip to the Brooks Range by Kaktovik Iñupiat in the early 1960s.

pace. By mimicking the animal's movements and timing his advance with the seal's short "naps," a capable hunter could approach to within a few feet.

Due to the time-consuming nature of these aboriginal techniques, the harpoon was replaced by a rifle whenever possible. Not only did it kill the seal more quickly, but the animal did not seem to be apprehensive at the crack of a rifle shot. Thus, the hunter could take several seal from the same location. One drawback, however, was that the rifle did not allow the seal to be easily retrieved.

On land, caribou was the most significant animal regularly hunted, although Dall mountain sheep were also highly valued. For centuries caribou provided a variety of food, sinew for sewing, antlers for making implements, and skins for clothing, tents, and bedding. Meat and skin were the most important of these items, with the latter still serving as crucial material for clothing.

In the summer, caribou were hunted near the coast where they were most easily accessible. In the fall, small groups of hunters traveled inland searching for small herds migrating back toward the interior mountains. Following a successful hunt, the meat was distributed by the women among the families of the hunters. Eaten throughout the year, caribou meat was a major nutrient in the Iñupiat diet. A full-time hunter with a family of five obtained an average of twenty-four caribou each year. In Wainwright, for example, Milan (1958:28) found that in the mid-1950s the average village-wide kill totaled 800 caribou a year.

Fish were another important food staple. In winter, they were caught through a hole in the ice with a line and lures made of ivory or metal. However, fishing was a much more important activity in summer and early fall. Iñupiat families not engaged in wage labor left their villages for fish camps along the coast or inland, setting their nets at the mouth of a stream or river. In a successful season, as many as fifty to seventy-five whitefish or other species were netted in a single day. Any fish not eaten at the time were dried and stored or frozen in ice cellars for use in winter.

This yearly cycle of Iñupiat subsistence activities continued into the 1960s. To the extent that village residents relied on hunting and fishing for much of their livelihood, the cooperative effort necessary for success in this activity served as a major form of community solidarity. As the desire, opportunity, and need to engage in wage labor became predominant, this integrative feature of village life was proportionately threatened. An ingenious way of resolving, at least temporarily, this dilemma was followed by Point Hope men who sought summer work in Fairbanks and other urban locations just long enough to qualify for unemployment compensation, at which point they would quit and go back to the village to hunt (VanStone 1960).[3]

GROWING UP

In the two decades following World War II, children continued to be a dominant feature of north Alaskan village life. An Iñupiat child was considered a vital part of the family and enjoyed much love and affection from both parents. Fathers seemed gentler and more demonstrative than those farther to the south. Families, most ranging in size from seven to twelve, were also much larger than in previous generations, due in large part to the more sedentary lifestyle and the lowered infant mortality rate brought on by improved health care services. Obviously, few parents had knowledge of ways to effectively limit the number of offspring. No strong preference was expressed for one sex as opposed to the other. Some families hoped the first-born would be a girl who could assist in caring for those who followed. Others wanted a boy because he could eventually be of assistance in hunting. A baby of either sex was welcomed on arrival with great affection.

Occasionally a family had more children than it could support. When this occurred, the infant was "offered" to another family that had fewer than it desired, or perhaps to grandparents. This form of adoption has a long history and is still prevalent today. A child also was adopted because the adoptive parents were childless, the parents had died, the biological parents were close friends with the adoptive parents, or because the child was illegitimate and could be given a better upbringing in a home with a father. Illegitimacy itself,

[3] A more detailed analysis of the impact of wage labor on the North Slope Iñupiat will be seen in later chapters.

however, carried none of the stigma characteristic of middle-class American society.[4]

Adoption was usually, though not necessarily, arranged between kin. An adopted child always used the terms "father" and "mother" for her or his foster parents even when closely related to them. The child's origin was never concealed and in many instances it was considered as belonging to both families. The child might even call the two sets of parents by the same terms and maintain as strong a bond with the biological parents and siblings as with the adoptive family. Whatever the reasons for adoption, parents treated the new child with as much warmth and affection as they did their own.

In earlier times numerous taboos relating to pregnancy had to be followed lest harm befall the mother, child, or both. For instance, a pregnant woman who walked backward out of a house could have a breech delivery; putting a pot over her head could cause extreme difficulty in delivering the placenta; sleeping at odd hours might give her a lazy child. Births also took place in a special parturition lodge, known as the *aanigutyak*. In winter, the husband built a snow house for this purpose, and the woman entered it as soon as she began labor. She gave birth in a kneeling position with the help of an assistant, usually a female relative with some experience in delivering babies.

By the 1950s and '60s, women without access to the public health hospital at Barrow had their children at home helped by specially trained midwives of which there were six at Point Hope. At Wainwright and Kaktovik, mothers were more likely to go to the Barrow hospital for their delivery. Still, numerous stories were told of the hardiness of Iñupiat women giving birth under difficult circumstances. VanStone (1962:79), for example, wrote of a woman traveling by small boat to Point Hope who asked to be put ashore "to go to the toilet." She gave birth after the craft had moved on without her, cutting the cord and scraping sand over the afterbirth. Then, putting the child in her parka, she ran along the beach to catch up with the boat.

By the time a child was a month old, it was customarily baptized by a missionary and given a name. Every child received an English and at least one Iñupiat name. Chosen by parents, they were almost always those of recently deceased relatives or highly respected individuals. When English names were introduced early in the twentieth century, Iñupiat ones often became family names. According to custom, the name given the child carried with it the qualities of the individual from whom it was taken. When an elderly living person's name was used, the person would give the child gifts. This action was prompted by the belief that after the older person's death, the donor's spirit would survive in the namesake.[5]

---

[4] An Iñupiat elder once told Ernest Burch that the fundamental stupidity of whites could be proven by two facts: First, they have to look at their watch to find out whether they are hungry; and second, they use the concept of "fatherless child" as though there really could be such a thing!

[5] Although sensitive to the skeptical attitudes of whites, many Iñupiat still carry on at least a vestige of this concept. Thus, on entering a house after playing outside, a child named after a maternal grandmother might be addressed, with a hint of amusement, by the mother or her sister, "Hello, grandmother!"

When the baby was two or three months old, the mother passed on some of the responsibility for its care to grandmothers, older siblings, and unmarried sisters and cousins. In these circumstances, a child soon became accustomed to having a variety of tenders, a pattern that continued until it could care for itself. Commonly, the baby was carried in the back of a parka by the mother or other female relative. If the mother was busy and no one else was available to carry it, she might put the child in a crib to play or sleep. If it cried, she would pick it up and play with it for several minutes. A few women, especially those strongly inculcated with middle-class American values, might complain that the baby wanted to be held "too much" and was "spoiled." Seldom, however, would any Iñupiat mother disregard her child's cries.

When outside, the mother customarily carried her baby until it was two years old or until another child was born. Strapped in place by a belt that went around the mother's waist and under the child's buttocks, it had little freedom of movement. Still, by the age of two, it had been given sufficient opportunity to move around that it was able to walk quite well. Sometimes a child older than two asked to be carried, and although the mother might fulfill the child's wish, siblings and friends were likely to discourage such requests through good-natured teasing.

The Iñupiat infant rarely had a set feeding or sleeping time, which was hardly surprising considering the similar lack of schedule of most adults. When the baby cried it was fed, whether by breast or bottle. Following World War II, bottle feeding was encouraged for those adults with sufficient cash income to obtain canned milk. By the age of one, all children were eating solid foods including homemade broths and premasticated meat. Weaning was a gradual process that might not be completed until the third or even fourth year. An older child rarely was rejected in favor of a younger one, and the transition occurred with little difficulty.

Toilet training, by contrast, was begun early, usually by the first birthday. The mother held the child on a pot or on her lap, blowing gently on its head. When the desired result had been achieved, she indicated her pleasure with a few kind words and playful movements. By the 1960s, the soft caribou skin and moss undergarments used by earlier Iñupiat mothers to clothe their children had been replaced by cloth diapers; and as a baby grew older, it was given "training pants" of cast-off clothing open at the crotch. Accidents and near misses were treated lightly, although they might bring a gentle rebuke. Even chronic bed-wetters were not punished, except among more acculturated families where the offender was made to stay in bed longer than usual. In general, there was no aura of shame or secrecy about excretory functions and no reticence in discussing them. During her field work, young girls might say to Jean Briggs[6] "don't look," but girls under four and all boys urinated unconcernedly anywhere out of doors.

---

[6] Jean Briggs, then a graduate student in anthropology at Harvard University, was an active participant in the research during the summers of 1961 and 1962. Much of the material on child-rearing has been drawn from her detailed field reports.

Photo 24. Children observing a young walrus.

Given the combination of large families and small houses, Iñupiat sleeping arrangements varied markedly from middle-class American patterns. Formerly, infants slept with their parents; but by the early 1960s, the youngest slept in cribs, the next oldest child or children with their parents, and still older ones with each other. As many as four siblings of both sexes might sleep in the same bed, all covered by the same large blanket. Youths received separate beds on reaching adolescence, and if the size of the room permitted, they might even have a cubbyhole or corner of a room to themselves. However, if the house was small and crowded, quite grown-up children slept in the same room with their parents. Only in the most affluent families would a child have a bed of its own.

Discipline was seldom imposed on the child before it was one year old. This was of little significance, however, since a child carried on the mother's back most of the time presented few problems. Only when it had sufficient freedom of movement to *pakak*—get into things it shouldn't—was it carefully observed.

Concepts of hygiene varied widely and appeared to be in direct proportion to the degree of association and identification with the outside world. But few mothers expressed concern about a baby putting a dirty object from the floor in its mouth or passing a bottle from a sick child to a well one. In short, infant care consisted primarily of keeping the baby happy. For the baby this meant being cuddled, fed, rested, warmed, and kept dry.

"How have the Eskimo managed to raise their children so well?" The woman asking me the question was a new teacher in Barrow. She spoke warmly of her pupils' good humor, liveliness, resourcefulness, and well-behaved manner. Although she later learned that Iñupiat children have their difficulties and conflicts, that they can be fretful, cruel, and petulant, her first impression had merit. Patient and obedient yet outgoing and enthusiastic, these young people seemed quick to offer help when needed. In so doing, they exemplified qualities that other American parents would like to see in their own children. To rephrase the teacher's question, what were the experiences of Iñupiat upbringing that favored the development of these attributes?

Certainly the warmth and affection given infants by parents, siblings, and other relatives provided them with a deep sense of well-being and security. Young children also felt important because they learned early that they were expected to be useful, working members of the family. While this included a number of tedious chores, involvement in the daily round of activities nevertheless enhanced their feeling of family participation and cohesion. Parents rarely denied children their company or excluded them from the adult world.

This pattern reflected the parents' views of child rearing. Adults felt that they had more experience in living and that it was their responsibility to share this experience with their children, "to tell them how to live." Children had to be told repeatedly because they tended to forget. Misbehavior was due to a child's forgetfulness, or to improper teaching in the first place. There was rarely any thought that the child was basically nasty, willful, or sinful. Where most Americans applauded children for their good behavior, the Iñupiaq praised them for remembering. One was able to see this attitude reflected in many situations. A father once was observed lecturing in Iñupiaq to his children before they set out on a short camping trip. Asked to expand on his remarks, he said:

> We stir them up a little to live right. Tell them to obey the parents; do what people tell them to do. And like now, when they go on a camping trip, not to take a new pillow. It gets dirty on the trip. Take the old one. They are young. They don't know what to do. We tell them how to do things. Like our parents used to tell us. Same as they used to talk to us. We used to talk a lot like that but we haven't lately. We begin again. Stir them up. They forget.

Another man discussed his nephew's helpless panic during a hunting trip when a storm threatened to wipe out the camp. Waking at night to find the tent blowing away and their boat temporarily lost, the boy had become frozen with fear. Never suggesting that he was cowardly or weak, the man was critical of the nephew's behavior but explained it in terms of his not having had sufficient experience to know what to do.

Fathers actively participated in the daily life of the family, and in disciplinary matters appeared to fulfill a function similar to that existing in many other American homes. Thus, a mother might say to a recalcitrant child, "Wait till I tell your father!" or "Wait till your father comes home. You gonna get a licking!" Among less acculturated families, the father retained a more dominant, rather than equal-participant, role. Here, the child was expected to be restrained, quiet, and respectful in his father's presence.

By the time children reached the age of three or four, the parents' earlier demonstrativeness had become tempered with an increased interest in their activities and skill level. They watched them play with obvious pleasure, responded warmly to their conversation, and made jokes with them. Though children were given considerable autonomy and their wishes were treated with respect, they were nevertheless taught to obey all older people. To an outsider unfamiliar with parent-child relations, the tone of Iñupiat commands and admonitions sometimes sounded harsh and angry. Yet in few instances did a child respond as if he or she had been addressed with hostility. This was due to the fact that admonitions tended to be indirect and general rather than geared to the specific individual.

A youngster who whined, sulked, cried, or expressed some other unacceptable emotion was told flatly, "Be nice!" If the child appeared to be getting into mischief, he was warned, "Don't *pakak!*" There were other frequently offered admonitions: "Don't *ipagak!*" meaning do not play in the water or on the beach; "shut the door," to keep out the cold; "put your parka on," guaranteeing adequate dress for outside; "don't go in someone else's house when no one is at home," reflecting concern for others' property. Most common was, "Don't fight!" which was directed not only against personal assaults and rock throwing but also verbal quarrels.

Certain acts like "taking without asking" and those involving potential danger did lead to punishment. If admonitions were unsuccessful, threats of such a fearsome creature as an *iñuqugauzat* (little spirit people), a *nanuq* (polar bear), or *tanik* (white man) were brought in for support. Or the threat might be unspecified, as in, "Somebody out there, somebody gonna get you." If this didn't work, the misbehaving child was dealt with more severely. The adult would shout, threaten, or actually strike the child, although physical punishment was relatively rare. More likely, the child would be isolated, a form of punishment reserved for serious breaches like fighting or playing with water in below-freezing temperatures. In keeping with the attitude that children were ignorant and forgetful, punishment was accompanied by explanation and reasoning. Seldom was anything more than mild humiliation or teasing used as a negative sanction.

A child's reaction to any of these treatments ranged from compliance, temporary fears, and unhappy looks—all of which were usually ignored—to sulking, rebellious shrieks, or silent resistance. This latter took the form of ignoring orders or repeating the behavior to see if the adult would notice. It was rare indeed to hear a child talk back, verbally refuse to perform the action, or say petulantly, "I don't want to." Sometimes a child did threaten vengeance—when it was angry at another child or an outsider such as a tanik— but it was most unusual to hear threats directed at parents or adult relatives. By adolescence, discipline seemed to consist entirely of lectures, though still delivered in the harsh tone characterizing Iñupiat cautions.

After the age of five, a child was less restricted in its activities in and around the village although walking on the beach or ice still required an adult. During the dark winter season, the child remained indoors or stayed close to the house to prevent it from getting lost and to protect it from polar bears that occasionally entered a village looking for food. In summer, children played at all hours of the day and "night," or at least until their parents went to bed.

By the eighth year, some of the responsibility for a child's socialization had been passed from adults to peers. Children frequently lectured each other using the same admonitions earlier told them: "Don't fight," "Don't pakak," "You supposed to knock," and "Shut the door." Rule-breaking might also be reported to a nearby adult: "Mom. Sammy ipagak." Tattling was not depreciated to the extent that it had once been (Spencer 1959:240). Still, while older children regularly "played parent" in which they imposed adult rulings on younger ones, all children instructed each other regardless of their age. Such instruction was generally taken in good spirit. Thus, when a younger child reminded an older one, "You supposed to knock," the latter was likely to smile sheepishly, go out of the room, knock, and enter again.

Although not burdened with responsibility, both boys and girls were expected to take an active role in family activities. In the early years, these were shared, depending on who was available. It was important for a child to know how to perform a wide variety of tasks and give assistance when needed. Both sexes collected and chopped wood, got water, helped carry meat and other supplies, oversaw younger siblings, ran errands for adults, fed the dogs, and burned trash.

As children grew older, more specific responsibilities were allocated according to gender. Boys as young as seven might be given an opportunity to shoot a .22 rifle, and at least a few boys in every village had taken their first caribou by the time they were ten or eleven.

Young girls, and to a lesser extent young boys, learned techniques of butchering while on hunting trips with older siblings and adults. In most instances, however, neither girls nor boys became at all proficient in this skill until their late teens or early twenties. Prior to compulsory school attendance and the hospitalization of large numbers of youths for tuberculosis, such knowledge was attained at an earlier age. A girl, especially, learned butchering as a young teen-ager since this skill was essential in attracting a good husband. By the 1960s, the skill was more likely to be picked up after marriage, and not always then.

It became clear over the course of the field work that while a gender division of labor among youths was clearly recognized by the Iñupiat, it was far from rigid. Boys occasionally swept the house and helped with cooking. Girls and their mothers went on fishing and duck-hunting trips, and sometimes caribou hunting as well. Each gender learned that it could assume the responsibilities of the other when the occasion arose, albeit in an auxiliary role.

Siblings played together more happily than is often the case in American society, but sibling rivalry was not completely absent. Hostility was generally

Photo 25. A young man's first caribou.

cxpressed by tattling or engaging in some form of minor physical abuse. However, anyone indulging in hard pushing, elbowing, pinching, or hitting was told immediately to stop. Rather than fight back, the injured party was more likely to request help from an older sibling or near-adult. Verbal abuse also was rare.

By contrast, competitiveness, derived from pride of achievement or skill attainment, characterized many children's activities. In games involving athletic prowess, a child would say, "Look how far I can throw the stone," rather than, "I can throw the stone farther than you." When rivalry was more direct, it was expected that the game be undertaken in good spirit and the skills of one participant not be flaunted at the expense of the other. Aggressive competitiveness was explicitly condemned, as when a father chided his son, "Why are you always wanting to win?"

Only very young children limited their play to those of like age. After reaching five or six, the age range of playmates widened considerably. Team games such as "Eskimo football" were particularly popular and had as participants children of both sexes ranging in age from five to twelve. The game combined elements of soccer and "keepaway" and, when played by older boys, elements of rugby as well. It was not until adolescence that a young person actively set herself or himself apart from other children. Youths of this age group briefly watched youngsters play volleyball or some other game, but seldom participated. Adults encouraged this separation, and when they saw a teen-aged boy or girl playing with younger children, they would say, "That person is a little slow in his (or her) development."

Many other popular games were played. Some, involving feats of skill and

Photo 26. Woman butchering an ugruk *while her daughter watches.*

strength such as hand wrestling, have had a long history among the Iñupiat. Others such as kick-the-can, London Bridge, volleyball, and board games like Monopoly and Scrabble were introduced by whites. Still other games combined elements of both. *Haku*, an Iñupiat team game in which the object was to make the members of the opposite team laugh, included the offering of amusing portraits of Hawaiian and Spanish dances, done, if possible, with a straight face. A few traditional Iñupiat games like *putigarok*, a form of tag where the person who was "it" tried to touch another on the same spot on the body in which he or she was tagged, closely resembled the western game of tag. Kaktovik children occasionally played a fantasy game called "polar bear" in which one child took the role of an old woman who fell asleep. The polar bear came and took away her child. She then woke up and attempted to discover where the bear had hidden it. At Barrow, Iñupiat children played a slightly different version of the same game called "old woman." A youth played the role of an old woman who pretended to be blind. When several of her possessions were stolen, she "accused" other children of taking them.

This game required a fair amount of verbal exchange. The more able the talker, the more likely the winner.

Storytelling was one of the most popular forms of Iñupiat entertainment, especially during the winter months when outside activity was sharply diminished. Typical stories involved autobiographical or biographical accounts of unusual incidents, accidents, hunting trips, or other events deemed interesting to the listener. Following the evening meal, a father might call all the children around him and recount his last whale hunt or how he shot his first polar bear. A good storyteller acted out part of the tale, demonstrating how he threw the harpoon at the whale's back or how the bear scooped up the lead dog and sent him flying across the ice. Other stories described life long ago before the taniks arrived. Myths and folk tales portrayed exploits of northern animals and birds endowed with supernatural qualities.

Children, too, liked to tell stories to each other. These short tales usually described some recent activity, real or imagined. Young Iñupiat were passionately fond of horror stories, and a vivid description of raw heads and bloody bones quickly elicited delighted screams of fear from the listeners. If the teller acted out part of the story, so much the better.

The Iñupiat child's creative imagination was reflected in all the activities of storytelling, imitating others, playing store, and inventing new games. Young girls turned a bolt of cloth into a regal gown they wore to an imaginary ball. Boys of four or five climbed under a worn blanket with make-believe airplanes to practice night flying. Charging over the tundra with sharply pointed sticks, a pair of six-year-olds cornered their supposed furry opponent. This kind of spontaneity, supported by flexible routines and a minimum of rules, continued until the early teens when events of the real world begun to offer greater challenges. Only in the classroom did these children find their psychic freedom curtailed.

All Iñupiat children from six to sixteen were required to attend local Bureau of Indian Affairs (BIA) schools. Parents generally agreed that school was a necessary part of the modern child's education, and the children themselves enjoyed the contrast of school and home. Still, the themes addressed in the classroom differed markedly from those of everyday Iñupiat life, and many a youth would have preferred lessons in hunting and skin sewing to those in arithmetic, geography, social studies, and English. Nor did they see much benefit in following newly arrived BIA teachers' admonitions that they learn to "Be prompt," "Work hard to achieve success," "Learn the values of banking and budgeting," and particularly "Keep clean," for such middle-class American values had little meaning for life at home.

The school term in Kaktovik and other North Slope villages began in late August and continued for 180 days, the number required by the government. Acknowledging the limitations placed on the student's behavior, it was still possible to characterize Iñupiat childhood at that time as one of relative independence. Participation in simple household tasks permitted boys and girls large amounts of free time. Only gradually did they have to assume the more adult responsibilities of cleaning house, caring for younger siblings, hunting and preparing food. Thus, apart from the school experience, there was no sharp break in the continuity of learning between infancy, childhood, and the beginning of adolescence.

In one special sense, there was an even greater blending of these age-grades than in the past. In aboriginal times, changes in clothing delineated a transition from childhood to adolescence. When a boy's voice changed, he was given a different style of short trousers. Later, when a father or male guardian decided the young man was ready for marriage, a minor operation was performed by cutting two slits at the corners of his mouth. Once the wounds were cleansed, decorative labrets were placed in the openings, thereby signifying that the boy had become a man and was ready for marriage. A girl's transition to adolescence came with her first menstruation, at which time she was placed in temporary isolation for up to a month or longer. With further maturation, marked by the growth of her breasts, she exchanged the clothes of childhood for those of the adult woman. Women were tattooed by making a series of closely drawn parallel lines extending from the center of the lower lip to the chin. In the early 1960s, a few women of sixty-five or more still carried these symbols of early womanhood; but by then the custom of marking differences in age and gender had become obsolete.

Much of the Iñupiaq child's upbringing was designed to prepare the young person to assume the skills and values of an adult. Children were made to feel that their contributions and participation were important to the overall life of the family. They were taught how to draw their subsistence from land and sea, what responsibilities needed to be undertaken in the home, and what cultural traditions they should follow. In spite of this background, and in part because of it, many adolescents felt unprepared to assume the responsibilities of life in a rapidly changing world only partially understood by their parents. Due to diverse models of adulthood offered by school teachers, missionaries, and their own kin, it was difficult for young men or women to choose how best to structure their adult lives. As a result, the process of becoming an Iñupiaq adult was fraught with turmoil and insecurity.

Taught from childhood that an Iñupiaq male should be self-reliant and a good hunter, boys observed their fathers seeking wage labor at a government or military installation. After obtaining such a position, these men could hunt only on occasional days off or during short two-or three-week vacations. They were also more likely to take chances by having to hunt in bad weather since that was the only time they could obtain subsistence foods for their families. The frustration and ambivalence felt by a father who was limited in his ability to provide this Native food quickly carried down to the son. So, too, girls regularly observed their mother's confusion as they tried to comprehend the economic, educational, religious, and other changes occurring within their spheres of activity. In many respects, the difficulties faced by Iñupiat women were somewhat greater than those of the men. In terms of the amount of energy that had to be expended, the larger families, a product of steadily improving health care, added significantly to the work required around the home. Furthermore, to this practical problem was added another having to do with ideological redefinitions of gender.

As noted previously, prior to the colonial period, Iñupiat women and men made decisions about the activities for which they were largely responsible. Thus, Iñupiat women maintained direct autonomy in many areas having to do with the production and distribution of food, skin sewing, and similar endeavors essential to survival of the group. Men, too, were dominant decision-makers in their important spheres of activity, most of which centered around subsistence hunting. But men were not dominators in the sense that, as a group, they tried to subjugate, command, or control the actions of women. Thus, the social relations between Iñupiat women and men prior to their colonial encounter with Europe and America were relatively egalitarian in nature. This, of course, was hardly in keeping with the definition of womanhood held by incoming colonizers. From their perspective, the position of women was clearly subordinate to that of men. Eventually, the undermining of women's autonomy took hold, thereby seriously reducing their ability to cope with many new and complex problems they had to face. Needless to say, the continuing stresses brought on by these changed social relations were closely watched by adolescent daughters seeking models to emulate.

In schools, too, adolescents of both sexes came to understand that the Iñupiat were a small and relatively unimportant segment of the world's population and that much of what transpired in national and international affairs passed them by without a glance. This knowledge, contrasting sharply with the earlier Iñupiat perception of themselves as a capable and self-reliant people, did little to enhance the students' pride and self-worth.

Though the village school was highly informative about the outside world, it did not prepare Iñupiat youth to live with it or in it. Primary-school children learned to speak English and if they completed the elementary curriculum, they could read and write. But to enter a high school or technical school, youths had to leave their villages for up to four years and travel to Sitka, Anchorage, Fairbanks, or some other city in Kansas or Oregon about which they knew little. Young men who chose not to continue schooling—and the choice was almost always left up to them—soon found their lack of skills placed them at a disadvantage when competing with whites for northern jobs. For young Iñupiat women, however, there were no jobs for them even if they did obtain the necessary skills. At that time in the early 1960s, any secretarial or other service-oriented training offered women in high schools could be utilized only in areas far removed from the villages. Thus, Iñupiat teen-agers of both sexes were trapped by the economic, social, and cultural environment in which they found themselves. There were few incentives to follow the ways of the past and little opportunity for skill training that could help prepare for the future. It was hardly surprising, therefore, that most adolescents devoted their time and energy to matters of the present.

This problem was compounded by the freedom given the youths by their parents and other relatives. As noted earlier, Iñupiat childhood became more peer centered with increasing age. With the sharp increase in number of living children (due to improvements in health care), older siblings were regularly called upon to assist their busy parents. They also took on greater responsibility for socialization of the young. Thus, by the time a child reached adolescence, most of her or his time was spent with those of similar age. This long-standing cultural pattern, continuing into the 1960s, meant that the parents' knowledge of their adolescent children's thoughts and behavior was often quite limited. Not surprisingly, when pressed to comment on a son and daughter's plans for continuing school outside the village, a father would say, "I don't know. They haven't told us yet." This lack of communication between parents and adolescents, coming at a time when the latter were searching for new models of behavior enabling them to "live in both worlds," did little to resolve their feelings of insecurity and isolation.

YOUTH AND COURTSHIP

Given this insecurity about themselves and their place in the world, Iñupiat teen-agers derived their strongest emotional ties from one another, and in many respects formed a closed social group. Spending almost all of their time together, they wore western clothes, used western slang expressions and emulated mannerisms largely western in origin. The only Iñupiat clothing regularly worn were fur parkas and, less often, *kamiks* (boots). Boys wore slacks of denim or wool, sport shirts and sweaters, shoepacks and rubber boots, and even black leather jackets with names emblazoned on the back. Girls liked slacks or wool skirts, slips, brassieres, sweaters, and wool jackets or coats. For parties they enjoyed wearing nylon stockings, dresses, and high-heeled shoes. Jewelry and cosmetics, and sometimes even a home permanent, completed the picture.

Girls paid a great deal of attention to their clothes. They would work and rework them, changing a hem here, fixing a cuff there, polishing and cleaning. Some even changed their attire several times a day, and, in contrast to married women and children, almost all dressed up for evening church services or other events at which boys were present. Teen-age slang came straight out of the lower 48 states. "Man, I don't go for parkas," "Crazy, man," "Yeah, hey," and similar expressions of the decade startled many whites on their initial visit to Arctic coastal villages. Contemporary dance steps and popular songs of the day were learned from radio programs, movies, magazines, white friends, and individuals who had taken trips south.

Another major influence was the antituberculosis campaign of the 1950s that sent many young North Slope Iñupiat to sanitoriums in Alaska and as far away as Washington state. This experience added greatly to their knowledge of American culture. By 1960, twelve of the fifty-odd Kaktovik adolescents had spent between nine months and two years in these sanitoriums. Other North Slope villages had similar temporary emigrations. Although the effect of hospital life depended largely on the age of the patient, the severity of the illness, and the length of stay, all Iñupiat returned with a greater awareness of the outside world, which was then passed on to others. Some Iñupiat children who had spent several years in the hospital returned no longer able to speak Iñupiaq. Others no longer cared.

In addition to school and hospital experiences, travel encouraged the spread of the new culture. Each year, youths took trips from their villages to Fairbanks, Anchorage, and farther south to visit friends and relatives who had migrated to these urban centers. When they returned home, their less experienced peers served as avid audiences for stories of their travels. Barrow itself was an important center of American culture and influence, due particularly to the extensive medical, educational, church, military, and other governmental facilities present in the area. Barrow also had become large enough to have its own movie theatre, which showed commercial films several times a week. Wainwright and other smaller villages were similary affected. Newspapers, mail-order catalogues, teen magazines, religious tracts, comics, radios, records, tape recordings, and even an occasional *True Confessions* or *TV Guide* found their way into Iñupiat homes in North Slope villages and were thoroughly absorbed by the young. Movies, whether obtained from outside, nearby military sites, or religious groups, were immensely popular.

By the early 1960s, strong emotional bonds between teen-agers, enhanced by their common school experiences, stays in hospitals, and sharing of popular culture generated by the mass media, had seriously affected their ability and that of their parents to maintain effective channels of communication. Seldom did Iñupiat youths voluntarily engage in activities other than those associated with household chores or hunting, with their parents and older relatives. Adolescent participation in Sunday school and similar church activities dropped off significantly. By 14, they had considerable freedom in making their own decisions even though the rest of the household might suffer some hardship resulting from it. Those wishing to attend private schools such as Sheldon Jackson Junior College in Sitka, Alaska, were indulged, even when the family's income could hardly cover the $500 tuition.

Because most Iñupiat adolescents identified with American ideas and concepts generated in the south, they frequently found themselves with little to do, and as a result became bored. This restlessness was expressed in phrases such as, "There is nothing to do" or "The day goes so slowly at home." Of course, definitions of boredom differed among individuals and locales. Adolescents in more isolated villages like Anaktuvuk Pass wished for the more active life of Barrow. Barrow youths were restless because they didn't have sufficient access to new movies, dancing, parties, and similar activities found in Fairbanks and Anchorage. Girls and young women wondered whether taniks might make better marriage partners than local youths. At Kaktovik, where Air Force personnel once lived adjacent to the village, several young women wished for the days " . . . when we used to have lots of white boyfriends, have lots of fun, and go for walks together." Dissatisfied youths from isolated villages like Kaktovik were heard to comment: "I think I will go to Barrow. There, they have movies all the time and the streets are full of people."

Still others were discontented with the seeming isolation of village life for quite a different reason. They felt left behind in the sweep of trends. These youths were older, had limited schooling, and never lived or visited outside the village. Sitting on the sidelines at parties, they would say wistfully, "Gee, I feel lonely" or "I wish they would play games I know how to play." Though less identified with the outside world, neither were they committed to earlier Iñupiat ways. Trying to bridge the gap, they, too, found few friends outside their own group.

When not occupied with home or school responsibilities, most teen-agers spent their time together playing cards, singing, or going for walks. Group singing, often with guitar accompaniment, was especially popular. Following an evening church service, eight or ten young people would get together to sing hymns and popular songs. Then they would go for a walk or join others at a local coffee shop. In places like Barrow, dances and parties were scheduled several times a year at the National Guard Armory or other community building. Movies were always well patronized no matter what the subject matter, and in summer organized ball games attracted numerous participants and spectators. Making tapes became a kind of recreation—kin or friendship groups recorded songs, news, and stories that were mailed to friends and relatives in other villages who then recorded and sent their own "tape letters" back.

Still, these new activities did not diminish interest in some of the more traditional pastimes such as hunting, fishing, camping, and boating. Groups of boys and girls often went on all-day outings. If they learned that a young married couple was camping along the coast, arrangements were made to visit them over night or for a weekend. Other young people staying at summer fish camps could also count on regular visits from these teen-agers. Finally, there was the simple activity of staying up all night. Adolescent youths considered such an event an entertainment in itself. When deciding how to spend an evening, the suggestion might be made, "Let's stay up," in the same manner as the proposal, "Let's make a tape" or "Let's go for a walk."

Boys and girls in their early teens rarely paired off, most social contacts being sought with the group rather then a given individual. Youths might tease each other with the comment, "You interested in him, right?" but it was not until the age of 15 or 16 that Iñupiat young people developed a strong interest in members of the opposite sex. At this time, boys began to seek out a particular girl, pay special attention to her, talk with her more than with others, sit beside her in church, and in other ways let her know of his interest. However, except in the most sophisticated segment of the Barrow teen-age world, physical demonstrativeness in front of others was deemed improper. And even in Barrow, putting an arm around a girl's shoulder or giving her a squeeze was done in a joking manner—any open evidence of affection would embarrass the girl and her friends.

Boys rarely visited girls in their homes unless other family members were there, and it was even less common for a girl to visit a boy's home. But as male youths became older, they attempted to arrange clandestine meetings by passing notes at school suggesting a time and place. By the middle teens, girls were very much aware of boys' attentions. Their conversations centered around boys and their activities; they dressed for them, giggled about them, and showed each other secret pictures of their favorite boyfriends. The late teens brought more sexual experimentation. A few boys had intercourse by the age of 15, and most by 20. Girls did not regularly solicit this degree of involvement, but once involved, usually continued. Finding a secluded meeting place presented problems, particularly in winter. Homes of young married couples were often available, although privacy was limited. Parents sometimes expressed concern over this kind of activity but seldom voiced such opinions. Religious precepts did not condone premarital sex, but this seemed to have little effect on behavior. In earlier times, no clearly defined restrictions were imposed. At infancy, children became aware of others engaging in intercourse. Masturbation was not forbidden. By puberty, young men and women occasionally traveled together away from the village, at which time they might contract a quasi-married relationship. Trial marriages were also common, though unbridled promiscuity was viewed with disapproval.

In summary, the youth of the early 1960s faced a difficult future for which they had few skills. On the surface they exhibited a markedly middle-class American veneer. Underneath, they were unsure of themselves and what they wanted to become. Few planned realistically. Some spoke of going away to school for training in professional or semiprofessional work related to education, bookkeeping, cooking, or science. The desire to make money was a common goal of many regardless of the kind of position it entailed. And there was a rather unrealistic assumption that jobs would be available when needed. Significantly, most young people wanted to remain permanently in Arctic Alaska. Even those who planned on going away to school, planned to return.

MARRIAGE AND FAMILY

The bilateral extended family has always been the basic unit of Iñupiat social structure. Recognition of kin through at least three generations on both the mother and father's side of the family provided an interwoven pattern of kinship linking together family units. By means of economic partnerships, quasi-kin groups effectively extended cooperative ties to non-kin as well. Under this arrangement, all Iñupiat who called each other by real or fictive kinship terms assumed a relation of sharing and cooperation (the extent of obligation depending on degree of distance from ego) and were seen by outsiders as being responsible for the actions of the entire kin group.

By the 1960s, these extended family and economic partnerships had begun to decline. Economic interdependence also lessened as opportunities for individual wage labor increased. As the desire for economic gain drew Iñupiat away from their earlier settlements to more urbanized towns and cities, migrants felt less obligation to pass on the benefits of their newly obtained

Photo 27. Ties between close kin remained strong. Kaktovik, 1958.

income to more distant relatives beyond the immediate kin network. However, cooperative kin ties were maintained in local secondary economic activities such as baby-tending, butchering meat, setting and checking fish nets,
loading and unloading boats, constructing ice cellars, painting houses, and
sharing common household items. In each of these instances cooperation was
not only expected, but if a request went unheeded, the individual quickly
became an object of gossip.

Choice of marriage partner also changed. In smaller villages like Kaktovik
prior to World War II, marriage between cousins was fairly common. At
Barrow, it was far less so. After the war, young people paid little attention
to these earlier preference patterns. While possible deleterious effects of
cousin marriage on future children were occasionally raised, such marriages
were not considered immoral, and in small villages with a limited number of
eligible spouses, they were almost necessary.

Spouse exchange, on the other hand, which had earlier established long-
distance reciprocity and given spouse-like recognition between two couples,

had not been practiced for years. Female partners in spouse exchange called each other *aipariik*, "the second." The four partners were collectively referred to as *nuliaqatigiik* and their children used the reciprocal term *qatangutigiik* for each other (Burch 1975). Significantly, those individuals who were *qatang* had definite obligations toward one another similar to those between brothers and sisters. But by the early 1960s, those Iñupiat using these terms were well into their 40s or older (Milan 1959:50).

Although formalized spouse-exchange disappeared, sexual mores of the time remained relatively free. As viewed by local missionaries, Iñupiat attitudes were "halfway between the old and the new." Although more conservative elders and other leaders of local churches in North Slope villages encouraged their young people to marry before they became sexually involved, the advice was largely disregarded and many young couples did not marry until they had a child. This pattern was closely linked to two factors. First, economic responsibilities of marriage as defined within the revised gender division of labor made demands that young Iñupiat men found difficult to meet. Second, young men and women did not feel they needed a marriage bond to fulfill their sexual interests.

When a couple decided to marry, they made arrangements with the local missionary to hold the ceremony in the village church. Even in remote inland villages most couples were joined in marriage by a minister or priest. In north Alaska, the older custom where a young man and woman regularly moved into the household of one of their parents for some time before becoming legally married had largely disappeared by the late 1950s. Even older couples whose common-law arrangement was accepted by the missionaries and other whites in the community were encouraged to go through the legal process to ensure the inheritance rights of their children.

Changes in courtship and marriage patterns were closely related to opportunities for wage employment and the greater mobility of young people. In this rapidly changing economic environment, prestige and eligibility as a suitor were measured more by the young man's wage-earning abilities than by his skill as a hunter. Thus, some young men left their communities for jobs in Barrow, Fairbanks, or Anchorage in order to enhance their suitability as potential spouses. Needless to say, this mobility seriously disturbed the gender ratio of smaller villages.

Following marriage, young couples often moved in with the family of the bride or groom. This arrangement eased the economic responsibilities of the newly married pair and also helped them learn the techniques and skills necessary in supporting and maintaining a family. It was at this time that young couples came to appreciate the need to become competent in subsistence skills associated with hunting, fishing, and the butchering of meat.

In keeping with the new responsibilities of maintaining larger households, women spent much of their day-to-day lives tending babies, washing dishes and clothes, cleaning, cooking, getting water, chopping wood, and burning trash. In tasks such as obtaining wood and water, male household members also helped. In addition, men assisted in the heavy work of setting up tents and building drying racks, making windbreaks for butchering meat, filling fuel tanks, and starting stubborn washing machines. Women, however, spent far less time in skin sewing and, given the reduced hunting activity of their employed spouses, in butchering and distributing meat as well. Still, the cultural expectations associated with the older Iñupiat gender division of labor could be recognized in the comments of an elderly Iñupiat male from Barrow:

> Women are supposed to take care of the house. A man does the hunting; a woman takes care of the kids and the food. She should know how much they got left, how much food there is for the kids. They always check the food. The man is always asking his wife, "How much have you got left?" And the woman says, "We have so much to last us for so many days or weeks." The woman always takes care of the food, and sews or patches clothes for the husband and the kids. She also scrapes all the caribou skin, seal, or whatever the skin is. But the man must help, too, once in a while. When we are a little short of food, the man spends most of his time hunting. The man never cooks or feeds the children because he hunts every day. Although the women are supposed to take care of the house and kids, they sometimes help the men, too. Women go upriver to hunt the ptarmigan while the men are hunting the caribou. My wife was always known as a good shooter. She killed lots of ptarmigan and even went seal hunting with me sometimes. Once in a while when women do not have a lot of children to take care of, they may even go out by themselves and hunt the caribou in summertime. In winter, when the children are inside, women don't do much hunting.

Although economic considerations played a major role in consolidating the marriage relationship, the bond between spouses was not limited to this sphere. In many instances, couples enjoyed one another's companionship and held each other in mutual affection and respect. They also instructed one another in various activities. Young men taught their wives how to shoot or flense a caribou while a wife might offer pointers on how to improve the butchering of a seal or ugruk. This cooperative teaching was found in all North Slope Iñupiat villages regardless of the degree of family acculturation.

Outside the economic sphere, separation of the sexes in village social life was more pronounced. Couples seldom went visiting together, although in the course of an evening social round, both husband and wife might find themselves in the same house. Nor did they entertain friends jointly. In predominantly female gatherings, men were usually ignored except for an occasional comment or joke. If several women entered a home, the men often got up and left. In predominantly male situations, the women assumed a passive role and remained in the background. A woman whose husband was entertaining friends would serve tea or coffee, listen to the conversation, laugh at appropriate occasions, and perhaps ask a question, but she rarely became actively engaged in the discussion. If the group was more or less evenly mixed, as when people were invited to hear a recorded tape-letter from a friend or relative, companionable exchanges most commonly took place among members of the same sex.

Still, informal visiting was an important feature of day-to-day family life. A friend would drop in on a neighbor, perhaps stand around for a few minutes, and then leave with little or no announcement of her or his departure. Visitors might enter a house and, after giving an initial greeting, ignore its occupants. Or they might sit and read a mail-order magazine or religious tract, or simply watch the activities of the household. Though efforts to entertain the guest were minimal, one could always expect the offer of a cup of tea, coffee, or crackers.

In conclusion, given the immense changes that had occurred in Arctic Alaska in the century leading up to the 1950s, Iñupiat kin ties had remained surprisingly strong. Indeed, as the anthropologist Robert Spencer (1959:364) wrote following his study of North Slope villages in 1951–52, "It would appear that only if the family system is disrupted will community disorganization on a large scale occur. For despite the cash income, the social organization of the aboriginal Eskimo is still a significant force." Unfortunately, a little more than a decade after his research was completed, that evaluation could no longer be made for Barrow. By the early 1960s, the ability of the kin network to cope with its emerging problems was strained to the limit. One factor had to do with the swelling of Barrow's population brought on by the sharp increase in the birthrate and the desire of more distant Iñupiat to take advantage of seasonal wage employment in construction and at the nearby military DEW line site. Newcomers also wanted better access to the local Public Health Service hospital for themselves and better education for their children. The influx of these new residents from as far away as western Canada, some of whom had few if any close relatives in the village, limited the ability of the once tight-knit kinship system to deal with stress.

Barrow also was faced with a steady increase of white male military personnel, construction workers, scientists, and other outsiders assigned to Air Force installations, weather stations, and the Naval Arctic Research Laboratory, all of which had been built only a short distance from the town. These outsiders, more than a few of whom had little interest in or respect for the Iñupiat and their culture, simply saw the community as a place to unwind, seek bootleg liquor, "look at the Natives," and perhaps establish a relationship with one of the local women. Stories of earlier whalers' liaisons with female Iñupiat and American magazine cartoons poking fun at the supposed Eskimo custom of "wife-sharing" provided the basis for numerous jokes about "who was making out with whom" on any weekend sojourn into town. As these disparaging tanik stereotypes of the Iñupiat became widespread, linkages based on mutual respect and common understanding diminished sharply. Eventually, interracial tensions reached the point where members of the two groups lived in separate worlds, each ignoring the other. While it is important not to overemphasize the negative quality of these relationships, nor to disregard the few examples of positive ties that were maintained between Iñupiat and whites, the generally hostile atmosphere was nevertheless present in almost all aspects of local social life.

As Barrow's internal problems multiplied, its community leaders sought new ways of dealing with them. By 1962, juvenile delinquency and other minor crimes had reached such proportions that investigators from the Division of Youth and Adult Authority of the state Department of Health and Welfare were invited to Barrow to study the situation. They found drinking and theft were particularly common among male youths and adults, while charges of intoxication and sexual misdemeanors were regularly filed against young girls and some older women. Most offenses were committed by individuals rather than groups, although male teen-age gangs were beginning to emerge. In their report, the investigators stressed the difficulty of finding capable and experienced community leaders, ineffective methods of social control, boredom, and the lack of social cohesion as factors influencing the rising rate of deliquency and crime. Although the study team addressed internal factors within Iñupiat society promoting these conditions, such as the weakening of traditional kin relations and inapplicable socialization practices, little attention was given to larger questions concerning cultural enrichment and political self-determination, both of which could provide a greater sense of pride, purpose, and worth from which a new sense of well-being could spring.

5/Beyond Kin

As we have seen, the core of aboriginal Iñupiat life centered around the nuclear and extended family, a relationship continually reinforced by patterns of mutual aid and reciprocal obligation. Beyond this immediate circle, there existed additional relational groupings, some of them kin-based. Joking partners, for example, were usually cross-cousins. Hunting partners were often related, though not always. The qargi club houses, primarily used by extended families for educational and ceremonial purposes, also served as socializing centers for unrelated others. In the large whaling community of Barrow, there were once three qargit, each linked with a whaling captain and his crew, although other family members and their wives were not excluded. It was through participation in institutions such as the qargi that the Iñupiat developed a larger sense of identity with a particular locality or settlement.

At one time, the qargi was the meeting place of one of the most important aboriginal festivals held on the North Slope—the Messenger Feast. Usually organized in December, it was a ceremony with both social and economic significance. In early winter, an umialik of a given settlement sent messengers to a nearby locality to invite its residents to participate in an economic exchange. Because of the effort that had to be expended, no one group could afford to give such a feast each year. The choice of the invited settlement was based on the number of trading partners involved and the length of time lapsed since the previous invitation. Elaborate gift exchanges between residents added to the development of intercommunity solidarity, as did the opportunity for distant kin to re-establish social and economic ties while participating in the activities of the feast.

By the early 1960s, neither the qargi ceremonial centers nor the Messenger Feast were significant community institutions on the North Slope. No qargi remained at Barrow or Wainwright, and at Point Hope the two qargit were only meaningful to the extent that they affected the patterning of the Christmas and spring whaling feasts (VanStone 1962:102). Similarly, only a vestige of the Messenger Feast was held between Christmas and New Year's Day.[1]

The one important traditional ceremony still actively participated in through the 1960s (and continuing to the present) was the *nalukatak*, or spring

---

[1] At the end of the 1980s, an active effort was being made to revive both the qargi and the Messenger Feast (see: MacLean 1988b).

whaling festival. Arrangements for this celebration, which took place at the end of the whaling season, were made by the successful umialit and their families. If no whales were caught, there was no ceremony. Formerly, the festival took place in the qargi of the successful umialik. One of its purposes was to propitiate the spirits of the deceased whales and ensure through magical means the success of future hunting seasons. A modern adaptation of this religious belief is seen on those occasions when Christian prayers of thanksgiving are recited during the ceremony.

On the day chosen for the event, every boat crew that had killed one or more whales during the season hauled their umiaq out of the sea and dragged them to the ceremonial site. The boats were then turned on their side to serve as windbreaks and temporary shelter for the participants, and braced with paddles or forked sticks. Masts were erected at the bow and from the top were flown the small, bright flags of each umialik. Before Christian teaching changed the practice, the captain placed his hunting charms and amulets on these masts. When the site had been arranged and a prayer given, the families of the umialik cut off the flukes and other choice sections of a whale and distributed them along with tea, biscuits, and other food to invited guests.

After a period of general relaxation, informal conversation, and further serving of meat and tea, the nalukatak skin ("skin for tossing") was brought out. Of all the Iñupiat ceremonial customs, the nalukatak or "blanket toss" is probably the most well known to whites. It was an exciting affair to watch. After bringing out a skin made by sewing several walrus hides together, thirty or more Iñupiat took their places in a circle, grasping firmly with both hands the rope handgrips or rolled edge. The object of the game was to toss a person into the air as high as possible—sometimes more than twenty feet. Such people were expected to keep their balance and return upright to the blanket. Especially skilled individuals might do turns and flips. Usually the first to be tossed were the successful umialit. In earlier days, they were expected, while high in the air, to throw out gifts of baleen, tobacco and other items to the crowd. More recently, candy has been used as a substitute. Once an individual lost her or his footing, another took a turn until all had a chance to participate.

In the late afternoon or evening, a dance was scheduled. When a permanent dance floor or temporary board platform had been made ready, five or ten male drummers, supported by a chorus of men and women, announced the beginning of the dance. The first dance, called the *umialikit*, was obligatory for the umialik, his wife, and crew. All other crew members then danced in turn, followed by other men and women in the village. The affair usually lasted well into the night.

Christian and national holidays, including Thanksgiving, Christmas, New Year's Day, Easter, and Independence Day, were celebrated, too. On the Fourth of July, for example, there were foot races for the children, *qayaq* and other boat races for the men, and tug-of-war pulls for those in all age groups. In those villages located near military, weather, or other government installations, local whites were invited to participate. Winners received prizes of candy and canned fruit.

Photo 28. The nalukatak *continues to be a favorite Iñupiat ceremonial activity.*

Thanksgiving was celebrated by a feast in the local village church, followed by group singing, drumming, and dancing. Between Christmas and the New Year, there was a continuous round of games, feasts, church services, drum dances, and dog races. In the 1950s, missionaries from the Church of the Assembly of God established small congregations in Barrow, Kaktovik, and several other North Slope villages. In contrast to the more established Presbyterian Church, this Pentecostal group prohibited all forms of dancing for members, resulting in the separation of some popular social festivities along religious lines. This increase in religious diversification had a significant impact on village life in the decade that followed. The older Episcopal (at Point Hope) and Presbyterian and newer evangelical church groups differed markedly in the kinds of recreation and social activities they considered acceptable. Converts to the new denominations spent far more time in specific church activities than did members of the established congregations. In the early 1960s, for instance, services of the Assembly of God Church at Wainwright and Kaktovik were regularly held two to three hours a night six nights a week. Although meeting less frequently, Presbyterian members had their own prayer and study groups, sewing circles, and midweek services, which did not involve members of the other denominations.

Establishing a second church in three villages either created or more frequently formalized splits between segments of the population in such a manner that it reduced the villagers' ability to function as a unit. This situation was reflected in the remark of a Wainwright Presbyterian elder: "We used to have good parties until the other church came. We played Eskimo games, danced, played guitars, and sang. . . . They have a lo-o-o-t of commandments

Photo 29. Qayaq races provided fun for all on the Fourth of July, 1958.

over there—just like the Pharisees, yes?'' Converts to the new churches, on the other hand, viewed some Presbyterians as living a less than moral life. The apparently profound satisfaction with which these recent converts engaged in their religious affairs attested to their strong sense of what constituted correct behavior.

RELIGION AND HEALTH

Significantly, contradictions in the mind of the Iñupiat between traditional beliefs and those of Christianity were often minimal. Certainly, most adult villagers considered themselves to be staunch supporters of Christianity. But they also held other traditional beliefs that they knew taniks didn't share, and thus were cautious about discussing them with outsiders.

For example, many Iñupiat continued their belief in spirit people who inhabited the region (*iñuqun*), monsters (*makkiligaarok*), the ten-legged polar bear, and other supernatural creatures. Children spoke more openly of these creatures than did adults, but there was little doubt that the youngsters learned of them from their elders. Fear of these beings became noticeably stronger in the autumn when darkness increased. One iñuqun "incident" took place at Wainwright when a small girl failed to appear home at bedtime. Community members spent the night searching for her, certain that she had been carried off in some mysterious manner. Actually the girl, afraid of being punished for a misdeed, had run away from home and was asleep in a box under another house.

An excellent way to learn about earlier Iñupiat religious beliefs is to ask the elders to relate legends that have passed down from generation to generation. A commonly shared myth related by an elderly Barrow resident illustrates the animistic nature of Iñupiat religion:

> Once there was a poor hunter. He always went out but never got anything. Finally, one day he saw a polar bear. As he crawled toward it over the ice, the bear said to him, "Don't shoot me. If you follow me and do what I say, I will make it so you will always be able to get whatever animals you think about." The bear told the man to climb on his back and close his eyes. "Do not open them until I tell you to." Then the man and the bear went down into the sea a long way. "Do not open your eyes," the bear reminded him. Finally, they came back up and the man saw an igloo along the edge of the ice pack. They went inside and the man saw another bear with a spear in his haunch. The first bear said, "If you can take that spear out of the bear and make him well, you will become a good hunter." The man broke off the shaft, eased the spear point out of the bear's haunch, and the wound began to heal. Then the first bear took off his bearskin "parka" and became a man. After the wound had healed completely, the bear-man put back on his bearskin "parka," told the poor hunter to climb on his back and close his eyes, and together they went back into the sea. When the bear finally stopped, he asked the man to open his eyes. Looking around, the man realized he had been returned to the spot from which he began his journey. He thought he had only been gone a day, but on arriving home, he found that he had been away a month. From then on, the man was always a good hunter.

In this, as in many other myths, animal spirits represented the controlling powers. Essentially, the Iñupiat saw the universe as a place where the various supernatural forces were largely hostile toward human beings. By means of ritual and magic, however, the Iñupiat could influence the supernatural forces toward a desired end, be it influencing the weather and food supply, ensuring protection against illness, or curing illness when it struck. The power to influence these events came from the use of charms, amulets, and magical formulas, observance of taboos, and the practice of sorcery.

Although all individuals had access to supernatural power, some were considered to be especially endowed. With proper training, these individuals could become a practicing shaman, or *angatqaq*. The Iñupiat angatqaq was a dominant personality and powerful leader, as he, or to a lesser extent she, has been in every society supporting this type of religious practice. Due to his great intimacy with the world of the supernatural, the shaman was considered particularly qualified to cure the sick, control the forces of nature, and predict events. At the same time, he was believed to have the power to bring illness, either to avenge some actual or imagined wrong, or to profit materially from its subsequent cure.

The Iñupiat of this region traditionally saw illness as resulting from the loss of one's soul or the intrusion of a foreign object. A person's soul could wander away during sleep, be taken by a malevolent shaman, or leave because the individual failed to follow certain restrictions placed by a shaman or the culture in general. Illness caused by intrusion was usually the work of a hostile shaman, but in either case, an effective cure for a serious illness could only be achieved through the services of a competent Native curer (Spencer 1959:327–330).

Although the shaman had extensive powers, lay Iñupiat were not without their own sources of supernatural influence. By means of songs, charms, magical incantations, and even names, individuals could ensure the desired end. The acquisition of these instruments of supernatural power came through inheritance, purchase, or trade, with charms and songs changing hands most easily and often. The major difference between the shaman and the lay Iñupiat was the greater degree of supernatural power assumed to be held by the former. The shaman did have one particular advantage, however—access to a *tuungaq* ("helping spirit"). Similar to the concept of a guardian spirit found throughout many North American Indian tribes, the tuungaq was commonly an animal spirit, often a land mammal that could be called upon to assist the shaman. When it was to the shaman's advantage, it was believed that he might turn himself into the animal represented by the spirit.

The showmanship skills of the shaman were no less dramatic than his apparent supernatural ones. During the months of winter darkness, shamans were most active, frequently demonstrating their powers in a qargi or patient's home. Called in to cure an illness, the shaman began by placing himself in a trance. While in this trance, he could speak with a deceased relative of the patient, fly through the air in search of a soul, do battle with the spirit of another shaman, or otherwise demonstrate the extent of his supernatural powers. In the 1880s, Charles Brower, a well-known trader living at Barrow, observed a Point Hope shaman at work and wrote: "Without waiting for dim lights or any such frills, he proceeded to work himself into a trance on the spot. As I stood by watching his dark, contorted features while he writhed on the floor, it wasn't hard to believe that the instructions issuing forth came straight from the devil in person." (Brower 1942:57)

Although these seances characteristically contained ventriloquism, sleight of hand, and induced frenzy, there is reason to assume that in most instances an Iñupiaq angatquq sincerely believed in his own supernatural power. Throughout Alaska and all of the western Arctic, the shaman seldom sought out the position. Rather, an older shaman selected as an apprentice a youth who exhibited behavior that might qualify him for the role. The youth could decline the invitation. If he accepted, he was trained in the profession, acquired the appropriate songs, and began his practice. If he was of unstable personality—not a common occurrence—the role at least gave him the opportunity to channel his behavior in an acceptable fashion.

The influence of the shaman began to decline following the arrival of white whalers who, without regard for the numerous taboos rigidly enforced by the Iñupiat shamans, consistently killed large numbers of whales. Native converts to Christianity, holding the Bible aloft, also flaunted traditional taboos without suffering. By the early 1960s, shamanism was rarely practiced in northern Alaska. This does not mean, however, that individuals once known to be shamans, or capable of becoming shamans, were ignored. On the contrary, the Iñupiat felt quite uneasy about such people.

The reason for this fear was related to the syncretic blending of aboriginal and Christian beliefs. The modern Iñupiat conceived of the supernatural world as being composed of God, Satan, and numerous vaguely defined devils. The belief in many devils was not only an aboriginal residue but was actually in perfect conformity with the version of Christianity presented by many missionaries. Furthermore, the Iñupiat believed that a shaman's helping powers (*tuungaqs*) were real spirits and, by implication, that the shamans actually performed the feats they claimed. It followed, therefore, that a shaman who became a Christian did not reveal himself as having been an imposter, nor did he necessarily stop being a shaman. Rather he was expected to exorcise his powers, "send away" the helping spirits, or in some other way, "get rid of them." (see: Burch 1971) By equating the tuungaqs with devils in modern Christian cosmology, it was hardly surprising that the traditional attitude of uneasiness toward shamans was still manifest in the 1950s. This syncretism was further seen in the belief that some psychotic episodes were attributed to possession by devils. At Wainwright, for example, an Iñupiat minister was once called in to pray over an individual who had a "fit" in an attempt to exorcise his devils—a request not unlike that made of a shaman seventy-five years ago.

By the 1960s, the Presbyterian, Catholic, and Episcopal churches on the North Slope had been joined by new denominations including the Assembly of God in Barrow and Kaktovik and, to a lesser extent, the Evangelical Friends in the area of Point Hope. All of these church groups stressed the efficacy of prayer, that is, the immediate intervention of God in daily affairs. This intervention was usually asked in two major areas: hunting and health. The churches preached that God could heal directly, although the evangelical churches put forward this doctrine more forcefully. Presbyterians, for example, used prayer as a supplement to medicine whereas the Assembly of God members frequently reversed the emphasis. In the Presbyterian Church, the minister or congregation as a whole might be asked to pray for an ill member. In the Assembly of God Church, any small group of members regardless of status were commonly called upon to help "lay on (healing) hands" when someone was sick.

Faith healing was an integral part of evangelical doctrine and examples of success were frequently reported by Iñupiat converts. A young boy mangled in the threads of a tractor and given up for dead was prayed over, after which it was reported he got up and walked home seemingly without ill effect. A woman seriously ill with tuberculosis was sent to the hospital for further examination and rest. After prayers were said for her, the illness went into remission. A man, caught in an avalanche of snow in the mountains, prayed and was saved from death. Films portraying the faith healing of Oral Roberts and other evangelical ministers were occasionally shown by local missionaries or lay Iñupiat preachers, and they dramatically reinforced belief in the immediate power of prayer.

Services differed significantly according to the church in question. The more formal service of the Presbyterian and Episcopal churches de-emphasized individual participation, whereas the evangelical churches encouraged personal expression. A typical Assembly of God service began with the singing of revival hymns to the accompaniment of an organ or guitar. Individual and group prayers and the offering of personal testimonials followed. As many as 75 percent of the congregation might speak in one evening. Offering their remarks in emotion-laden voices, they would relate the story of their "salvation," enumerating in detail such past sins as drinking, dancing, playing cards, and smoking (women tended to be less specific than men in this regard), and why they were going to refrain from committing such acts in the future.

Prior to the arrival of the evangelical and sect missionaries, each village had one established church. There is little question that the homogeneity of religious belief arising from this arrangement encouraged a sense of identity within the village as well as with the Judeo-Christian world. Regular services brought together most village residents in a common ritual. The establishment of local church offices provided a structure for the emergence of leaders. And a common doctrine set a standard by which Iñupiat could measure their own religious and moral behavior. So, too, resentment against others within or outside the community found expression in the act of refusing to attend church—an action that was quite effective since attendance was one of the few activities expected of all village residents. Only salaried employees could be considered exempt, and even then, the more religious felt considerable qualms about working on the Sabbath.

LAW AND SOCIAL CONTROL

Traditional Iñupiat society was characterized as being quite limited in the development of social institutions beyond the family. Thus, in many respects, settlements and villages represented a community of interest rather than a corporate unit. Since there was no political organization, various social sanctions, customary law, common goals, and norms had to provide the essential fabric of settled life. Individuals had great freedom of choice in their actions, but their security lay in cooperating and sharing with one another.

Nonconforming individuals, such as an aggressive bully or persistent womanizer, presented a problem. If nonconformists could not be curbed by kin or the force of public opinion, the remaining alternative was to exclude them from the community's economic and social life—an effective sanction given the unpredictable conditions of Arctic existence. If severe interpersonal conflicts arose between one or more members of different kin groups, the villagers were faced with a more serious dilemma, for no technique existed for resolving feuds. It was not until long after the government had assigned U.S. marshals to police this northern area that interfamily feuds resulting in bloodshed disappeared entirely.

As long as Iñupiat economic and social security depended on the assistance and support of others, gossip, ridicule, and ostracism was quite effective in ensuring conformity. Iñupiat socialization, emphasizing as it did rapid fulfillment of the child's needs and wants, freedom of action in many spheres, early participation in adult-like responsibilities with appropriate recognition for achievement, and the rejection of violence in any form also encouraged the formation of a conforming rather than a rebellious personality type. However, this method of social control was considerably weakened when family groups became less cohesive, when greater opportunities for wage labor brought increased economic independence, and when substantial value conflicts began occurring between generations. All of these trends had become fully developed by the late 1950s.

Also, temporarily broken homes were a serious problem in the early years of this decade as the U.S. Public Health Service undertook a major effort to reduce the incidence of active tuberculosis in Alaskan villages. The impact this hospitalization campaign had on community life was pronounced. In Kaktovik, for example, approximately 25 percent of the adult population had to leave the village for up to two years. In some other northern villages, the rate was even higher. Of these, 6 percent were parents. Admission rates were strikingly high in other villages, too, requiring in each instance a pronounced family readjustment. Fortunately, by the late 1950s, advances in drug therapy had allowed most patients to be treated in their own communities.

Family life also suffered as a result of other factors. Fathers and sons left their communities in search of seasonal jobs in major employment centers. Other sons and daughters left to attend boarding schools. And there was a significant increase in binge drinking in village and home with a corresponding rise in physical abuse within the family. By the 1960s, the latter problem was of such magnitude that it was a common topic of conversation in church, at village council meetings, and at informal gatherings.

Given these changes, it was hardly surprising that traditional mechanisms of social control had lost much of their effectiveness. As adults became less dependent on others, they were less bound by public opinion. In 1961, a long-term Iñupiat male employee at a military site expressed his feelings: "No one is going to tell me not to drink. I've got a steady, paying job and I can do whatever I want." Some of the more alienated youths offered similar opinions. After a short visit to Wainwright, one teenager from Barrow spoke of the strict curfew in effect there:

> When I visited the village, I didn't know about the midnight curfew for young people. I went out until about three in the morning with a local girl. I went out late the next night, and on the following day a village council member spoke to me at the post office about the curfew. I told him I was a visitor from Barrow and I shouldn't have to obey the curfew. He said I did, but I kept going out late anyway. Finally, the whole council called me in and told me I could not go out after twelve o'clock anymore, and I said, "This is America, not Russia, and I can go out as much as I like." The council didn't like that, but there was nothing they could do. I left soon afterwards, though. That Wainwright is a strict place.

After a similar visit to Kaktovik, this same youth gave further insight into his negative attitude toward the more isolated Iñupiat villages:

> After living in the States, I can't stand this place for very long. The people here, they don't know what it is like outside. Some of the boys brag about how good they are, but I just keep quiet, laughing inside. They haven't seen anything like I have. And another thing, they don't have any respect for privacy. Why, they just come into your house without being invited and drink your coffee, or anything. The people at Barrow don't do things like that. They have much better manners and aren't so backward.

While these comments reflect an especially strong alienation derived in large part from his acceptance of Euro-American stereotypes learned during his life in the "States," many youths in the 1960s showed lessened regard for old Iñupiat ways and, after leaving home, simply ignored the traditional pressures to conform. When their actions disrupted village life, as was the case of individuals who became aggressive after drinking, they might be brought before the village council. But the effectiveness of the council as a deterrent depended largely on the prestige of the council members, their experience, the type of problem brought before them, and the degree of support given by local whites.

A few village councils such as the one at Point Hope were organized as early as the 1920s when they were encouraged by resident missionaries, but at best they were only nominally effective. The only significant legal authority they had was the ability to file a complaint with the U.S. Marshal. The major impetus for the development of local self-government—Euro-American style—on the North Slope came in the mid-1930s after governmental responsibility for the Iñupiat had been placed under the jurisdiction of the Bureau of Indian Affairs (although one or more councils had been organized 20 years earlier farther south in the Kotzebue area). With the passing of the Indian Reorganization Act (IRA), the Iñupiat and other Native Americans were urged to draft village constitutions and bylaws, ratify them by majority vote, and submit them for approval to the U.S. Secretary of the Interior. By 1960, all Iñupiat villages with a population of 100 or more had some form of self-government. Most were organized formally with an elected president, vice-president, secretary, treasurer, and several council members. They met at regular intervals and took action on such common problems as supervising the operation of Native cooperative stores, spring village clean-up, promoting civic improvements, and making and enforcing local regulations. In every instance, elected officials were Iñupiat men.

One of the difficult problems facing the council members was that of coordinating community activity, such as village clean-up. Not only did these village leaders have to contend with lack of precedent, but they had to be careful not to identify themselves too closely with white power figures for fear other village members would conclude they no longer represented Iñupiat interests. Leaders who ceased sharing the norms, objectives, and aspirations of the larger group ceased being leaders. Nor could they assume an authoritarian or aggressive stance in their actions for such behavior went directly against traditional Iñupiat values.[2]

An illustration of how these factors resulted in the replacement of a village leader at Point Hope is reflected in the efforts to build a community-wide electric power plant. Most local residents favored obtaining a power plant, but they had little knowledge of how to implement such a plan. Nevertheless, with the urging of the council president, arrangements were made and the plant constructed. Problems arose immediately, most of them linked to monthly charges each family had to pay for electricity. Locally designated "bill collectors" refused to press for these payments, at which point the council president, faced with the possibility of bankruptcy, aggressively reminded the villagers of what happened to white Americans who refused to pay their bills. Although the installation of meters eventually resolved the immediate financial problem, this leader lost much of his influence and was not re-elected to the council. Similar problems emerged elsewhere as the primary qualification for election to village councils began shifting from older prestigious community leaders who had the respect of the community to younger, more educated individuals who had the ability to speak and write good English but had little other knowledge or experience.

But it was in the area of law enforcement that the councils faced their greatest woes. Having established regulations against the importation of intoxicating beverages, the members had no way of enforcing their rulings. The same problem occurred with gambling, curfews, and the confinement of dogs. With the exception of Barrow, by 1960 no community had obtained sufficient funds to hire an outside law enforcement officer, and few local whites, even if requested, had any interest in taking on such a responsibility.

When an individual disregarded a local regulation, he or she was usually approached by a council member, reminded of the ruling, and told to conform. If the individual persisted, the person was brought before the council and asked to account for the behavior. This practice was most effective with village youths but was pursued with adults as well. For more serious offenses like minor theft, a combination of council and family pressures would be applied to the offender, who was usually a teen-ager. Before the 1960s, theft was uncommon among the Iñupiat, and adults spoke of this misdemeanor with strong feelings of indignation. However, by this time the problem had become of sufficient concern that in most Arctic villages, householders locked their doors on leaving home for any length of time.

The issues that the councils were least able to resolve concerned drinking and the curfew. Although liquor was forbidden by local ordinances, moderate drinkers were seldom criticized as long as they indulged in their own homes. Beer and alcohol were obtained by air freight from Fairbanks through a

[2] Distrust of village council members assuming the roles of leader was also common among Yup'ik villages in southwest Alaska. At this time, the Yup'ik word for village council member (*angaayuqaruaq*) was "pretend boss," suggesting that those who took such organizational responsibilities were not recognized as the real leaders (Vaudrin 1974:79). Significantly, present-day leaders are more likely to be elected officials.

resident white or from a friend recently returned from the "outside." Drinking was considered a problem when it resulted in such open hostility as destruction of property, picking a fight, or wife-beating. There were also instances of young Iñupiat who under the influence of liquor, killed the lead dog of another hunter, destroyed furniture and other household items, and broke into government buildings for purposes of theft. Generally, under such circumstances, public opinion did not support taking firm sanctions against the offender. This was largely due to the Iñupiat perception that those who drank were not responsible for their actions, and thus, couldn't be held accountable. That is, "being drunk" was not only an explanation for damaging behavior, it was also a justifiable excuse.

Problems with alcohol were particularly severe in Barrow. According to a middle-aged Iñupiat:

> When I got out of the Army in 1946 and went to Barrow, there was almost no drinking going on there. But now there is quite a lot. Eskimos go crazy when they drink. They just don't know how to hold their liquor. Kaktovik, for example, is a much smaller village and there is more control over the people. Leaders are also much more effective in counseling those who drink. At Barrow, it isn't anywhere near as effective. There are too many people here who just don't care.

In most instances, Barrow teen-agers ignored the curfew. They knew the council had little legal power to enforce its ruling, and therefore prohibitions they didn't like were disregarded. In an attempt to combat this problem, Wainwright eventually tried to raise sufficient funds through household assessments to incorporate the village, thus giving greater legal status to the council's rulings.

Given this increase in social problems, the Iñupiat still maintained a common set of standards covering a wide range of behavior and, with few exceptions, actively conformed to these standards. In the villages, there was no overall sense of lawlessness, no rampant vandalism, delinquency, crime, sexual misconduct, or alcoholism. However, what did disturb village leaders deeply was the realization that, if future generational differences of what constituted right and wrong became more sharply drawn—resulting in a polarization of what constituted approved behavior—the problems they faced could become far more serious.

CONCEPTS AND IDEAS

Ideas that are affectively charged and collectively held are important cultural markers influencing alternative courses of behavior. By analyzing these ideas, it is possible to improve our understanding of how human groups define their world, express their feelings, and make their judgments. In the distant past, regional Iñupiat culture was relatively homogeneous. With the Iñupiat having to devote much of their energies to gaining a living, differences in thought and behavior were frequently directed toward experimentation, which might better satisfy the long-term needs of all of the people. Thus, in the aboriginal context, Iñupiat desires tended to parallel the cultural definition of the desirable—necessity and possibility were closely intertwined.

In spite of the relative homogeneity of this way of life, a thorough description of shared ideas held by the Iñupiat has always been difficult, partly because of their culturally prescribed tendency to keep their thoughts and feelings to themselves. In his study of the Barrow Iñupiat in the early 1950s, Robert Spencer (1959:249) commented on this practice: "No one could feel free to indicate to others that he might be out of sorts. This was true in all interpersonal relationships. People talked, and still do, of the weather, hunting, food. (But) there was no attempt to evaluate situations or to pass judgment on them." Thus, the Iñupiat often underplayed or concealed their unhappy states of mind (though disapproval was certainly conveyed in other ways). Nor did they appear to pay much overt attention to others' problems, not because they were unaware of them, but because it was tactful not to notice. It is the lack of *expression* of negative feelings (but not of sensitivity), coupled with the limited choice of alternatives found throughout much of their history that has made the task of analyzing Iñupiat concepts and ideas difficult—a fact no doubt contributing to the minimal discussion of the topic.[3]

Still, some Iñupiat ideas have long been recognized. One set is closely related to the tentativeness of life, the constant presence of unforeseen contingencies, and the lack of control over matters pertaining to subsistence and health that characterized so much of the Iñupiat past. This fact was brought home to a missionary trained in linguistics who, in the early 1960s, spent time on the North Slope studying the Iñupiaq language. In the course of his investigation, he noted continual use of the word "if" rather than "when" with reference to the future. Traditional Iñupiaq does not provide a choice between "if" or "when-in-the-future." With some frustration the missionary regularly heard the phrase "when Jesus comes" translated into Iñupiaq as "Jesus *kaitpan*," meaning "if Jesus comes."

Similar qualifying expressions found among Iñupiat speakers included "maybe," in regard to the future, or "we're all right so far," in answer to an inquiry concerning the health of a relative. Even more explicit reference to life's tenuousness was contained in the common expression, "If I'm still alive," when commenting about some future action. Vincent Nageak's response to the author's remark about returning to Kaktovik after 1961—"but I might not be here when you get back"—is another case in point. In each of these instances, the Iñupiat perspective reflected a fatalistic outlook on the world. However, it was not a fatalism of resignation, of "giving up" in the face of difficulty, but of the realization that one had little control over the natural course of events. To outsiders who saw the forces of nature as something to

---

[3] In many respects, these traditional views continue. For example, in the late 1980s Edna MacLean (1988a:30), a respected Iñupiaq from Barrow now serving as a professor of Native languages at the University of Alaska at Fairbanks, spoke of her difficulty in writing about her study of Iñupiat values: "This has not been an easy article for me to write. By talking about myself, I am bordering on breaking one of the cultural mores of being Iñupiaq."

be controlled, this attitude was often quite disturbing. Reflecting on Iñupiat attitudes toward life and death in the 1950s, a public health nurse assigned to the Alaska's northern region once said:

> I am always surprised to see their easy acceptance of death. On many occasions, I have visited Eskimo villages to find that I arrived too late, that a child had died a day or two before. The usual response to this was, "Nurse arrived too late and the child died." There was never any thought, "If only she had come earlier," but a simple acceptance of fate.

A similar perspective is reflected in the traditional Iñupiat approach to health and illness. Much greater emphasis was placed on keeping well rather than getting well. Under the conditions of Arctic life, the people had few illusions regarding their ability to cure serious illnesses—other than through the services of a shaman. Even in the late 1950s, village "health teams" were only partially effective in implementing sanitation and other illness prevention programs among the young, largely because of the lack of support of older residents who were less knowledgeable regarding the need for modern health practices.

Nevertheless, this fatalism was not accompanied by lassitude. On the contrary, hard work and industriousness were considered prime virtues. In every village, adults were active much of the time, butchering meat, repairing fish nets, mending clothing, building boats and sleds, improving ice cellars. Those adults who arose late or in other ways gave the impression of having little to do would be admonished by kin with the remark, "How do you ever get your work done?" While lazy people could be found in every village, their actions were actively condemned, criticisms usually taking the form of gossip.

Hard work was not considered an end in itself, however. Nor was there any guiding principle that one should "work first and play later." Both work and relaxation were considered important, and a person should not indulge in one too long without the other. The western concept of the "coffee break" was a popular part of any work gathering, even where there was pressure to finish a given task. While some jobs required immediate attention, such as storing food in ice cellars before a storm, most work was viewed more casually, without any feeling that it must be completed within a specific time. A girl hanging up laundry might stop halfway through and turn to some other activity, perhaps not returning until the following day. A young man might paint part of his bedroom wall and then take a nap. Someone else might work for 12 hours straight butchering and hauling home a large kill of caribou.

This lack of stress placed on finishing a job for the sake of its immediate completion presented problems for those Iñupiat employed in wage labor. The remark by the radar station superintendent at Kaktovik that the Iñupiat like to "take off and go hunting whenever they want to" is a good illustration. It was not that the Iñupiat didn't have a clear sense of job completion. What differed was the work setting in which the concept applied. Of course, boats needed to be secured before a storm; sufficient driftwood or other fuel had to be stored for winter; wounded game should be tracked down and killed.

Photo 30. Repairing fish nets along the shore.

But the Iñupiat saw no need to fill up the gas tank of a Jeep at the end of a day or automatically rewind a movie film after using it.

Fatalism was also tempered by the stress placed on self-reliance. Given the severity of the environment and the limited food supply, this emphasis has always had an important integrative aspect, the ability to care for one's self serving as a prerequisite for survival. This was especially noticeable in Iñupiat attitudes toward illness. Only with the greatest reluctance would individuals be willing to pass on their responsibilities temporarily to another. An Iñupiat with an illness considered quite debilitating in Euro-American society was far more likely to continue her or his work without complaint. This acceptance of illness as a normal part of the life cycle had its roots in the traditional cultural pattern where attitudes of patience and endurance were basic to survival. Actually, those who chose to work steadily, keeping hunting and other gear in repair and maintaining an accurate account of needed goods, were not only being self-reliant; they were also exerting greater control over the world around them, and in so doing, leaving less to fate.

With the continued emphasis placed on cooperation and sharing, one could nevertheless detect a strong current of individualism flowing through much of Iñupiat culture. This was reflected in comments such as: "Nobody ever tells an Eskimo what to do. But some people are smarter than others and they can give good advice. They are the leaders." This individualism was particularly pronounced in the permissiveness of child rearing, which stressed respect for the thoughts and feelings of the young. The way and extent to which a man fulfilled his responsibilities in providing game was an individual one. So, too, a woman was free to make many decisions whether she would accompany her husband on a long hunting trip or visit relatives in another village or town. Prestige was more commonly gained through individual achievement than through association in a particular group.

In aboriginal times, an Iñupiaq's relation with the supernatural was viewed as personal. The shaman, too, gained his power through individualized experiences, rather than in the context of group ritual. Nor did the status of umialik carry any clearly defined authority over others, his role as leader being determined almost wholly by his own qualities and skills and the willingness of others to accept his leadership. Except perhaps within the family, commands were not expected from others, and an authoritarian person met great resentment. Most interpersonal conflicts were settled between the individuals concerned with little outside mediation. Only rarely did an influential village leader speak out authoritatively on behalf of those to whom he was not related by kin, and in such instances there was no assurance that his prescriptions would be carried out. Given such an approach, it is easy to see how difficult it was for leaders in Barrow and other communities to address the rising problems of delinquency and alcohol abuse found among members of different families.

A sense of competition further highlighted the emphasis placed on individualism. Iñupiat games regularly matched one man against another as in foot, boat, and dog races, tests of strength, song duels, dancing, and storytelling. Even kickball, a team effort, featured individual skill with the ball. Betting which hunter would obtain the largest number of seals in a given season also was popular. Competitions were held to determine who could make the best harpoon, kayak, and other material objects. Women competed in skin sewing, making clothing, baskets, and the like. This type of competition continued to be common into the 1960s, and as such provided a reminder of the need to perform well. Not only might physical survival someday depend on it, but competitiveness in the demonstration of skills motivated others to do even better, thereby providing the potential for improving techniques. White employers, too, saw as advantageous Iñupiat ingenuity in using available resources to solve technical problems.

Competition, of course, could get out of hand. Rivalry was expected to be of the good-natured kind, never psychologically injurious to any specific person. Modesty being an important virtue made it less likely that one would flaunt one's skills before another or recount one's achievements in a boasting manner. This was not a self-effacing type of modesty but one that allowed individuals to admit their own merits in a matter-of-fact tone as in, "I make good *mukluks*." Pseudo-self-effacement was occasionally used to draw attention to one's self. Thus, a good hunter who had returned from a hunt with an unusually large supply of meat might remark, "Oh, it was nothing. Anybody could have done it!"

Before the introduction of Christianity, shamans served as a check on the seemingly "too successful" man. The hunter who always got his kill or always appeared able to accomplish any task to which he set himself—*and* who boasted about it, or who refused to share the results—soon incurred the displeasure of the shaman as well as everyone else. If the man by his actions threatened the shaman's leadership, the latter would use his own techniques to plot the successful individual's downfall. Sanctions such as these had the cultural effect of assuring a uniformity of status, which paved the way for the expression of another important idea—cooperation and reciprocal exchange.

As noted earlier, cooperation was instilled in the child at an early age and backed with responsibilities that put these ideas into practice. In addition, children were encouraged to emulate those older than themselves in such a way that they became important symbols of identification. Girls were urged to learn from older sisters and mothers how to sew skins, butcher meat, make clothes, and complete household chores. Boys learned how to hunt, prepare skins, make boats, and carry out similar male-oriented endeavors. Upon achieving adulthood, young men and women were expected to maintain strong ties with their kin; in so doing, they subordinated their own interests to the welfare of the group. Given these conditions, it was easy to understand why the "poorest" Iñupiat was defined as an orphan—a person without kin and, thus, an individual who had no one to turn to in time of need. Economic and social security were largely drawn from the extended family where the giving and receiving of assistance was expected.

Yet if cooperation was still an important ideal for many families in the 1950s and early 1960s, the increased geographical mobility of many village residents reduced the opportunity for its active expression. In families where traditional subsistence pursuits were regularly followed, expectations regarding labor exchange, borrowing, and sharing continued to be reinforced. Men hunted together and shared their catch. Women assisted each other with baby tending, carrying water, and similar household-related responsibilities. Members of related families helped each other, constructing, repairing, and painting houses, borrowing another's boat, sled or dogs, and sharing the use of electric generators. However, as more individuals left their communities for seasonal or year-round employment elsewhere, this cooperative pattern became steadily harder to follow.

Seasonal migration was evident in all Arctic villages. Men left home for summer jobs as soon as spring seal hunting was over in early June. Many sought jobs in central and southern Alaska, or at one of the military sites scattered throughout the newly formed state. Often they were hired on as common laborers or cannery workers, although a few became skilled carpenters, heavy equipment operators, fire fighters, and mechanics. Those joining a union found summer jobs through the employment office in Fairbanks, thereby enabling them to leave directly for their work site. Working "outside" also brought expectations that at least part of the wages would be sent home, an arrangement that was upheld by older married men far more often than by younger single adults.

In other villages like Barrow and Kaktovik, jobs were available locally. But even here, the nature of the work left inadequate amounts of time for subsistence hunting and fishing. Working a six-day week, few individuals could give more than minimal assistance to others and therefore could expect little in return. With sufficient cash income to purchase most of their food and other required goods, it might have been possible to share these items with the full-time hunter in exchange for fresh meat, fish, and other traditional food products. But this modern version of reciprocal exchange was unusual, and the transaction most often occurred through the medium of the village Native store.

Many Iñupiat expressed concern over this turn of events, on the one hand wanting the material advantages of a cash income, and on the other, disliking the penalty that it seemed to require. As the importance of the extended family continued to decline, further reductions in the traditional patterns of cooperation occurred. Could the expression of this value find another institutional base outside the extended family? Non-kin-based institutions carrying the greatest meaning for the majority of adult Iñupiat were the Christian churches. Here, members contributed freely of their time and energy in support of religious activities ranging from weekday services and Mother's Club meetings to summer Bible schools. Similar efforts went into the maintenance of church buildings, missionary residences, and the like. But few thought such collective endeavors could replace the deteriorating cooperative ties linking families and generations.

There was general agreement that while religious institutions could help in providing a sense of identity and purpose for the devout, they were simply not designed to address the mounting economic problems facing Arctic Alaskans and other Native peoples within the state. Just how serious were these problems? In the mid-1960s, the federal government undertook a comprehensive study to find out. In a lengthy report, *Alaska Natives and the Land*, the U.S. Federal Field Committee for Development Planning in Alaska (1968:12–13) concluded:

> Among Alaska Natives generally, more persons are unemployed or are seasonally employed than have permanent jobs. More than half of the work force is jobless most of the year; for them, food gathering activities provide basic subsistence. Only one-fourth of the work force has continuing employment . . . 50 to 60 percent are jobless in March and September. . . . At these times only half of those employed have permanent jobs. In the summers, when no estimates are compiled, joblessness among Natives across the state may drop to 20 or 25 percent. . . . Year round jobs in most villages are few. Typically the opportunities are limited to positions such as school maintenance man, postmaster, airline station agent, village store manager, and possibly school cook or teacher aide. In these places, other adults gain income through the sale of furs, fish, or arts and crafts; find seasonal employment away from the villages as firefighters, cannery workers, or construction laborers; depend upon welfare payments, make their National Guard income stretch mightily; or, as usually is the case, (1) provide for the bulk of their food supply by fishing, hunting and trapping, and other activities of food gathering; and (2) rely upon a combination of means to obtain the cash needed for fuel, some food staples, and for tools and supplies necessary to the harvest of fish and wildlife.

THE ECONOMICS OF DEPENDENCY

The 1960 U.S. census report placed the number of Alaska Natives at approximately 53,000, of which 52 percent were Iñupiat and Yup'ik, and 14 percent Aleut. More than 70 percent of this population lived in 178 villages or rural towns predominantly Native in composition. Half of these were communities of 155 people or less. Over the next few years some of these rural residents migrated to urban centers. However, between 1950 and 1967, 80 percent of the villages grew, many expanding more rapidly than the rate of net annual increase. The expectation by outsiders that Iñupiat and other Native villages would disappear in the 1960s simply did not materialize. Most Iñupiat continued to live in village communities far removed from areas of rapid economic growth. Did those Iñupiat and other Alaska Natives who chose to migrate from their isolated settlements to the growth centers of interior and south-central Alaska improve their economic and social conditions? Not really. A detailed economic study comparing in part the statistics of the 1960 census with a later Department of Interior report concluded that "the relative well-being of the Native people in all of these regions does not vary significantly." (Rogers 1972:177–210)

Other state and federally sponsored research undertaken at the same time determined that high levels of poverty found among the Iñupiat and other Alaska Natives in the 1960 census continued through the decade while income levels for non-Native Alaskans grew steadily. Even taking into account the free health and social services available to Native Alaskans and the value associated with subsistence hunting and fishing, the rich were getting richer while the Natives were getting poorer.[4]

Under the aegis of President Lyndon Johnson's "Great Society" program, additional studies were undertaken of what to do about this widening economic gap. Anticipating significant economic development from power projects, oil and gas exploration, timber and other natural resources, a key U.S. Department of the Interior (1967:25–26) report concluded that future employment opportunities would enable Natives "to make the transition from their present subsistence existence to a more self-supporting one with adequate income and employment." However, instead of stressing assimilation, as had been common in the past, emphasis was placed on "equal opportunity," "equal standards of living," and "equal participation in Alaska's growth and development." Explicit in this and related government documents was the judgment that equal opportunity was the crucial ingredient for Iñupiat and other Native development. More implicit was the qualifier that *if* the Iñupiat and other Natives had equal qualifications, then they should have the same opportunities for advancement. However, this view disregarded the earlier

---

[4] As stated by the Federal Field Commission (1968:528): "The economic position of Alaska Natives, and of the communities in which they live, is steadily falling further behind statewide averages.

history of disadvantageous relationships between Alaska's Native population and white Alaskans.

The concept of equality carried another hidden assumption. It subtly eroded the principle of "unequal" allocation of funds to Iñupiat and other Native groups facing serious economic difficulty. Thus, critics of government policy began promoting the principle that given the history of economic disadvantage, a strong case could be made for preferential rather than equal treatment of Natives in job opportunities and educational programs. That is, where past events provided the Iñupiat and other Alaskan Natives with less than equal qualifications, they deserved a better than equal opportunity now.

Finally, the concept of equal opportunity raised the issue of the Natives' right to develop their distinct culture as well as participate in the economic life of the state. Full access to white industrial society was not an option available to most Natives. If it were, the implication was still that the urban sector of American society had all the advantages and that these should be shared with the minority population. This subtle form of white paternalism was not infrequently a hidden feature of the "full participation" policy, a paternalism that continued to devalue the present and future contributions of Native Alaskans to the rest of American society. In so doing, negative stereotyping and feelings of self-disparagement were further encouraged.

This attitude was reflected in a letter written by an Iñupiat from northwest Alaska to his legislator expressing deep concern over the economic future of the people of his village:

> Again spring is here with us, and work or jobs are pretty dim in our area. Last year, all the men were without work all summer long. My total earnings for 1967 were less than $300 and that worries a man with a family of eight. We hate to get welfare but it is our only solution. It is tough without work and hunting only does not meet our needs. Sometimes we have bad luck even tho we hunt. We have to worry what our next meal will be. But I really thank the BIA office in Nome for giving us help when help is most needed. Even tho we hate to ask for help, our children give us courage to write and ask for help. There are over 25 men in our village and not even one has work prospects. Only three men have steady jobs in our village—that's the store manager, postmaster, and BIA janitor, plus one BIA cook. We need help to get work. I know labor market is scarce. But we should get training for older men without high school education. (Arnold 1969:18)

The problems posed by this Iñupiaq were characteristic of many older village residents in the 1960s. Possible solutions were viewed as being closely tied to the potential contained in exploiting Alaska's natural resources. In the next few years, as the projections for Alaska's oil and gas resources became more clearly understood, the state's future economic growth appeared highly promising. However, this positive outlook did not include the state's rural segment, most of whom were Natives. According to the Federal Field Committee Report (1968:521): "The leading growth industry—oil and gas—is one of the most capital intensive and technology intensive of all commodity-producing industries and employs almost no unskilled or semi-skilled labor." Although Alaska's economic growth would create new jobs at minimum entry levels, the report also stated that these new positions "may well be more than offset by the disappearance of unskilled and semi-skilled jobs in declining industries or trades, and resulting from automation, modernization, and up-grading of work in general. Under these circumstances, programs to place additional Natives in minimum-entry jobs may succeed only to the extent they *redistribute* unemployment rather than alleviate it." (ibid: 521)

The results of this study made it clear that the geographical mobility of the Iñupiat to new growth centers would not ensure their active involvement in Alaska's economic development. To fit the occupational needs of a rapidly modernizing state, the Iñupiat and other Native groups had to have at least the equivalent of a high school education. While such an education was not seen as a sufficient condition for effective Iñupiat and other Native partici-pation, it was regarded as a necessary prerequisite.

The severity of educational needs for the Iñupiat and other Alaska Es-kimos, Indians, and Aleuts was highlighted by the Governor's Commission on Cross-cultural Education (1970:5), which stated that due to improved comprehensive health services and an increased birth rate, the median age of the Native population had become 16.3 years. Of the approximately 16,000 elementary students, more than 11,000 lived in predominantly rural Native communities[5] where school overcrowding was endemic. At Barrow, for ex-ample, buildings constructed to expand the secondary school program had to be used for primary-level students.

Secondary educational facilities were even more limited. As reported by the Governor's Commission, of the seventy-seven village schools operated by the state, only six offered work beyond the eighth grade. Of the seventy-three federally operated BIA village schools, only four offered ninth-grade courses, and only two offered tenth-grade courses. Thus, high school edu-cation for almost all rural youth had to be obtained away from home. By the late 1960s, of the 4600 Alaska Natives attending secondary schools, more than one thousand were sent outside the state for their education, primarily to Oregon and Oklahoma. As increased pressure was placed on the two in-state BIA schools to accept more secondary students, Iñupiat and other Native youths were forced into already overcrowded boarding home programs for borough high schools in Fairbanks and Anchorage (Kleinfeld 1973). Consid-ering the mounting interest of Iñupiat and other Native students in attending high school and the lack of adequate facilities, the prospects for a minimally adequate secondary education were far from satisfactory.

In order to improve the quality of existing schools, personnel at the senior levels of the BIA and state school systems became increasingly interested in supporting new teacher preparation programs, introducing bicultural and bi-lingual materials into the schools, and encouraging more Native participation at the local level. However, an important counterforce was the continuing influence of Social Darwinian views found among whites and inculcated into

---

[5] Though the statistics did not differentiate between Eskimo, Indian and Aleut populations, many of these young students were obviously Iñupiat.

the thinking of some Iñupiat and other Native Alaskans. Belief in the supremacy of white middle-class values and institutions set the stage for outright rejection of Native peoples, or at least the necessity of making them become like whites. Institutionally, this view was reflected in the success-failure orientation of those schools perceived as important in that they provided a ladder where the "most fit" could gain access to the white world. Where middle-class uniformity rather than cultural plurality was the desired end product of the school system, "unsuccessful" students were left with strong feelings of inferiority and ambivalance about the outside world.

With few exceptions, federal and state agency efforts to incorporate local and regional Iñupiat and other Native Alaskans into the educational decision-making process were also a failure. Reasons for this rejection were varied. They included questioning the Iñupiat's ability to make good judgments, simplistic ethnocentric views regarding the benefits of assimilation, problems of a centralized bureaucracy attempting to bring change to small rural villages, the threat of diffused decision-making on the professional status of administrators and teachers, and conscious and unconscious feelings of racism.[6]

This failure also can be attributed to the ambivalence felt by the Iñupiat in promoting their own ideas and plans for educational improvement. As explained by an important Iñupiaq leader from Barrow: "Many Iñupiat think of themselves as quite capable of dealing with whites in community affairs. But when it comes to school matters such as curriculum changes, teacher recruitment, and financial problems, they feel very inadequate."

Even when participation was sought, effective consensus was often hampered by cultural, historic, and generational differences that hampered cooperation between Eskimo, Aleut, and Indian. In addition, wide ranges of opinion were expressed regarding the nature and purpose of education. So, too, state and federal policy-makers, operating in a central bureaucracy and only minimally influenced by recommendations of Iñupiat and other Native advisory school boards, found it difficult to evaluate the degree of importance of these diverse perspectives in undertaking their long-range planning.

However, by the mid-1960s, one could feel the political winds beginning to blow as the Iñupiat began putting out new, articulate, and militant proposals in support of decent education for their students. Typifying this trend was a statement by Barrow's town leaders:

> We, the people of Alaska's Arctic Slope Region, wish to point out the greatest needs of our people. . . . We have societal needs in the areas of communication, transportation, economic viability, health and sanitation, political recognition, social welfare, recreation and many others. We have, however, a rich resource. Our resource is the people of the Arctic Slope Region. On the basis of their

---

[6] Such perspectives were not only found among educational administrators and teachers. Arctic bush pilot Bud Helmericks (1952:221), writing about his life on the North Slope, quotes Jack O'Conner, for 25 years the head of Alaska's Game Commission: "Generations of living off the country have taught the natives to kill today, for tomorrow the game may be gone. Kill anything that moves, as tomorrow it may move out of reach is the natural reaction of such limited intelligence as they possess."

character and ability, our needs and problems can be met. This greatest need, therefore, and the key to solving many of our own problems, is the need for community-wide, quality education. The terms "adequate," "minimum," and "basic" are not acceptable in the general sense when referring to the pre-school, primary, elementary, secondary, and adult education needs of our people.

Ever since the Organic Act of 1884, governmental efforts to assimilate the Iñupiat by providing an education that could enable them to enter the wage economy on an equal footing with whites had failed. Prospects for participation in Alaska's economic future appeared minimal. Social problems within the villages were increasing. And most important of all, following statehood in 1959, Native land holdings were being challenged. The Statehood Act specified that the state should select approximately 103 million acres within 25 years. Since Congress had never determined conclusively the status of Native land rights, this action posed a severe threat of land expropriation. It countered the Organic Act, which stipulated that Natives would not be disturbed in the use or occupancy of their land and that the determination of their title would be reserved to Congress. What could be done? The answer was clear—organize politically. If the Iñupiat and other Alaska Natives wanted to keep their land, they would have to fight for it. Some Native leaders went further, stating that the question of land ownership was only part of a larger struggle involving the right of political and cultural "self-determination." It is issues such as these that we will address in Part Three: *Politics, Petroleum, and Profit.*

PART THREE | Politics, Petroleum, and Profit

Sharing is what has made our culture strong. Only through sharing have we survived as a people in this land.

Eileen Panigeo-Maclean, Inupiaq (1988)

The great lesson of this period in our history is that while the forces of supply and demand are imperfect, and sometimes slow to respond, ultimately they prevail.

C.C. Gavin, Jr., Chairman, Exxon Corporation (1986)

6/Claiming the Land

THREATS TO NATIVE RIGHTS

One afternoon in early August of 1958, while standing on the bluff overlooking the Beaufort Sea, I saw an umiaq with two men in it heading toward Kaktovik from the northwest. Propelled by a large outboard motor, the skin boat slowly made its way past the lagoon, eventually reaching the shore directly in front of my tent. A tall, well-built man leapt from the bow and, anchor in hand, deftly drove its point firmly into the sand. Joined by the other Iñupiaq, both men began unloading food and supplies on to the beach. Soon, the visitors were surrounded by excited villagers of all ages, many of whom greeted them with considerable enthusiasm. Stories had been circulating for some time that two people from Point Hope were planning to make the long journey north to Barrow and then 300 miles east to Kaktovik. One of these expected voyagers was Dan Lisburne, a well-known leader from Point Hope. Now, he and his partner had finally arrived.

I, too, was looking forward to meeting these visitors from far away. Situated at the end of a long spit of land projecting out into the Chukchi Sea 125 miles above the Arctic Circle, Point Hope was the farthest from Kaktovik of any Iñupiat settlement on the North Slope. It also had a deserved reputation as a close-knit community with strong leadership and local spirit, Lisburne had taken the trip partly for enjoyment but more significantly because he wanted to share his experiences and learn those of other villagers living along the Arctic coast. Thus, one issue discussed with the Kaktovik Iñupiat concerned problems they were facing following the forced relocations of their village by the Air Force. Of greater long-range concern was the withdrawal of 4500 acres of land for a military reserve—an area encompassing the entire surface of Barter Island including the village and cemetery. As one local villager, Daniel Akootchook, described the event later on: "No one knew what this was about, or why. We were just told to move. . . . If I had known English then, as I do now, I would have fought to keep the village. . . . We got nothing for having to move. . . . It was not fair of them to do this."

While in Kaktovik, Lisburne shared a similar apprehension about the possibility of the government taking over land south of Point Hope. This concern had arisen two months earlier, after several Iñupiat returned home

141

Photo 31. The arrival of two Point Hope Iñupiat at Kaktovik.

from a hunting trip to Ogotoruk Creek, 30 miles southeast of the village. Lisburne indicated that the Ogotoruk Creek Valley was an important hunting ground for Point Hope people, providing them with large numbers of caribou. While in the area, the Iñupiat had come across government scientists undertaking a survey. The surveyors told the hunters they were engaged in geologic research for the U.S. Atomic Energy Commission (AEC). Not knowing why scientists from the AEC were interested in Ogotoruk Creek, the Point Hope residents were curious. This curiosity soon turned to anxiety as rumors spread that Ogotoruk Creek had been chosen by the AEC as the site for detonation of a large nuclear bomb.

Later that summer, while at the Naval Arctic Research Laboratory in Barrow, I also heard reports about the AEC-sponsored geologic and geographical studies being undertaken in the Cape Thompson area. Although precise information was unavailable, the rumors appeared to be true. The Atomic Energy Commission was indeed actively exploring the detonation of a massive atomic device. The blast, expected to be 100 times more powerful than the one at Hiroshima, was tentatively scheduled to take place in 1962. Ground Zero was Ogotoruk Creek, 31.5 miles southeast of Point Hope.

On returning to my university in the fall of 1958, I learned more. Partly in response to broad popular opposition to the hazards of above-ground testing of atomic weapons by both the U.S. and the U.S.S.R., the AEC had decided it could improve its public image by establishing a program called "Operation Plowshare," drawing on the biblical narrative in which swords were beaten into plowshares. From this peaceful use of the atom, suggested the AEC, would come "a new age of atomic progress."[1] The program was inaugurated June 19, 1957. Still, no specific plan had as yet emerged.

In October of that year, following Russia's launch of Sputnik I, the American scientific community came under pressure to achieve a major technological accomplishment of its own. At the University of California's Lawrence Radiation Laboratory, scientists responded by recommending to the AEC that earth excavation offered the "highest probability of early beneficial success" in the Plowshare program (Brooks 1971:64). Actively supporting the proposal, Dr. Edward Teller, "father of the hydrogen bomb" and director of the radiation laboratory, suggested that the AEC detonate a 2.4-megaton atomic device on the northwest coast of Alaska in the region of Cape Thompson.[2] Such an explosion would create a deep water hole to be used as a harbor for the eventual shipment of coal, oil, and other nonrenewable resources thought to exist along this part of the coast. After exploring other possibilities, the AEC accepted Teller's proposal and on June 9, 1958, publicly gave it a name—"Project Chariot." Four days previously, unknown to the people of Point Hope and other nearby Iñupiat villages, Lewis Strauss, then chairman of the AEC, had requested the withdrawal from the public domain of 1600 square miles of land and water in the Cape Thompson area, including land villagers had earlier sought under the Alaska Native Allotment Act.

That summer, while scientists surveyed the area surrounding Cape Thompson, nuclear physicist Teller and others connected with the AEC and California's Lawrence Radiation Laboratory made speeches in Alaskan cities pointing out the financial benefits the state would receive from the multimillion-dollar investment of federal funds. Further assuring his audiences, Teller told them that "the blast will not be performed until it can be economically justified." Gaining support of the press, Teller and his associates were less successful in getting an endorsement by the state's financial leaders. Some doubted the commercial viability of mineral deposits thought to be available along the coast. Others rejected the idea that a harbor was needed to ship out whatever minerals were found. Still other dissenters associated with the science faculty of the University of Alaska at Fairbanks, concerned citizens, environmentalists, and a few government officials were more vocal in their criticism of the blast itself and its implications for the safety of the people and wildlife of the region. But Dan Lisburne and other Iñupiat leaders from Point Hope, Noatak, and Kivalina, the villages closest to the proposed blast, were not informed and thus remained largely ignorant about the plan. It wasn't until the spring of 1959, after watching a local movie, that Point Hope residents were called to an impromptu meeting by a visiting missionary from Kotzebue and told the rumor about the blast was true.

Although AEC officials excluded Iñupiat villagers from early discussions

---

[1] Some critics of the commission questioned these peaceful intentions, pointing out that from its beginning in 1957 until August of 1961, Plowshare was in fact administered by the AEC's "weapons branch," a division of military application (Davis and Zannis 1973:143).

[2] Later, revised estimates called for a chain of five atomic bombs to be detonated, the largest of which would be ten times more powerful than that set off at Hiroshima.

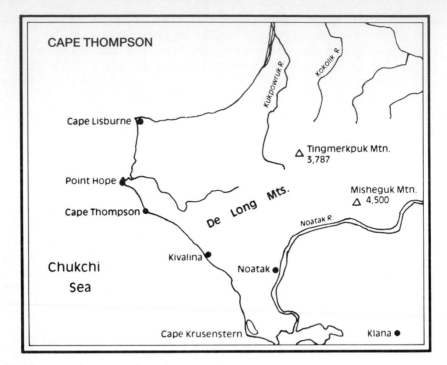

Map 6. Cape Thompson and nearby Iñupiat villages.

about Project Chariot, they did continue to promote it before Alaska's financial community and state legislature, knowing support here was essential. After holding numerous discussions with public officials and private industrial leaders, the commission succeeded in gaining approval from the state as well as Fairbanks and other city chambers of commerce. Plans for the detonation progressed. Acknowledging the skepticism of those questioning the project's accruing any commercial benefit, the AEC shifted its argument for the detonation away from possible economic advantages and toward the experimental, calling it a massive test in "geographical engineering."[3] Under the revised plan, in June 1959 the Environmental Studies Program would try " . . . to determine the effects of a nuclear explosion on the environment—its rock substrata, soils, atmosphere, and biota, including man." (Wilimovsky 1966).

That fall, Don Charles Foote, a young geographer working under contract to the AEC's Environmental Studies Program, was asked by commission staff to explain what he knew of Project Chariot to the Point Hope village council. But it was not until the spring of 1960 that official representatives of the AEC

[3] As John A. McCone, the AEC's newly appointed chairman, testified before the U.S. Congress Joint Committee on Atomic Energy, "We are seeking an alternative to the harbor in Alaska because, as I said to the committee once before, we couldn't find a customer for the harbor."

came to the village to explain details of the proposed blast. Foote (1961:9–10) described what happened in his follow-up report to the AEC:

"To the detriment of the Commission and Project Chariot, the officials who spoke in March, 1960, made several statements which could not be substantiated in fact. Among other things, the Point Hope people were told that the fish in and around the Pacific Proving Grounds were not made radio-active by nuclear weapons tests and [there would not be] . . . any danger to anyone if the fish were utilized; that the effects of nuclear weapons testing never injured any people, anywhere; that once the severely exposed Japanese people recovered from radiation sickness . . . there were no side effects; that the residents of Point Hope would not feel any seismic shock at all from Project Chariot; and that copies of the Environmental Program studies would be made immediately available to the Point Hope council upon the return of the AEC officials to California."[4]

Foote's report went on to describe the AEC delegation's evaluation of how Project Chariot would affect the people of Point Hope. They were told that although there was no need to restrict the area where the men hunted and that the detonation would occur at a time outside the normal caribou hunting cycle, it would be essential that hunters and dogs remain clear of "any remotely dangerous area"; it would be days, weeks, or months before hunters could pass through Ogotoruk Creek. And finally, the residents were informed that, although the AEC would compensate them for damage to structures, there was little possibility, short of long and costly lawsuits, that awards could be made for personal or property damages. Still, a statement was made that some direct compensation would be forthcoming to the villagers prior to the explosion.[5]

Not surprisingly, assurances that Chariot would not be a hazard to the subsistence way of life of the Point Hope Iñupiat were sharply rejected by the village council. Immediately following the close of the meeting, the council voted unanimously to oppose detonation of the bomb. As Foote summarized the results of the meeting: "The net result of the first official presentation of Project Chariot to the people of Point Hope was to produce a profound lack of confidence in the sincerity of the AEC."[6]

Protests soon became more widespread. William Pruitt and other scientists at the University of Alaska, along with those working within the AEC itself,

[4] Many details concerning Project Chariot, Don Foote's role in it, and his overall summary of its impact on the people of Point Hope were later shared with the author while we were colleagues at McGill University.

[5] Several years later, Howard Rock (1962:13), a Point Hope Iñupiat and editor of the newly published Native newspaper, Tundra Times, described how the people were offered material enticements if they were willing to support the project: "Since 1958 there were attempts to lull us, the people of Noatak, Kivalina, and Point Hope. We were wheedled with rewards of acclaim from science and the peoples of the world if we would agree to go along with Project Chariot. Model housing programs were dangled before our eyes if we would move for a year into a newly built housing center, either at Nome or Kotzebue. After a year we would be moved back, not to our home villages, but to a combined spanking new housing center close to the harbor area."

[6] This negative appraisal was greatly reinforced the following August when the editor of the Fairbanks Jessen's Weekly (Gregory 1960) wrote that a leading AEC official had reported that Point Hope men had not hunted in the Ogotoruk Creek area for many years prior to 1959–60.

pointed out that the tundra's food chain was peculiarly susceptible to radio-active fallout from recent atomic testing. Alaska's caribou, for example, were found to contain approximately seven times as much strontium 90 as the meat of domestic cattle in the southern part of the United States. This was because caribou fed on lichens, rootless plants deriving their nutriment from the dust in the air as it was carried down by rain and snow, thus directly absorbing the radioactive fallout before it became diluted in the soil (Brooks 1971:70). Since the Iñupiat ate the caribou, they already had a considerably greater intake of strontium 90 than other Americans. Further above-ground testing would only add to the already existing danger. The inland Iñupiat of An-aktuvuk Pass, several hundred miles northeast of Cape Thompson, also spoke out sharply against additional testing. Located high in the Brooks Range, they relied more heavily on the caribou for their subsistence than did other Arctic villagers. In a plea to the outside world, Simon Paneak, head of the village council, noted that the radiation levels " . . . keep getting higher and higher, and we just don't know what to do."[7]

While the conflicts generated by Project Chariot continued, another government-imposed threat to Native subsistence was just beginning. In May of 1961, at Barrow village 200 miles north of Point Hope, John Nusunginya, an Iñupiat and member of the state legislature, was hunting eider ducks. These ducks have always served as an important part of the Iñupiat diet, especially in spring when other forms of Native foods are limited. However, a 1916 international Migratory Bird Treaty between the United States, Can-ada, and Mexico, banned the hunting of waterfowl from March to Septem-ber—the only time they spent in the Arctic. Until 1961, no attempt was made to enforce this convention in Alaska. But after poachers farther south violated the treaty, game wardens in the Bureau of Sport Fisheries and Wildlife of the Department of the Interior were ordered by the Interior Secretary to see that the treaty was obeyed. As a result, on Saturday, May 31, 1961, Nusun-ginya was arrested by Harry Pinkham, a federal warden. Several other Iñupiat were arrested as well. All day Sunday and Monday, the villagers planned their response.

Monday evening, a delegation of Iñupiat leaders asked warden Pinkham to meet with other local residents at a town meeting in the nearby community hall. Arriving at the hall, Pinkham was greeted by more than 300 Iñupiat, 138 of them holding eider ducks along with a written statement that the individual hunter had taken the duck out of season. As the warden watched, all those present signed a petition addressed to President Kennedy demanding

[7] On March 3, 1961, the Point Hope village health council finally wrote to President John Kennedy opposing the proposed chain explosion, stating that such a detonation would be " . . . too close to our hunting and fishing areas. We read about the cumulative and retained isotope burden in man that must be considered. We also know about strontium 90, how it might harm people if too much of it gets into our body. . . . We are deeply concerned about the health of our people now and for the future that is coming." The Iñupiat of this and other Arctic villages all feared that the successful conclusion of Project Chariot would cause serious health hazards, thus making the region and the way of life no longer tenable.

that he allow the continued hunting of migratory waterfowl for subsistence food at any time. The petition was handed to the warden with a request that it be given to the U.S. President with the explanation that when the season legally opened, ducks would have already left the Arctic for warmer climates. If the government was saying that the Iñupiat could not utilize waterfowl for their subsistence hunting, it should also know that "hunger knows no law." By 1961, all charges against the 139 defendants were dropped. The treaty was never changed but neither have further arrests been made.

EMERGING POLITICAL ASSOCIATIONS

Alarmed by increasing threats to their land and livelihood, Iñupiat Eskimos from the north and Yup'ik Eskimos in the south decided to undertake more explicit political action. With funds obtained from the national Association on American Indian Affairs, a major conference was held at Barrow in November 1961. From this gathering emerged the *Iñupiat Paitot* (People's Heritage), the first political organization in the Alaskan Arctic designed to protect aboriginal Native land rights. In discussing Project Chariot, the conference claimed that the proposed site of the detonation belonged to the Eskimo people and that because the government had no right to undertake research there without their approval, the Department of the Interior should revoke the license of land withdrawal given to the AEC. Additionally, criticism was directed at treaties limiting the subsistence hunting of waterfowl. The opening statement of the conference set the tone for the discussion that followed:

> We the Iñupiat have come together for the first time ever in all the years of our history. We had to come together in meeting from our villages from the Lower Kuskokwim to Point Barrow. We had to come from so far together for this reason. We always thought our *Iñupiat Paitot* [aboriginal hunting rights] was safe to be passed down to our future generations as our fathers passed down to us. Our *Iñupiat Paitot* is our land around the whole Arctic world where the Iñupiat live.

Within a year, Chariot was set aside by the AEC, due in large part to the rising chorus of protest mounted against the project by organizations across the United States, including Alaska's northern Natives and their recently formed Iñupiat Paitot. Nevertheless, other problems of greater severity were rapidly developing. Of particular concern to Alaska's Natives were actions flowing from passage of the 1958 Alaska Statehood Act. This legislation, while acknowledging the right of Natives to lands they used and occupied, nevertheless authorized the new state government to select and obtain title to 103 million acres from the territory's public domain. With each selection by the state, more Native lands were placed in jeopardy.

The question of how to resolve this conflict was presented to the U.S. Department of Interior's Bureau of Land Management (BLM) in 1961 by

Athabascan Indians living in the Minto Lakes region of interior Alaska, south of the Arctic Circle. Seeing the site as potentially profitable for future oil production and immediately valuable as a recreation area, the state requested a large parcel of land near Minto Village. Further arrangements were made to build an access road to the area for Fairbanks residents and other visiting sportsmen. The Minto Athabascans filed a protest with the U.S. Department of Interior asking it to protect their rights by rejecting the state's application. Shortly thereafter, sportsmen, conservationists, biologists, and other interested parties joined in the debate. Finally, in 1963, all the groups involved sat down with state representatives to seek a solution. At this gathering, the Minto village chief, Richard Frank, argued that the proposed recreational development would destroy the Native way of life and suggested that the project be undertaken elsewhere, where increased hunting pressure would not threaten local subsistence. "A village is at stake," he said. "Ask yourself this question: Is a recreation area worth the future of a village?" No answer was forthcoming, everyone eventually recognizing that the issue of who was to control the land could only be decided at the federal level. As the state continued selecting lands in other sections of Alaska, similar protests were filed by Native villages and associations. In 1963 alone, a thousand Natives from 24 villages petitioned Interior Secretary Stewart Udall to install a "land freeze" on all land transfers from the federal government to the state until Native rights had been clarified.

Nor was the state selection of public domain land the only threat faced by Alaska's Native population. The U.S. Army Corps of Engineers had proposed that public domain land be withdrawn along the Yukon River for the construction of the immense Rampart Dam, behind which a lake "greater than Lake Erie or larger than the state of New Jersey" would be formed (Brooks 1971:79). At a cost of several billion dollars, this dam would produce five million kilowatts of power, thereby attracting industry to the area, particularly aluminum mining. Exploratory funds had already been provided by Congress. Support again came from Alaska's federal and state senators and congressmen, large private contractors, and urban mayors all desirous of "opening up vast areas to mineral and timber development." Nevertheless, active opposition to the dam quickly emerged from another federal agency, the U.S. Fish and Wildlife Service, which stated in its report to the Army Corps of Engineers: "Nowhere in the history of water development in North America have the fish and wildlife losses anticipated to result from a single project been so overwhelming. . . . We strongly oppose authorization of the Rampart Canyon Dam and Reservoir Project." Similarly, the 1200 Native villagers living in the Yukon Flats area where the dam was to be built offered their own assessment of the proposal by filing claims to more than a million acres of land adjacent to the river, stating: "We use an area of 1648 square miles for hunting, fishing, and for running our traplines. This is the way in which our fathers and forefathers made their living and we of this generation follow the same plan." (Arnold: 1976:103)

Like Project Chariot, the Rampart Dam proposal was eventually discarded following detailed federal and private studies that pointed out its economic and ecological weaknesses.

As pressure mounted on the federal government to resolve the issue of Native lands, Alaska's congressional delegation in Washington put forward a number of proposals. Senator Ernest Gruening recommended that the problem be taken up by the U.S. Court of Claims. Senator Bob Bartlett thought state land transfers should proceed without waiting for the land claims issue to be resolved—a proposition strongly endorsed by state officials. Leaders of the Association on American Indian Affairs, various religious groups, and similar supporters of Native American interests urged that no land transfers be awarded until the claims were settled. But still missing in this increasingly national debate was a forceful, articulate presentation from Alaska's Native people.

By 1965, several regional Native organizations, including the Tanana Chiefs and southwest Alaska Council of Village Presidents, the Fairbanks Native Association, and the Cook Inlet (Anchorage) Native Association, had been formed to address common interests including land, village housing, education, welfare, and the need for improved health facilities. A year later, at a meeting organized by a young Barrow Iñupiat, Charles "Etok" Edwardsen, Jr., the Arctic Native Slope Association came into being, its members immediately voting to place their claim on fifty-eight million acres— virtually all the land north of the Brooks Range—based on aboriginal use and occupancy. Board members of the association were elected from Kaktovik, Point Hope, Anaktuvuk, and other North Slope villages.

In the fall of 1966, more than 250 leaders from seventeen regional and local associations came together in the first statewide meeting of Alaska Natives. Most of the funding came from Tyonek, an Athabascan village that had earlier obtained almost $13 million from oil leases on its reserve. Overcoming a long history of distrust, the Eskimo, Indian and Aleut representatives at this meeting unanimously recommended that a freeze be imposed on all federal lands until Native claims were resolved; that Congress enact legislation settling the claims; and that there be consultation with Natives at all levels prior to any congressional action. In addition to gaining experience in how to overcome their differences, Native leaders at this conference also learned another important fact—unity brings political recognition and strength. Astonished at the attention given the conference by well-known state politicians, one Native leader observed, "If any delegate was seen paying for his own meal, it was probably because he chose to dine alone!" (Arnold 1976:115) Next year, following a series of additional meetings, the Alaska Federation of Natives (AFN) was formally brought into being, with offices located in Anchorage. While problems of cultural differences, distinct languages, regional vested interests, and limited funding would continue to plague the organization, it was nevertheless able to provide a convincing

Figure 5. Symbol of the Alaska Federation of Natives

united voice in the effort of Alaska's Natives to achieve a land claims settlement from the U.S. Congress.[8]

The first breakthrough for the Native population occurred later in 1966, when Interior Secretary Morris Udall imposed a "land freeze" on all federal land transfers to the state until Congress acted on the claims issue. Aghast, the Governor of Alaska filed a lawsuit requiring Udall to transfer lands to the state. Concurrently, further claims were made by other Native villages and associations. By 1967, 20 percent more Alaska land had been claimed than actually existed (Brewer 1975:264). Given the seriousness of the impasse, federal action had to be taken. In the summer of 1967, two bills were introduced to Congress to resolve the issue. One was sponsored by the Department of Interior. The other had the support of the Alaska Federation of Natives. Both requested money and land, but the former authorized a maximum of 50,000 acres per village while the latter made no mention of a maximum, the actual amount to be determined by the subsistence needs of the people in question.

The state, too, faced a potentially severe crisis. State revenues were declining, partly because the freeze prevented the issuance of oil leases on federal lands from which it was to receive 90 percent of federal revenue. It also recognized the growing political importance of the AFN and that Native claims would precede the obtaining of their remaining public domain lands. Thus, Governor Walter Hickel proposed that the two work together to achieve

---

[8]The Tundra Times newspaper and its able editor, Howard Rock, played a crucial role in disseminating knowledge and communicating differing views among Alaska's Native peoples. Still, disagreements such as those between northern Eskimos and southeastern Indians were common. Thus, whereas the southeast Alaska Native Brotherhood wished to obtain money for its lost lands in the U.S. Court of Claims, the Iñupiat and Yup'ik Eskimos wanted the land itself. In a July 1963 letter to the editor of the Tundra Times, Eben Hopson, the Iñupiat leader from Barrow, wrote of his concern: "I can just picture you and a handful of other Eskimos sitting at a conference table with a battery of members of the Alaska Native Brotherhood and being voted down on every proposal you might have." Editor Rock responded to Hopson's letter that what he had in mind was an "affiliation" rather than a "merger."

a satisfactory settlement for both.[9] The resulting state/AFN Land Claims Task Force report recommended that forty million acres of land be conveyed to Native villages in fee simple (full legal ownership); that all lands used for hunting and fishing continue to be available for that purpose for 100 years; that the Native Allotment Act remain in force; that 10 percent of income from oil sales/leases of certain lands be paid to Natives, the total of which would be at least $65 million; and that the settlement be carried out by business corporations organized by villages, regions, and one statewide. Senator Gruening introduced the task force bill into Congress in 1968 and arranged for public hearings by the Senate Interior Committee to be held in Anchorage. Encouraged to attend by the AFN and the *Tundra Times*, villagers from Barrow in the north to Ketchikan in the southeast selected spokespeople to attend. The resulting speeches by Natives from across the state were consistent in demanding rights to their land. Andrew Isaac, traditional chief of the interior village of Tanacross and a well-known Native leader, spoke for most rural villagers when he made his presentation:

> I saw my first white man in 1904. He was a preacher. During the course of the years I saw more white men. In the early 1940s, a highway was built near Tanacross, and white men have come on to our land more and more. . . . We made our claim in 1963 because the state came in and selected our land—everything, even our village and graveyard. This is not fair. We own our land. The white man does not.

Major opposition came from the Alaska Sportsmen's Council and the Alaska Miner's Association. The former objected to the granting of land but approved a cash settlement. A spokesman for the latter association was opposed to both, stating that " . . . neither the United States, the State of Alaska, nor any of us here gathered as individuals owes the Natives one acre of ground or one cent of the taxpayer's money." (Herbert 1970) Underlying the sportsmen's opposition was the threat of reduced access to hunting and fishing lands, whether for individual or commercial interest. Miners and others averse to a land settlement feared that the loss of forty million acres would dramatically reduce opportunities for the state's future economic development. No one, however, was fully prepared for the momentous discovery that was to occur shortly, hundreds of miles to the northeast, or how that event would reshape the debate over Alaska's land and the future of its people.

DISCOVERY AT PRUDHOE BAY

In the spring of 1907, a half-century prior to the land claims hearings, the eight-man crew of the Anglo-American Polar Expedition stood on the shore

---

[9]As Edgar Paul Boyko, the state's attorney general, put it, "The state needs land—the Natives need land. The state and the Natives should go into partnership." For a more in-depth discussion of this effort, see: Arnold (1978) and Naske and Slotnick (1987).

of Flaxman Island 100 miles west of Kaktovik, surveying the damage that had occurred to the schooner *Duchess of Bedford* during its winter layover. Observing caulking torn from the ship's seams, the consensus was that the vessel was no longer seaworthy, and thus the crew had no recourse but to return to Victoria, British Columbia, from whence they had begun their journey a year earlier. Most reached home by boarding a passing whaler. Another dog-sledded southwest across Alaska to the coastal port of Valdez. However, Ernest Leffingwell chose to remain and continue his geographic and geologic investigations.

Over the next few years, he and several Iñupiat assistants mapped the entire Arctic coast from Barrow to Herschel Island in western Canada. Eventually, Leffingwell returned to Washington, D.C., where under sponsorship of the U.S. Geological Survey, he completed in 1919 a detailed report on his investigations. In this monograph he identified a gray sandstone outcropping of rock found along the coast that he aptly named *Sadlerochit* formation, a name taken from an Iñupiaq word meaning "area outside the mountains." But what caught the greater attention of his readers was the description of petroleum seeping from the ground at Cape Simpson, fifty miles southeast of Point Barrow, and at Angun Point, thirty miles southeast of Kaktovik— locations the Iñupiat had visited for years, cutting out blocks of oil-soaked tundra for use as fuel.

The timing of Leffingwell's report coincided with the growing industrial needs of the United States for petroleum. The recently concluded World War I had demonstrated to American governmental and military leaders that a secure source of oil was essential if the nation was to maintain its growing status as a world power. Shortly thereafter, President Harding designated a large portion of Alaska's North Slope (approximately the size of Indiana) as a Naval Petroleum Reserve to be used in time of national emergency. That emergency came in December 1941, following Europe's blockade of oil to imperialist Japan and the latter's attack on Pearl Harbor. Two years later, $60 million was spent by the federal government to find and develop oil fields in the reserve. But success was limited. At Umiat, a short distance inland from the Colville River delta on the Arctic coast, thirty-six shallow wells were drilled, but only one produced any oil. Pumping 120 barrels a day, it was of no commercial value. Soon, Umiat was added to the long list of northern ghost towns.

Following World War II, the U.S. oil industry instituted an extensive search for Alaskan petroleum. In 1957, at Swanson River on the Kenai Peninsula not far from Anchorage, it succeeded. Richfield Oil Corporation drilled an important commercial well that was soon producing 900 barrels per day. This discovery, along with other encouraging petroleum and gas explorations, was crucial in helping convince Congress that the territory did indeed have the economic potential to become the forty-ninth state.

In the next decade, geologists explored most of Alaska's federal and state lands including those on the North Slope. Then, in the winter of 1965–66,

Photo 32. The abandoned site of Umiat in the summer of 1958.

after obtaining approval from the state, Exxon and Atlantic Richfield oil companies flew in drilling equipment to an isolated inland site 330 miles north of Fairbanks. There in January 1967, they drilled 13,517 feet without success. Pushing sixty miles northward, a second well was drilled at Prudhoe Bay on the Arctic coast. On December 26, 1967, in thirty-degree-below-zero weather, an Exxon geologist recalled what happened next: "We could hear the roar of natural gas like four jumbo jets flying right overhead . . . as flare from a two-inch pipe shot at least thirty feet straight into that wind. It was a mighty encouraging sign that something big was down below." (Rintoul 1986:22) That something big was oil-rich sadlerochit sand that had been deposited 200 million years before when the North Slope was a tropical wilderness. It represented the largest petroleum deposit ever encountered in North America, with an estimate of 9.6 billion barrels of recoverable oil.

Today on Flaxman Island, fifty miles east of Prudhoe Bay, one can still find the weathered cabin built by Ernest Leffingwell from the timbers of the *Duchess of Bedford*. On the outer wall of that structure, a cedar sign placed by the Alaska Division of Parks on authorization of the National Park Service's Office of Archeology and Historic Preservation states: "From this base camp geologist Ernest D.K. Leffingwell almost single-handedly mapped Alaska's Arctic coast during the years 1907–1914. He also identified the Sadlerochit—main reservoir of the Prudhoe Bay field."

The Iñupiat who travel to this area in search of game occasionally stop and observe the plaque on the cabin's weathered wall. Their relatives were the ones who helped Leffingwell map the Arctic coast, making it considerably more than an "almost singlehanded" effort. They also reported oil seeping from the ground near Barrow and Kaktovik. But neither that generation nor those following had any indication of the dramatic changes that would occur on the North Slope and elsewhere following the 1968 discovery of petroleum in the sadlerochit sands of Prudhoe Bay. Among those many changes was the assurance that settlement of Alaska's Native land claims would now be addressed with much greater urgency.

CHANGES IN LEADERSHIP

Steps to resolve Native claims were intimately related to the land freeze. It the two were separated, oil-rich areas could be developed with lessened regard to the claims issue. If the freeze remained in place, petroleum and gas would remain untapped. Thus, depending on one's political and economic interests, major attention was focused on either supporting or removing the freeze. With the 1968 election of Republican Richard Nixon to the presidency, Walter Hickel, Alaskan governor and successful commercial developer, was nominated to become Secretary of Interior. Hickel, a vocal critic of the freeze, was in turn viewed negatively by powerful conservation groups and their influential Washington lobbyists. To receive confirmation as Interior Secretary, he needed a broader base of support. The AFN, in turn, would give its support if Hickel agreed to continuing the freeze until the claims issue was resolved. Hickel finally agreed and was later confirmed. The AFN had obtained another victory in its effort to obtain greater political influence.

The Federation further enhanced its national image by obtaining former U.S. Supreme Court Justice Arthur Goldberg and former U.S. Attorney General Ramsey Clark as key legal advisers. This, however, caused considerable dismay within the ranks of the AFN, particularly among staff lawyers who had long represented regional Native interests. During this earlier period, the ability of the AFN to resolve its internal contradictions had been based largely on an understanding whereby board members meeting in Anchorage regularly consulted with regional lawyers. Following these contacts, proposals were then ratified at meetings of regional associations prior to any action being taken by the AFN Board. Though cumbersome, this was compatible with the Native value placed on consensus (Ervin 1976:61). But when Goldberg was brought on the team, lawyers for the regional associations believed their interests and those of their regions would be reduced in importance— an evaluation of some substance.

Similar changes were taking place within the Native leadership. In the beginning, regional associations were basically "grass-roots" organizations, formed by local village leaders as a means of resisting serious threats to their subsistence-oriented way of life. Then, with the emergence of the AFN, the struggles became increasingly complex. More highly educated urban-based

Natives began moving into positions of leadership.[10] Several of these new leaders had previously attended Mount Edgecumbe or other government-run Native residential boarding high schools. Such shared experiences not only gave them a broader perspective on the world but enhanced their ability to work together in tackling the issues arising within the AFN. Others had received their initial leadership training in federally funded programs such as Alaska's Rural Community Action Programs (RuralCAPs).[11]

Still, these new leaders faced an almost overwhelming set of responsibilities for which they had little preparation. Maintaining regular contact with federal and state politicians in Alaska and Washington, D.C., participating in congressional hearings, giving speeches to chambers of commerce and similar groups, and negotiating conflicts between the AFN and regional associations provided little time to deepen their understanding of the outlook and needs of their largely rural-based constituents. Travel funds, too, were limited. Eventually, as their links to regional and national seats of power strengthened, their ties to the villages diminished—a process that would lead to serious difficulties later on.

As the struggle to obtain a claims settlement continued, the AFN stepped up its campaign to reach supporters sensitive to the needs of Alaska Natives. The civil rights movements of the 1950s and 1960s had attuned many to the problems of poverty and systematic discrimination against America's non-European minority populations. By means of lobbying organizations, press releases, television appearances, speeches, and publications, Americans also came to learn that the Eskimo, Indian, and Aleut, who claimed more than two-thirds of Alaska, owned outright less than 500 acres and held in restricted title only an additional 15,000 acres. While 900 Native families shared the use of four million acres in twenty-three reserves run by the federal Bureau of Indian Affairs, all other rural Native families lived on the public domain (Federal Field Committee for Development Planning in Alaska 1968). For Native subsistence-oriented villagers, minimal cash income combined with the high cost of goods had resulted in a standard of living lower than that of many dispossessed ex-sharecroppers living in the Deep South.

The late 1960s was an era of intense organization by many constituencies seeking improved civil rights, Native rights, women's rights, and environmental quality, all competing for limited federal and state resources. Following the mechanization of southern agriculture and resulting mass migration

[10]At the forefront of this new leadership team were Emil Notti, an engineer of Athabascan descent and the first AFN president; John Borbridge, a Tlingit high school teacher and AFN vice-president; Flore Lekanof, an Aleut and also a teacher; Don Wright, a contractor and former union official; and William Hensley, an Iñupiaq state senator from Kotzebue. Eben Hopson from Barrow was also an important leader although he did not have a level of educational experience comparable to the others.

[11]One of the hallmarks of the 1960s "Great Society" strategy under President Johnson was to initiate a close working relationship between the federal government and the disadvantaged people themselves, thereby bypassing state and local governments that were frequently considered a hindrance to antipoverty efforts. Though this caused great turmoil in federal-state relations, it did provide minority leaders at the local level with an important institutional base from which to engage in advocacy programs.

of black Americans to northern cities, decades of poverty had finally exploded in racial violence. The Poor People's Campaign and its March on Washington drew further attention to severe economic deprivation in both city and countryside. Militants representing the American Indian Movement (AIM) were engaging in major protests from Washington, D.C., to Alcatraz Island near San Francisco in their demand for social justice. An unpopular conflict in Vietnam provoked massive demonstrations thoughout the nation. Thus, the call of Alaska's Native leaders was only one among many—each challenging the American people to re-evaluate the country's political, economic, and environmental goals.

DISCOURSES ON DEVELOPMENT

Several of these conflicting issues came together in late August 1969 at the 20th Alaska Science Conference, a division of the prestigious American Association for the Advancement of Science. Held at the University of Alaska at Fairbanks, the conference leaders had chosen as their theme "The Impact of Oil on the Future of Alaska." This broad perspective grew out of problems of the previous 1968 meeting, which had been the target of protests by student dissidents frustrated with the physical scientists' seeming lack of interest in matters of social and environmental concern. In part to counter the possibility of renewed demonstrations, several well-known social scientists from within and outside the state were invited to speak on the politics of petroleum, public policy and the environment, the ecological impact of Arctic development, and similar topics of a volatile nature. John Borbridge, Jr., a vice-president of the AFN, and I were asked to address the issue of social change in Alaska and its relation to Native peoples. The conference was scheduled for the week prior to the state sale of North Slope oil leases in Anchorage. An almost unbelievable figure of $1 billion was on many people's lips as the amount the oil companies might have to bid for rights to drill at Prudhoe Bay. A state rich in resources but poor in cash was about to receive a phenomenal windfall. Given this provocative atmosphere, the 300 people expected to attend the conference were joined by 700 others, along with a battery of reporters from major newspapers running front-page stories on a daily basis.

The first invited speaker, Robert Engler, a well-known critic of the oil industry, warned his large audience of the impact of the multinational oil corporations on the state's political, economic, and social institutions. He argued that wherever these enterprises had functioned, their concentrated economic power over the community—the most massive of any industry in the world—had been forged into political power as well. Law, public bureaucracies, political machinery, foreign policy, and public opinion, he said, have all been "harnessed for the private privileges of the international brotherhood of oil merchants." By various means, public relations specialists, lobbyists, and lawyers had kept the spotlight away from the penetrating powers of oil, focusing instead " . . . on the mystique of petroleum technology, corporate benevolence, and the possibility for an amenable public to be cut in on 'something for nothing.' " (Engler 1969:3)

A rejoinder to Engler's presentation was given by Frank Ikard, president of the American Petroleum Institute, the industry's key trade and lobbying organization. Ikard, rather than taking Engler on directly, spoke of the oil industry's desire to work with the citizens of the state in a joint venture that would enhance the lives of all concerned. Other oil company representatives addressed the need for a favorable price and tax structure if "a great and lasting oil industry here in Alaska can be developed."[12] James Galloway, vice-president of Humble Oil, a joint owner with Atlantic Richfield of the discovered well at Prudhoe Bay, addressed the environmental issue, saying that some Arctic land had to be torn up to get the oil out. "Let's not fool ourselves," Galloway reminded his audience. "This activity is far past the point of return."

Conservationists from the Sierra Club and similar organizations responded sharply, reminding the participants that Congress was about to pass the National Environmental Policy Act, which required the government to make a detailed public list of any adverse environmental effects of every project in which it was involved before action could be taken. Underlying much of the debate that followed was the question of whether Alaska could control the recovery of oil or whether the oil industry would end up controlling Alaska. Senator Ted Stevens, throwing away his prepared speech, spoke heatedly, saying, with appropriate gestures, "I am up to here with people who tell us how to develop our country." Federal regulations were not needed to govern construction of the proposed pipeline to Prudhoe Bay, Stevens told his audience. Such proposals suggesting that Alaskans were not to be trusted in managing their own affairs were "stupid, absolutely stupid." Compromises were also proposed suggesting that the state was new enough and rich enough to build its economy and use its resources "in ways that will not produce derelict landscapes."

In my presentation I briefly traced the problems arising from Alaska Native-Euro-American colonial contact over the past hundred years, suggesting in conclusion that only "by revising white assumptions about Native development will the Eskimo, Indian, and Aleut no longer be immune to Alaska's development." Audience response was not enthusiastic. Shortly thereafter, John Borbridge, Jr., the lone Native participant, addressed the conference. Speaking articulately and with intensity, he cautioned both the audience and the attending press:

> For the most part you have easily gotten used to the Alaska Native, because he had needed your help and your assistance, and a fairly large, complex "industry" has emerged based on his needs. The relationship between one who gives and one who receives when it has been institutionalized is very easy to accept, to adjust

[12]These and other statements that follow are drawn from key conference papers published in a book edited by Rogers (1970) and from the analysis of the politics of oil and Alaska Native land claims undertaken by Berry (1975).

to, and to forget. As long as the arrangement is accepted or tolerated, there is nothing that is disconcerting in this relationship. But what happens as the Alaska Native assumes his rightful place as an equal partner in the economic, political and other power structures of this state? What happens when instead of coming in and asking for help, he comes in by right and asserts his right to share equally in the opportunities and benefits of economic and social development? (Borbridge 1970:202)

The conclusion of his presentation was met with a brief sprinkling of polite applause. It was clear that an aggressive calling for equal rights by a Native northerner could stir less than positive responses in Alaska just as easily as it could further to the south.

After congratulating Borbridge on his paper and greeting several friends who had come to the session, I left the lecture hall and walked to my room at a nearby dormitory. Looking out across the lovely hillside campus, one could see the leaves of the aspen trees beginning to turn a pale yellow, a sure sign of coming fall. But I hardly noticed. On my mind were the sharply conflicting discourses that had been offered over the past few days. With the hindsight of the conference to draw upon, I recognized that my presentation was largely superfluous to the struggles that had unfolded at the lectern and in the hallways. Most participants were not the least interested in being reminded of a colonial past that only stirred guilt feelings among the sensitized and hostility among the unconcerned.

More significant in these debates was the implicit assumption that the land—tundra and forest, federal parks and wildlife refuges—belonged to the federal government and the state and by extension, its citizens. It was as if the claims of Alaska's Natives to the land were nonexistent—or at least an inappropriate topic for discussion at a scientific meeting. And yet, without a resolution of this issue, other struggles over petroleum development and environmental protection would have to wait.

On September 10, 1969, a week after the conference ended, the state of Alaska offered its petroleum lease sale on lands it had claimed in the Prudhoe Bay region. When the bidding was over, competing oil companies had paid more than $900 million to the state for the right to drill on selected lands. For many members of Congress, this major financial windfall to the state placed the whole land claims settlement issue in a new light. No longer did earlier monetary settlement proposals appear so high. The sale further demonstrated to Congress that the state could easily afford to share some of its mineral revenues with its Native people. But on that September day outside the hotel where the sale was taking place, Charlie Edwardsen, Jr., from Barrow, and other supporters calling themselves Concerned Alaska Native Citizens, carried picket signs and handed out leaflets proclaiming, "We are once again being cheated and robbed of our lands" and "Two billion dollar Native land robbery." Under the watchful eyes of both the Anchorage police and local reporters, the AFN president was asked what he thought of such efforts. They did not have the support of the "official Native organization," was his carefully phrased reply.

Photo 33. Picketing the oil lease sale in Anchorage, 1969.
Courtesy Ward Wells Collection, Anchorage Museum of History and Art

During the fall, state officials and private developers continued arguing over how best to develop Alaska. At a meeting organized by the state Legislative Council, Arlon Tussing, a young economist associated with the University of Alaska, offered an alternative view challenging the predominant theme of the day. Speaking at a well-attended Brookings Institution seminar, Tussing reminded his audience, "There is a philosophy of development for development's sake and almost everybody at this seminar shares that philosophy to one degree or another. But this is a set of attitudes peculiar to certain classes of people—businessmen, politicians, and upper-level civil servants, economists and the like. . . . The majority of Alaskans may not be for development for development's sake; most villagers are not, nor are the oil workers on the Slope, nor fishermen. . . . I even suspect that most of the 15- to 20-year-old children of the people here have little use for that philosophy." (Berry:1975:101)

At this same time, Alaska Natives intensified their own internal debate over the question of land rights. The North Slope Iñupiat were especially distraught over reports of the state Division of Lands approving the mooring of an oil company barge at the site of a Native home and cemetery. Using this event as an illustration, the Arctic Slope Native Association argued strongly that the AFN must take a more militant stand. Finally, in February 1970, AFN president Emil Notti made a speech that mentioned the possibility of establishing a "Native Nation." "If Congress cannot pass a bill that we think is fair, then . . . we will petition Congress and the United States to set up a separate Indian nation in the western half of Alaska." Barrow leader Eben Hopson, commenting in the *Tundra Times* on the background to Notti's threat, said, "It took him a long time to express himself in this manner . . . to perhaps fall into the same line that the Arctic Slope Native Association has been advocating all the time."

Elsewhere in the state, Natives were becoming increasingly frustrated over threats to their land. In hearing after hearing with government officials and in conversations with their own leaders, they argued that the land was theirs as it had been for centuries. They also anticipated receiving cash compensation from a claims settlement that could be used to stimulate local economic development and enhance their Native cultural integrity. Additionally, they sought ways to deal with growing social problems in the villages. And finally, they wanted greater political self-determination (Fienup-Riordan 1984a).

Given the volatility of Native American protests occurring across the nation, many of them focusing on federal government collusion with energy corporations, President Nixon was led to proclaim his own policy of "Indian self-determination." However, his definition was quite opposite to that espoused by most Native Americans including those in living in Alaska. Marvin Franklin, an "American of Indian descent," executive with the Phillips Petroleum Company, and acting Commissioner of the Bureau of Indian Affairs [BIA] in the early 1970s, supported Nixon's proposal:

> The psychology of the Indian is not mysterious and not too unlike that of other Americans. He wants a chance to put his skills to work and he wants more of a voice in his own affairs. His special handicap—let's call it a mixed blessing and handicap—is his inherited Indian culture. It has given him a strait jacket that makes it tough for him to compete on equal terms with his fellow citizens.
>
> The new program (of the BIA) will turn over to tribal government, as rapidly as possible, a maximum amount of *administration* for Indian affairs. Minimum control will be retained in Washington; policy will be set there, but administration

of that policy will be in the hands of tribal representatives or bureau superinten-dents (Franklin 1973; italics added).[13]

Basically, the government's "self-determination" policy meant that tribal governments and villages had reached the stage where they could carry out decisions made in Washington. Needless to say, this was quite different from the concept of self-determination held by Native Americans in Alaska and elsewhere that promoted the creation of democratic self-governing Native villages and regions.

Later in the year, the AFN challenged another bill put before Congress. Proposing a billion dollar settlement for the extinguishment of all land claims within the state, formal title would be given to only ten million acres, far less than that considered necessary for subsistence, let alone economic self-sufficiency. Other serious limitations included the possible termination within five years of BIA educational and social programs, their responsibilities to be turned over to the state for as long as the latter saw fit to fund and administer them. By contrast, the House Subcommittee on Indian Affairs proposed an alternative settlement involving forty million acres. This was more satisfactory. But could the financial settlement offered by the Senate bill be combined with the land settlement proposed by the House?

There were other unresolved problems, such as compensation for loss of aboriginal rights to fish and wildlife resources. Should such claims be specif-ically addressed in the settlement act? What conflicts were likely to emerge with the state over subsistence hunting and fishing on state land? After congressional hearings, three Alaska governors—Egan, Hickel, and Miller—affirmed that "the subsistence needs and reliance upon these resources by Alaska Natives would be met by the state of Alaska." (Hickok 1982:36) Congress then put aside the subsistence issue, not wishing to set in place any new law that might challenge the sensitive balance of legislative jurisdiction over fish and wildlife resources earlier established between the western states and Native American tribes in the region.[14]

Finally, there was the question of how to distribute settlement monies and land. Executive and legislative leaders wanted to solve the claims issue as quickly as possible so that future litigation would not interrupt construction of the TransAlaska pipeline. Secretary Hickel proposed a grant of $500 mil-lion. Senator Henry Jackson, chairman of the Senate Interior and Insular Affairs Committee, and Representative Wayne Aspinall, chairman of the House Interior and Insular Affairs Committee, were willing to include land,

[13]Later that year, a new BIA commissioner, Morris Thompson (1973), declared, "In a nut-shell, here is the federal government's policy today: It offers self-determination and self-government to Indian people as rapidly as Indians want it and can assume responsibility for it. In other words, tribes have the option of assuming control of their own federal programs whenever they wish to do so."

[14]As a result, the subsistence rights of Alaska Natives were never addressed in the final settlement act. A later bill, the Alaska National Interest Lands Conservation ACT (ANILCA), did contain protective legislation for subsistence hunting and fishing on federal lands. However, similar subsistence activities on state held land have generated considerable conflict in recent years (see: Chance:1987).

but they were opposed to seeing the BIA reservation system extended to Alaska. Rather, they and other congressmen wanted Alaska's Natives to become more actively assimilated into mainstream America. Out of this desire came the proposal that profit-making corporations be the means to achieve the settlement.

AFN leaders had no interest in Hickel's proposed distribution of cash since it disregarded the need for subsistence land. Furthermore, history suggested that any funds dispensed on a large scale would quickly disappear. Nor was there much enthusiasm for receiving the land "in trust," to be bureaucratically administered by the Bureau of Indian Affairs. Some AFN leaders, including vice president John Borbridge, Jr., were drawn to the suggestion that land previously held communally would be adapted to modern conditions by utilizing a corporate approach. Furthermore, Don Wright, then AFN president, was told that any proposed AFN alternative involving traditional governments or IRA councils would be discouraged by Congress.[15] Thus, while some actively argued for the corporate scheme, other AFN leaders felt obliged to support it.

This was not true, however, of the Arctic Slope Native Association. Its leaders had a different strategy. Having learned earlier about Congress' scheme to use profit-making corporations as the means for receiving settlement monies and lands, the ASNA put forward a proposal suggesting that the land be owned "tribally" through regional IRA councils.[16] But when this alternative went before the AFN, it was soundly defeated (Paul 1984:63–64; Upicksoun 1984:228).

THE CORPORATE OPTION

The one real strength of the Arctic Slope Native Association's IRA regional plan was that Native land, held "in trust" by the federal government, could never be lost through stock transfer, corporate sale, hostile takeover,

[15]As reported by Wright years later, "We were [also] told by major oil companies, by major timber representatives, major mining companies, even people from the chambers of commerce on tourism and things like that. They said, 'You will take what you get and be thankful for it.' So we would withdraw from time to time and try to re-evaluate and decide what really we should do. . . . I feel that the true meaning of ANCSA was exactly what happened. It was a smokescreen designed by big corporate influence over the Congress of the United States to expropriate private property from Alaska Native people." (Wright 1984:46)

[16]In 1934, Congress enacted the Indian Reorganization Act [IRA] designed to strengthen Indian tribes through the establishment of legally recognized self-governing bodies. Two years later, an amendment was passed expanding the concept of tribal protection to include non-"tribal" village Natives. It also permitted such residents to petition the Secretary of the Interior for incorporation. Although most IRA councils were established in unincorporated villages where they became a federally recognized government, it was also possible to form regional entities. The North Slope did just that, establishing the Iñupiat Community of the Arctic Slope [ICAS] in 1971, which in effect federated the region's earlier traditional village councils. Although IRAs are considered dependent sovereign entities by the federal government, they have not been formally recognized by state governments, which has led to numerous political and legal problems over the years.

or nonpayment of taxes. In the minds of those making the proposal, this was of great significance since as the villagers had stated so many times before, the land represented both the spirit and substance of their culture. Land was something to be shared, not individually owned. It was where their ancestors lived, where they grew up, where their grandchildren would live. Furthermore, the wildlife it contained was a renewable resource on which they could always depend. Thus, it provided both a cultural and economic bond between generations reaching into the past and projecting into the future. As long as the people and the land were one, the culture would survive. If the two became separated, it could easily wither and die. Finally, if Alaska Natives became shareholders in the exploitation of their own resources, rather than become self-determining Native communities with control over those resources, they would be giving up what was rightfully theirs.

While acknowledging the importance of safeguarding the land, most AFN leaders nevertheless strongly opposed the IRA as the means to achieve it. To protect the land was one thing. To have it permanently held "in trust" by a disliked Bureau of Indian Affairs was another. Dignity, too, was at issue. Federal and state educational institutions that had long ago restricted Native children from attending white schools, treating the students as inferior, were remembered by Native leaders who wanted to remove the shackles of second-class citizenship and forge their own destiny unimpeded by governmental constraints. Now the government wanted something that belonged to the Native people. "You want the land? Pay us a fair price for it. It's not a question of charity or a handout. We own it."

The lure of corporate power and wealth also held considerable appeal to some Native leaders who had been frustrated by years of political powerlessness and poverty. If the claims settlement meant opening the door to the economic mainstream and its increased standard of living, then it was time to learn how to use the tools of that structure. While the corporate model had real difficulties, its appeal for the majority of AFN leaders remained strong.

Thus, most urban-based Native leaders, in contrast to subsistence-dependent villagers, saw the land as the key to a brighter future. As expressed by Emil Notti, the AFN's first president, in corporate hands the land could serve as a vehicle enabling the Native population to actively participate in the economic development of the state (Fienup-Riordan 1984b:25). In similar manner, cash compensation flowing to the regional corporations could provide scholarships and in other ways help shareholders be more effective in adapting to modern economic life.

For reasons such as these, the AFN leaders eventually accepted the corporate model as the means for managing the land and the money to be obtained from the settlement. Turning then to the highly charged question of how such settlement monies and lands were to be distributed, a decision was made that the initial dispersal of funds should be allocated according to the population size of the twelve regions. However, the Arctic Slope Native Association was so opposed to this idea that it withdrew from the AFN,

executive director Charlie Edwardsen, Jr., accusing the organization of promoting "welfare legislation" rather than a land settlement. Only if the regions
with the most land area were to receive the largest amount of land and money
would the ASNA rejoin the federation. As Joe Upicksoun, association president, explained to the leaders of the other regions: "We realize each of you
has pride in his own land. By accident of nature, right now the eyes of the
nation and the world are centered on the North Slope. . . . Without intending
to belittle your land, the real reason for the entire settlement is the oil, which
by accident is on our land, not yours."

After further negotiation, the AFN offered to revise its plan, and the
Arctic Slope association returned to the fold. Under the new proposal, money
received from Congress was to be divided by size of land lost through the
extinguishment of title, while funds from future mineral developments would
be shared among the regions. Given this arrangement, the Arctic Slope would
retain half of the revenues it received from mineral development and distribute
the remainder to other regions based on population (Arnold 1976:136).

Finally, by 1971 it appeared that most parties in the debate were ready
to seek a resolution. The one additional factor required to shape the final
settlement was the support of the petroleum industry. Given the large financial
commitment made in oil exploration and bidding, the companies were anxious
to see a return on their investment. When their efforts to build a TransAlaska
pipeline from Prudhoe Bay to Valdez on Alaska's southwestern coast were
blocked by new Native claims, the industry realized that future profits were
dependent on the land question being resolved. Working closely with the
White House and in conjunction with the AFN, the industry applied its
powerful lobbying organizations to the problem. Soon, a congressional resolution was at hand.

In April 1971, President Nixon proposed to Congress a settlement in which
Alaska Natives were to receive 44 million acres of land, $500 million in
compensation from the federal treasury, and $500 million more in mineral
revenues from lands to which title was to be extinguished. Major recipients
would be the twelve regional corporations suggested earlier. After a summer
of rewriting, the Senate and House passed separate bills supporting the President's proposal. Following a final conference committee review, the Alaska
Native Claims Settlement Act was passed. Nixon, knowing that several pro-
visions, such as the issue of taxation, had been opposed by the AFN, wanted
a symbolic statement of Native support. The AFN called a meeting of 600
delegates and, at the conclusion of a lively debate, voted overwhelmingly for
the bill. Significantly, the one Native association voting no was from the Arctic
Slope. The "no" vote was in opposition to Congress' decision to use population as the key criterion for the allocation of land and money rather than
the size and value of the land. In a letter sent to President Nixon prior to the
signing of the act, the association's president and executive director said the
only method that " . . . even begins to approach the type of allocation a court
would make [is one] which would take into consideration not only the size
of the area claimed, but its value." Rejecting the appeal by the North Slope

Native Association, President Nixon signed the bill into law December 18, 1971.[17]

THE LAND CLAIMS SETTLEMENT

In the final version, claims to almost all of Alaska were extinguished in exchange for approximately one-ninth of the state's land plus $962.5 million in compensation. Of the latter, $462.5 million was to come from the federal treasury and the rest from mineral revenue-sharing. Settlement benefits would accrue to those with at least one-fourth Native ancestry. Of the approximately eighty thousand Natives enrolled under ANCSA, those living in villages (approximately two-thirds of the total) would receive 100 shares in both a village and a regional corporation. The remaining one-third would be "at-large" shareholders with 100 shares in a regional corporation plus additional rights to revenue from regional mineral and timber resources. The Alaska Native Allotment Act was revoked and as yet unborn Native children were excluded. The twelve regional corporations within the state would administer the settlement. A thirteenth corporation composed of nonresidents would receive monies but not land.

Along with cash compensation, these corporations could also earn income from their investments. However, the bill did not clarify whether the corporations were expected to redistribute the proceeds from their investment income to their shareholders or whether they could keep them for further investment (McBeath and Morehouse 1980:61). A "shared wealth" provision of the act (Section 7(i)) stipulated that 70 percent of income received by regional corporations from their resources was to be shared annually with the other corporations. To protect the land from estrangement, no Native corporate shares could be sold to non-Natives for twenty years, until 1991, at which time all special restrictions would be removed. Then, non-Natives would be eligible to become shareholders, lands would be liable for taxation by the state, and the regionals would be open to the possibility of hostile takeovers.

Under supervision of the regionals, village-level corporations would also select lands and administer local monies received under the settlement act. Although village corporations could choose to be nonprofit entities, all selected the profit-making category.

The President's signature on the settlement act forever transformed the relationship between the Native peoples of Alaska and the land. No longer was ownership directly linked to Native government. Instead, by conveying land title to the twelve regional corporations and 200 local village ones chartered under the laws of the state of Alaska, all ties to traditional or IRA

[17] It should be noted that while the AFN gave its support to the settlement act, these leaders were never officially designated as representatives of legally designated traditional councils or IRA tribal entities. Thus, it has been argued that village and tribal resources were distributed to non-village/tribal entities without their consent (Conn 1985:44).

"tribal" governments were bypassed. With a stroke of the President's pen, the Iñupiat and other Native Alaskans whose earlier use and occupancy had made them co-owners of shared land now became shareholders in corporate-owned land. Having obtained fee simple title to more land than was held "in trust" by the government for all other Native Americans, these new share-holders were land rich. But as individuals and families, they were landless. Thus, from this moment on, their future was intimately linked to that of the corporate world.

Most Native people were unaware of the complexities of the bill, but they looked forward to having their own land and additional monies that could be used to improve their low standard of living. Alaska Federation of Natives leaders were enthusiastic at the large settlement, feeling they had achieved a considerable accomplishment under highly adverse conditions. The limitations in the bill stemmed primarily from pressures placed on them by the government and petroleum industry, forcing them to make compromises not of their choosing. They also saw the corporate solution both as a way to remove themselves from the bureaucratic yoke of the Bureau of Indian Affairs, thereby regaining greater control over their lives, and as a new tool in the fight to maintain their culture. Indeed, the theme of 1971 AFN convention was *"In the White Man's Society, We Need White Man's Tools."* Charlie Edwardsen, Jr., the activist leader from Barrow, used the expression "the new harpoon" that could be utilized "for the maximum gain of all our people." (Edwardsen 1974:252)

Not all, however, took an optimistic view. Critics of the AFN vote suggested that eventually, the regionals could become conduits for larger multinational corporations, enabling the latter to take over valuable lands and resources currently held in Native hands. Loss of this land would then be followed by destruction of Native culture and the rise of new class relations mirroring those of the larger society. By this means, the government's long-term goal of assimilating Alaska's Native population into the larger mainstream would finally be achieved. As summed up by Fred Bigjim, an Iñupiat educator from Nome who had once been a close aide of Eben Hopson, "What is happening to Native people in Alaska is not a new story; it is a new chapter in an old story." (Bigjim and Ito-Adler 1974:8)

Still, whether one supported the bill or opposed it, all agreed that the implications of the land claims settlement for Alaska's Natives were profound. Given the discovery of oil at Prudhoe Bay, even more pronounced changes were to occur on the North Slope. For due to this circumstance, the Iñupiat were able to bring into being a unique development strategy, one which combined elements of both adaptation and resistance to the steadily mounting pressures coming from what they once called the world "outside."

7/Taking Control

CORPORATE STRATEGIES AND VILLAGE VALUES

The leadership experience gained by Iñupiat working in the Native association and the AFN was immensely helpful in organizing the Arctic Slope Regional Corporation [ASRC], the North Slope Borough [NSB], and the federally recognized IRA regional "tribal" council—the Iñupiat Community of the Arctic Slope [ICAS]. Some Iñupiat took on the political task of developing the borough. Others worked with the recently formed ICAS. Still others concentrated on the long and difficult process of selecting land. Although the ASRC was to be the primary recipient, village corporations were involved as well. Thus, in the spring of 1972, at Barrow and in other villages, members of local land selection committees stood before huge maps on the walls of their elementary schools trying to decide which land to claim. What were the best fishing sites? Where were the caribou most likely to migrate? Locations for harvesting berries? Obtaining coal? Launching a umiaq? And in the back of the people's minds was the issue of whether today's choices would meet the needs of generations yet to come.

Questions of even greater magnitude faced the regional corporation, for it was responsibile for selecting approximately 4.5 million acres of subsurface as well as surface lands. This was the entitlement figure allocated of the fifteen million acres initially claimed by the Arctic Slope Native Association. The corporation immediately recognized two distinct needs: some lands should be selected for their traditional-use value, and others for their potential wealth in oil, gas, and minerals. Enlisting the assistance of village elders, traditional land selection was begun. For the rest, the corporation needed the input of highly skilled geologists familiar with the region's oil, gas, and mineral potential. Thus, the corporation's directors soon found themselves working closely with petroleum companies seeking the same resources. However, large sections of land were exempt from consideration, including the four million-acre federal National Petroleum Reserve just south of Barrow, the nine million-acre Arctic Wildlife Refuge surrounding Kaktovik, and other lands claimed by the state. Such difficulties forced the ASRC to extend its land selection to less familiar locations in the western and south-central portions of the region west of Anaktuvuk Pass. This, in turn, brought on years of litigation with other Native corporations applying for the same land, the kind of conflicts that eventually led one Iñupiat leader, Oliver Leavitt, to call the whole land claims settlement "a breadbasket for the lawyers."

The $46 million financial settlement to be received by ASRC raised equally complex issues about investment and profit-sharing. Should these funds be used to generate short-term profits? Invest in conservative stocks and bonds? Make local capital improvements? Set up subsidiary corporations that could provide local employment, businesses, and needed services for shareholders? How much income, if any, should be passed on to these shareholders and how much should be used to generate more profit? As the issues multiplied, so did the conflicts.

At the heart of the matter lay several key questions. One pertained to the relationship between the people and the land. For both the Iñupiat and Yup'ik Eskimo, the issue of land ownership had always been one of "relation" rather than possession (Fienup-Riordan 1987:143). That is, the right to use a given site was based on one's relation to previous generations of kin who hunted in the area and to the animals located there. In modern times, land continued to be held in common for the benefit of its members. Thus, no villager could sell or otherwise dispose of any portion of that which was collectively shared. Private property with its alienability and inheritability was simply not an issue. As Barrow elder Roxy Ekowana expressed it, "I did not sign up for a (government) allotment because it went against my grain of thought to own a piece of land—even though I did have a hunting area."

Corporate land, on the other hand, is viewed differently. Under this arrangement, the corporation, not the shareholders owns the land. Shareholders are owners of the corporation, but each shareholder only owns an interest in it. Furthermore, these individual shares only entitle the shareholder to a portion of the equity if the corporation is broken up. Whether the proceeds of a land sale, for example, are passed on to individual shareholders is a decision to be made by the board of directors. Thus, corporations could sell land at fair market value without shareholder approval. Stockholders could then receive or not receive a dividend based on the sale. If the shareholders did not like the sale, all they could do was vote the directors out of office after the fact. While the settlement act postponed the stock alienability feature until 1991, a fundamental point was clear: Native lands were in serious jeopardy.[1]

Given the value placed on sharing the proceeds of land held in common, the introduction of a corporate form of ownership created enormous tension among the Iñupiat. The greatest fear, of course, was that the corporate structure embraced by ANCSA might one day become the means of their own destruction. Could the people own land and stock as individual shareholders and still maintain their cultural identity as Iñupiat? That is, could a historically

---

[1] Corporate shares, however, were not alienable until 1991. It soon becomes obvious to anyone delving more deeply into ANCSA that legal aspects around the land issue are complex in the extreme. For a clarifying discussion of some of the problems associated with the corporate aspects of ANCSA, and of the 1988 amendments to ANCSA, see: Flanders (1989a; 1989b). These 1988 amendments are taken up briefly in the next chapter.

cooperative economic system based on sharing, reciprocity, and redistribution through exchange prevail when conjoined with one based on competition, one which concentrated its attention on the accumulation of wealth? Or, as an alternative, was it possible to circumvent limitations imposed by the corporate structure and maintain a commitment to the rights and obligations that bound people together through reciprocity?

This latter issue was closely linked to another set of questions. Given the fact that a requirement of the settlement act was that ASRC be a profit-making corporation, did it also have an additional social responsibility to its Iñupiat shareholders? Legally, once the regional corporation selected the 4.5 million acres of land and received the $48 million allotted from the settlement, the land and money became economic assets under state law, to be utilized like any other assets in the furtherance of profit-making. But was that all? Not as far as subsistence-oriented villagers were concerned. To them, financial gain was important, but it was not their bottom line. They wanted to be assured that the land with its subsistence resources and cultural significance would not be jeopardized. Land, rather than financial gain, was the issue.[2]

Most newly elected regional corporation leaders viewed the contradiction differently. For them, the primary purpose of the regional corporation was, first, to receive and disperse money available to it under the act; second, to select, own, and manage lands available under the act; and third, to conduct business for profit for the benefit of its shareholders. As a senior ASRC official expressed it more than a decade later.

> "The Alaska state corporate structure has no governmental powers. It's business, just [like] General Motors and Ford Motors.   How does that relate to maintaining our culture and providing our people with their lifestyle, their own original aboriginal lifestyle? We don't have those powers. . . . The framers of the state constitution [said] we wouldn't be stuck with delivering those services which we had no business doing, except make a profit and issue dividends and be the stewards for our stockholders. . . . We can make monies available for scholarship loans and grants for our students to go to college. But we have to make a profit before we can actually make monies available to them." (Upicksoun 1984:228–229)

The newly formed village corporations of the North Slope also chose the for-profit status enabling them to receive income for investments. But in their specific cases, control of the corporations lay in the hands of village-based Iñupiat. Since these leaders were intimately involved in local community affairs, they tended to be more sensitive to their constituents' views, including those that emphasized protecting the subsistence and sharing way of life. As stated by the Barrow Ukpeagvik Iñupiat Corporation [UIC] president in the early 1980s, "We are at home with these people; we are not just a paper

---

[2] As it turns out, financial gain for Alaska Natives overall has been limited. In the draft report of a study directed by the U.S. Department of the Interior (1985), it was determined that although there were substantial differences between regions, of the total $962.5 million received by the regional corporations as part of the settlement, an average of $410 was passed on to each of the approximately 80,000 shareholders. The study found that dividends paid to these shareholders over the past twelve years averaged 35 cents a share.

corporation. We know their problems and have to fight for their rights." Such efforts included participation in lawsuits designed to prevent oil development that would threaten subsistence hunting and fishing in coastal areas, and the providing of social, cultural, and recreational services for elders. Economic benefits, in addition to those sought from financial investments, included reduced energy costs achieved by undertaking a joint venture to produce liquefied natural gas and electrification for the town. By 1980, the UIC had yet to declare a dividend. But due to its taking a coordinated approach that addressed the social needs of the community as well as profit-making, it continued to receive active support of village shareholders.

One other important institution was established on the North Slope at this time—the Iñupiat Community of the Arctic Slope [ICAS]. Formed in 1971 as a regional Native government constituted under the amended federal Indian Reorganization Act of 1936, the major purpose of ICAS was to provide a shelter to protect Native lands and to furnish governmental and social services to the region's Iñupiat population. Although it did engage in lawsuits (such as *Edwardsen v. Morton*, which asked for trespass damages to Native residences, fishing and hunting areas resulting from oil exploration on the Slope), it was only minimally active until 1975. Then, following passage of the U.S. Indian Self-Determination and Education Assistance Act, the BIA provided ICAS with funds not available to the state-affiliated borough. The amount flowing to ICAS from the BIA's health and human services program was small in comparison with state transfer payments to the borough, but it did enable this regional IRA to establish welfare assistance programs and expand health services.

Far more significant, however, was the potential contained within the ICAS to serve as a *federally recognized* Native government for the North Slope Iñupiat. Given ICAS's political nature, it wasn't long before difficulties arose between it and the NSB. As a Native organization to which only Natives could belong, ICAS, from its beginning, served as a significant political base for those Iñupiat holding the view that sovereignty remained the key issue for Alaska's Natives. And to the most militant of these, the North Slope Borough was simply "the illegitimate child" of the United States and the state of Alaska. As one activist leader expressed it, "In 1867, the Russians sold to the United States the right to trade with Eskimos, Aleuts, and Indians. They could not sell Eskimos, let alone their private property, and most of all the sovereign rights of my ancestors." (Neokok 1984:81)

Local spending irregularities eventually led to a loss of federal funding for ICAS. However, its political potential as a legal structure for establishing an Iñupiat "homeland" continues to remain highly significant. To use a federally recognized, BIA-sponsored institution as a structural base for establishing greater political autonomy may have its ironies. But that is secondary for those who continue to emphasize that the fundamental strength of the regional IRA council lies in its Iñupiat control. As summed up by James Stotts (1984:337), corporate treasurer of ASRC and ex-assembly president of the North Slope Borough, "IRA councils . . . are more representative of the

Iñupiat perspective than the state municipal corporations. The reason is very simple: It's because membership in the village and regional IRAs is restricted only to the Iñupiat."

Eventually, differing pathways taken by the regional corporation, the North Slope Borough, the village corporations, ICAS, and subsistence-oriented villagers led to open conflict. In one instance, after scrutinizing an environmental impact statement attached to the proposed Joint Federal/State Beaufort Sea Oil and Gas Lease Sale of 1979, the North Slope Borough allied with village corporations from Kaktovik and Nuiqsut and brought suit against the government. Already worried about possible deleterious effects of an oil spill on the fish and sea mammal resources of the mid-Beaufort Sea region, the borough had earlier prepared its own Coastal Management Program to safeguard the subsistence economy on which many residents depended. It was to be accomplished by dividing the coastal areas into four no-development classes based on their importance as wildlife habitats and two development zones based on their suitability for short- and long-term petroleum development.

North Slope elders, too, had expressed deep concern over changes occurring along the Beaufort Sea near Prudhoe Bay. At an annual elders conference held in Barrow, Ernie Frankson, a respected leader of an earlier generation, said: an oil spill "will devastate our animals if (the oil companies) have an accident." Others, aware of the research then being undertaken on the environmental impact of oil spills, responded in like manner. "These white people who were talking, these scientists with much knowledge, their job covers a lot of things; about animals and small living organisms in the ocean, . . . But it is the animals, these fish, the source of our livelihood which are located out east over there which I worry about, thinking they may destroy them." (Bodfish 1981:438) Not long afterwards, the borough's planning department prepared a zoning ordinance to regulate land and water uses in the area until the Coastal Management Program could be approved.

At the same time the borough was putting forward its plan, ASRC, with most of its land holdings in place, was entering into lease agreements with Chevron, Union-Amoco, Shell, and Texaco—an arrangement that would yield more than $29 million from land rentals and bonuses. Thus, in the spring of 1979, when borough and ASRC officials met in Washington to discuss the lease sale, the latter urged that in view of its business relationship with Chevron and Texaco, both of which were anxious to bid in the offshore sale, any attempt to block the sale would be against the corporation's best interest. The borough, on the other hand, saw the sale as compromising the needs of its subsistence-oriented residents. Following the meeting and over the objection of the NSB, the ASRC voted 9 to 1 to issue a public statement in support of the sale. The press release appearing August 17, 1979, was received with enthusiasm by the petroleum industry and the state. However, when asked to explain the corporation's position at the next elders conference, the ASRC president found it difficult to respond satisfactorily to the questions put to him by the frustrated members of his audience.

Later in the year, after the borough's legislative assembly had given its conceptual approval to the Mid-Beaufort Coastal Management Program, it was submitted to the Alaska Coastal Policy Council for approval. But opposition by the petroleum industry and critical reviews by several state agencies was so pronounced that the assembly president withdrew the plan. To continue at that time would have involved lengthy, costly, and politically damaging litigation.

As for the tensions between the NSB and the ASRC, the two organizations eventually came to a compromise in which both agreed that since nearshore drilling along the barrier islands could not be stopped, they should undertake a joint effort to control these operations as much as possible. Yet the underlying political and economic forces shaping the struggle remained largely unchanged. The borough's mayor, Eben Hopson, in a speech to the Canadian government's Mackenzie Pipeline Inquiry in 1977, addressed the problem:

> There will be a tug-of-war between those of us who want to maximize state oil income for needed investment in our Arctic cities and villages, and those who want to help the oil industry avoid taxation. I do not want to see this tug-of-war split Alaska's Native leadership as it appears to be doing. I do not believe that letting oil corporations explore our land for oil obliges us to adopt the policies of the oil corporations. This tendency to assist the oil corporations avoid taxes may extend even to the point that our regional Native corporations will oppose the development of home-rule government in Alaska. Rather than fight for local self-determination for our people, the influence of the oil corporations may lead our regional corporations to fight against it.

Thus, in Hopson's view, oil interests wanting to tap the Arctic's natural resources would always draw to their side those sectors of the Native leadership most closely linked to the corporate world. For the regional corporation, sensitive to the needs of its shareholders as well as its corporate interests, the contradiction was indeed difficult to resolve. A senior ASRC officer, seeing the problems that lay ahead for many regional corporations, once commented: "If the corporations are bankrupted or if the stock is bought up so that it is no longer in control by Native stockholders, then I guess you can say that we have lost it all. Then we will have nothing. We will be worse off than before ANCSA, because when we started, at least we had our land rights intact."[3]

However, the ASRC leadership, viewing the immediate future of their own region, saw no such concern. The corporation's 1979 annual report, listed record earnings of more than $29 million, the value amounting to $8.69 per share. Corporation assets increased to $36.9 million. The ASRC also redistributed more than $9 million (70 percent of its subsurface revenue) to the other eleven regional corporations in keeping with the 7[i] "shared wealth" clause of the settlement act; the funds were sorely needed by those regional

---

[3] In a 1985 ASRC-sponsored attitude survey, 84 percent of the North Slope stockholders opposed selling their stock to anyone, including non-Natives, after 1991 (Hellenthal 1985:3).

corporations then facing serious financial difficulties. Finally, the corporation provided a growing number of jobs for its shareholders while its Arctic Education Foundation presented 75 scholarships to qualified North Slope Iñupiat wishing to pursue higher education.

If the new corporate life of the North Slope was largely controlled by the ASRC, political life was not. Quite a different kind of structure was needed to address the complexities of political governance in a region where the federal and state government, energy industry, and environmental interests were competing to enhance their control over the land's resources. Numerous proposals emerged, but on one central point, there was complete unanimity: While the land they had claimed was rich in oil and gas, the quality of housing, education, sanitation, and public services of the people was poor. And while the rest of America was relatively poor in oil and gas, the standard of living of its people was far higher. The time had finally arrived when Alaska's most northern Iñupiat could throw off this legacy of the past and build a modern Arctic community on the North Slope.

THE NORTH SLOPE BOROUGH

The idea for establishing a borough form of government was proposed in 1969 by Fred Paul, attorney for the ASNA, to Eben Hopson, then executive director of the AFN. Paul recommended that a borough be organized covering the whole of Arctic Alaska including Kotzebue and perhaps even Nome. Hopson was enthusiastic, stating that "this is perhaps the only way we can have some assurance of control."

Choosing to limit the proposed borough to the 88,000 square miles defining the boundaries of the Arctic Slope Native Association, Hopson urged the village leaders to support a plan in which the region would control its own education and health facilities, hiring outside teachers, skilled health personnel, and similar professionals as needed. The local leaders agreed and by 1971 had obtained the necessary petition signatures from their constituent populations. Application was then made to the state's Local Boundary Commission for status as a first-class borough, a category that also carried the right to establish a home rule charter.

At a 1971 hearing in Barrow, ASNA president Joe Upicksoun stated that the basic reason for the petition was to achieve a "maximum amount of self-determination for the people." He reminded the assembled commissioners that the social and economic conditions on the North Slope were deplorable; that few jobs were available and that village residents had to live without water and sewage systems, fire protection, and adequate housing. He further pointed out that federal agencies had been the worst violators of the environment; that the state had not provided land-use planning; that the lack of local government threatened to cause the kinds of depredations that had already occurred in Nome, Fairbanks, and other cities. Finally, since school facilities were available only up to the ninth grade, high school students had to attend boarding schools far from home, an unsatisfactory situation for both children and parents.[4]

In statements presented later to the Local Boundary Commission, British Petroleum, Atlantic Richfield, Humble, and Mobil oil companies charged that the request for a borough form of government was inappropriate for a location such as the North Slope; that Prudhoe Bay would contribute most of the borough's taxes while receiving no benefits; and that once incorporated, the borough would no longer "have to run the gauntlet of state government."[5] Hopson responded that "local government is resisted at every turn by the oil industry in the name of tax avoidance. Oil corporations are not people, even though politicians and bankers often behave as if they were. A corporation has no ideological commitment to the development of democratic self-determination."

Eventually, the state commission approved the request to form the North Slope Borough with areawide powers of education, taxation, planning, and zoning. Then, in a vote of 593 to 33, the region's villagers agreed to become a part of the new local government. One major benefit of having a borough was to utilize state and federal "transfer funds" to improve educational programs, health facilities, and public utilities. A lingering worry, however, especially in the eyes of those Iñupiat wishing to maintain full political control over the region, was the realization that some time in the future, borough leadership could fall to non-Natives.[6]

On July 2, 1972, in a regional election, Eben Hopson was chosen mayor. In a speech shortly after his victory, Hopson assured the petroleum industry that it would not be taxed excessively on the output of oil at Prudhoe Bay. Such an oral commitment, however, hardly satisfied the oil companies. Instead, following the borough's formation, they introduced a new tactic by threatening to stop construction of the pipeline from Prudhoe Bay south to Valdez unless the state's tax laws were repealed or substantially altered.

Governor Egan called a special session of the legislature to consider bills that would effectively deprive the North Slope Borough of most of its authority to tax oil company property. The borough, in turn, hired a state lobbyist who successfully negotiated a compromise enabling it to tax the Prudhoe Bay operation but limiting the amount. Shortly thereafter, borough leaders and petroleum industry officials worked out a compromise in which the former

---

[4] For a fuller treatment of the early functioning of the North Slope Borough from which some of the above is drawn, see McBeath and Morehouse (1980), McBeath (1981), and Morehouse, McBeath, and Leask (1984).

[5] The reference to freedom from state control alluded to the "home rule" concept contained within the Alaska Constitution, which provides a souce of authority independent of state government. For example, such authority could enable the borough to exempt from taxation all property valued at less than $20,000—more than the value of most Native homes—and design special use taxes that would apply only to heavy equipment such as that found at Prudhoe Bay.

[6] The concern was justified. In the 1970 census, the population of Barrow, the North Slope's largest town, was 91 percent Iñupiat. By 1985, that segment had dropped to 61 percent; for those between 30 and 50, non-Natives outnumbered the Iñupiat (Worl and Smythe 1986:373).

agreed to a temporary suspension of a sales and use tax and the latter agreed not to oppose the borough's Capital Improvement Program and municipal bond sales.

At this same time, Hopson requested that the eight North Slope villages (two of which, Atqasuk and Point Lay, were too small even to be incorporated) transfer their municipal powers to the borough on the assumption that this increased centralization would improve its bargaining power with the state and the oil companies. The villages concurred with the request by passing on many, although not all, of their municipal powers to the borough. Nevertheless, conflicts between the villagers and the borough soon arose.

At Anaktuvuk Pass, for example, villagers became dissatisfied with the slow construction and poor design of a $2.5 million school being built under the direction of the NSB; they threatened to secede from the borough if prompt action was not taken. In 1975 at Point Hope, a similar arrangement made with the borough to obtain new housing and schools hit a snag, which was exacerbated when the construction company contracted to do the job failed to consult local residents about the buildings. The Point Hope Iñupiat chartered a plane and flew to Barrow, demonstrating their anger at a borough assembly meeting. The city of Barrow, too, resisted turning over some of its powers to the borough, feeling that its local interests might not be served by the larger political body. Still, throughout the 1970s and well into the 1980s, the borough was seen by most residents as effectively using its centralized powers in support of Iñupiat interests. These interests focused on three fundamental concerns: defending subsistence hunting and fishing rights; enhancing Iñupiat culture; and promoting a Capital Improvement Program.

DEFENDING SUBSISTENCE RIGHTS

Subsistence rights of the Iñupiat and other Alaska Natives have a long unwritten history closely linked to customs and codes ensuring the survivability of individuals, families, and villages; respect for their culture's relationship with the land; and the need to conserve resources. Increasingly, state and federal wildlife regulations have interfered with these subsistence activities, and this is especially true in the villages.[7]

On the North Slope, federal government restrictions on subsistence hunting were first encountered in 1964, culminating in Barrow's famous "duck-in" demonstration. Following passage of the settlement act, aboriginal hunting and fishing rights were extinguished throughout Alaska. This enabled the

---

[7] Federal laws recognizing the right of Alaska Natives to use wildlife for their subsistence have existed ever since 1870 when a federal act exempted the Aleuts from killing fur seals on the Pribilof Islands as long as the animals were used for food and clothing. This policy was reinforced with the Marine Mammal Protection Act of 1972 in which Natives again were allowed to hunt walrus, polar bear, sea otter, beluga, sea lion, and five species of seal for subsistence purposes without restriction. Other regulations, however, have been more stringent, such as those associated with the fur seal treaty, where Native harvesting is limited to "traditional means," excluding the use of firearms and power boats.

state's Fish and Game Department to enforce its rules for restricting hunting and fishing without regard to the cultural heritage of its citizens. On federal lands, differing laws were in effect. But in neither instance were Alaska's Eskimos, Indians, and Aleuts able to enjoy the special rights of subsistence hunting and fishing characteristic of many Native American tribes farther to the south.

Then, in 1976, following the study of a decline in the northern caribou population, the state Fish and Game Department issued a moratorium on caribou hunting for all of the North Slope and much of northwest Alaska. While such action had little effect on sports hunters, its impact on the Iñupiat was considerable. Hardships were particularly pronounced in inland villages where caribou meat was a main source of protein. The state's response to the nutritional problem was to offer a $68,000 grant through RurAL CAP to replace the loss of meat. Allocated on a per-capita basis to the affected villages, Nuiqsut's share, for example (some $3,000 of the $28,000 of the North Slope portion), went for beef and chicken and the cost of air freight— an amount providing a little more than two meals per family.

Responding to the crisis, the North Slope Borough undertook its own research study of the caribou population, which suggested that there were many more caribou in the area than previously reported. Through letters of protest, the borough put pressure on the Fish and Game Department to rescind its action. In addition, the NSB took responsibility for distributing additional emergency supplies to those in need. Two years later, following another survey, the Fish and Game Department allowed the harvesting of one caribou per license.

A more far-reaching crisis occurred in 1977 when the International Whaling Commission (IWC) proposed a moratorium on hunting the bowhead whale. This action was taken partly as a result of the demands of several national conservation organizations, which, given an apparent decline in the whale population, demanded that the IWC oppose any hunting of the bowhead at all. Recognizing the immense economic and cultural importance of this animal to North Slope whaling communities, the borough administration, together with the Arctic Slope Regional Corporation, organized a major campaign designed to get the IWC to rescind the moratorium. Films and recordings emphasizing the economic and cultural importance of whaling were produced by the borough and made available to schools and television stations. Press releases were sent to the major news services. Native organizations from western Canada to Greenland handed out statements stressing that the aboriginal harvest of the bowhead by Arctic peoples was a basic human right taking precedence over any national or international agreement. Influential environmental organizations such as the Sierra Club and Friends of the Earth offered their active support as well.

Called to a meeting in Barrow, seventy whaling captains from the nine Arctic whaling villages formed the Alaska Eskimo Whaling Commission (AEWC). The commission, working closely with the NSB and the ASRC, challenged the IWC moratorium policy. Detailed biological studies utilizing the latest bioacoustic technology were undertaken by the AEWC to determine the actual number of whales migrating along the northern coast. The results suggested that the bowhead population included between 10,000 and 12,000 whales rather than the less than 1000 previously estimated. Members of the commission also attended international meetings of the IWC, contributing this and other scientific data to assist the commissioners in their deliberations.

Finally in 1978, at a special session of the IWC conference in Tokyo, the United States delegation—with members of the AEWC at their side—persuaded the commission to lift the moratorium in exchange for an agreement by Alaskan Eskimos that they would limit their annual subsistence hunting to twelve bowheads killed or eighteen struck. The AEWC agreed, conditional upon the establishment of a cooperative management plan dealing with federal and AEWC regulations; research on improved equipment; AEWC participation in IWC decisions; and a U.S. commitment to seek full restoration of the subsistence harvest. Even though the International Whaling Convention of 1946 allowed a special exemption enabling Alaska Natives and aboriginal peoples in other nations to hunt whales for subsistence (Berger 1985:63), this self-governance of whale hunting has continued to the present time. Still, in the minds of the Iñupiat (and the St. Lawrence Island Yup'ik whale hunters), the subsistence harvest of these animals should not be constrained by federal laws or international conventions.[8]

While these negotiations were going on, the borough also was opposing the 1979 Joint Federal/State Beaufort Sea Oil and Gas Lease Sale. Finally successful in restricting offshore leases to within the Barrier Islands, the borough nevertheless paid a substantial penalty by becoming the target of a massive public relations campaign by the oil and gas industry. Utilizing television, newspapers and radio, their publicity departments depicted the NSB as being opposed to development, disinterested in the nation's national security needs, and generally obstructionist in blocking efforts of the petroleum corporations to provide new energy sources for the American people.

In 1980, through the combined efforts of Native and environmental lobbying organizations, Congress passed and President Carter signed into law the Alaska National Interest Lands Conservation Act (ANILCA), which explicitly provided federal protection for subsistence hunting and fishing on federal lands.[9] One premise underlying this act was of crucial importance to the Iñupiat and other Native Alaskans for it clearly affirmed a federal commitment to protect Native Alaskans' subsistence interests: "The Congress

---

[8] In the spring of 1988, whaling captain Percy Nusunginya, refusing to abide by the quota jointly established between the AEWC and the National Oceanic and Atmospheric Administration (NOAA), took a bowhead whale off the Barrow coast. This act of civil disobedience followed 24 years after Percy's brother, John, had been arrested in the famous "duck-in" protest. Arraigned in Anchorage, Percy pleaded not guilty and was released on a $5,000 bond. The case is important in that it challenges the federal government to consider Native subsistence whaling rights based on the 1946 (and other) international whaling conventions.

[9] The state had passed its own legislation pertaining to subsistence rights two years earlier, but without distinguishing between Native and non-Native residents. This was done partly in response to impending federal legislation.

finds and declares that the continuation of the opportunity for subsistence uses by rural residents of Alaska, including both Natives and non-Natives, on the public lands and by Alaska Natives on Native lands is essential to Native physical, economic, traditional, and *cultural* existence, and to non-Natives physical, economic, traditional, and *social* existence." (cited in Berger 1984:64; emphasis added).

This declaration made a significant distinction between Native *cultural* and non-Native *social* subsistence needs—a difference placing federal and state policies at odds. A Kotzebue Iñupiat, Suzy Erlich, summed up the conflict at a local meeting of the Alaska Native Review Commission[10] in 1984:

> Subsistence, as it is used nowadays, merely lumps us in. The state of Alaska cannot discriminate, so subsistence is everyone's right. We use the word subsistence as a politically separate term, and in fact, when the state uses subsistence, it is a privilege. To us, subsistence is our inherent right because that is how we have always been and, I believe, that is how we will always be.

Although the ANILCA declaration represented a commitment by the federal government to assure the continuation of aboriginal subsistence hunting and fishing rights on federal lands in Alaska, these lands were largely multipurpose in nature. Subsistence needs, although recognized, were considered secondary to those of mineral development, conservation, tourism, and the like. Therefore, each time a restriction was placed on Iñupiat subsistence activities, the ability to depend on this aspect of their economic way of life was subtly eroded.

ENHANCING CULTURAL IDENTITY

A second major goal of the borough was to enhance Iñupiat cultural identity. It especially wanted to establish an independent school district, for by this means the people could control their own budget, elect their own school board, hire their own teachers and superintendent, and shape their own curriculum. In borough villages, new schools, including high schools, were planned, constructed, and staffed with funding derived from federal and state transfer payments.[11] Bilingual and bicultural educational programs were given particular attention in an effort to strengthen knowledge of Iñupiat

[10] Sponsored by the Inuit Circumpolar Conference (see below) and the World Council of Indigenous Peoples, the Alaska Native Review Commission [1983–85] was formed to investigate the impact of the Land Claims Settlement Act on Alaska Natives and offer recommendations for appropriate changes. Testimony was gathered from Natives in many Alaska villages. Along with other agencies and foundations, major financial support was provided by the North Slope Borough. A summary of the report and its recommendations is contained in an important book, *Village Journey*, written by Justice Thomas R. Berger (1985).

[11] This shift in educational commitment by the state to support high schools even in small villages was the result of a 1976 suit (Hootch v. Lind) brought against the state demanding that high schools be built in rural villages so the students would not have to leave home to complete their education. The state settled out of court, following which new school programs were introduced in ninety-five communities throughout rural Alaska.

history, language, and culture. A cultural heritage program, funded in part through local and federal Indian education grants, stressed learning from the past and included active participation of Iñupiat elders in classroom discussion.

Well aware that the Iñupiaq language had suffered greatly as a result of earlier educational policies, instruction in Iñupiaq became a required part of the curriculum from kindergarten through grade six and optional for students in grades seven through twelve. Further efforts to revive the language included the introduction of scientific terms and abstract concepts. In this manner, contemporary developments and ideas could be spoken in Iñupiaq as well as English and in so doing demonstrate that one's Native tongue need not be thought of as inapplicable or out-of-date. As a further incentive to strengthen Iñupiat cultural knowledge, more than 100 local teacher aides were hired in the villages to supplement the work of "regular" teachers, most of whom came from outside the region. Vocational and recreational adult education courses were offered and an experimental center for higher education established for a brief period.

The borough also formed a Commission on History, Language, and Culture, which published a series of highly respected books and monographs dealing with Iñupiat archeology, oral, and cultural history. Anthropologists, archeologists, and historians played a particularly active role in these endeavors, undertaking collaborative research and writing up the results with the assistance of local elders. The commission also sponsored mapping projects documenting traditional names and including traditional land use inventories that told how and for what purpose the people had earlier used the land. Other activities included the development of a large photo library and plans for the establishment of a North Slope museum.

While the revised educational curriculum focused on strengthening Iñupiat history, language, and culture, Eben Hopson called for creation of an international environmental regime in which all Arctic nations would agree to following similar rules of industrial development. Meeting in Barrow in June 1977, he and other Inuit (Eskimo) leaders from Greenland, Canada, and the United States presided over the birth of the Inuit Circumpolar Conference (ICC). Given the ecological interdependence of the entire circumpolar region, the delegates began working on an Arctic policy designed to resolve pressing problems associated with the expanding oil and gas industry, including drilling on the Outer Continental Shelf.

While in basic support of economic development in the Arctic, the delegates nevertheless favored a cautious approach in which the Inuit would be actively involved in the decision-making process, and in which the economic benefits accruing from this development would not seriously jeopardize either the environment or the culture of the largely Native population. Further attention was directed toward protection of the subsistence economy and the renewable resources that would have to sustain the people long after petroleum and minerals had been depleted from their particular regions. Resolutions on these topics were adopted along with others calling for the development of educational exchange programs, improved village health training, expansion of village communication technologies, and designating the Arctic and sub-Arctic as a nuclear-free zone.

At the conclusion of the conference, a permanent international organization was formed with the understanding that further meetings of the ICC would be held on a regular basis. The absence of invited Siberian delegates was noted, and plans were made to seek their involvement in future gatherings. This effort to unite all of the circumpolar peoples was perceived by Eben Hopson and other ICC leaders as one of immense importance for it not only extended the ideal of local and regional self-determination to its fullest international extent, but it affirmed the desirability of establishing a viable northern Native political entity able to transcend the artificial boundaries imposed by the western nations.[12]

CAPITAL IMPROVEMENT PROGRAM

The third major thrust of the borough in the 1970s and 1980s was to undertake a Capital Improvement Program (CIP) designed to dramatically upgrade the education, health, and standard of living of its members communities. Along with improved educational facilities, the program called for the construction of housing, health care services, sanitation and water supply systems, public safety buildings, and public roads. The initial plan, introduced in 1975, had a projected financial outlay of $60 million. Within five years it was to rise far above that.

The borough's basic strategy was to transform petroleum property tax revenues into local jobs adapted to meet Iñupiat needs. This was to be done through a policy of Native hire. Soon, Iñupiat men began taking jobs in CIP projects as construction workers while women became clerks, secretaries, teacher and health aides. The Arctic Slope Regional Corporation and local village corporations also hired Iñupiat men and women in their various economic enterprises and administrative bodies. By 1977, approximately 50 percent of the jobs held by the North Slope Iñupiat were financed through the borough while an additional 25 percent came from the regional corporation.[13]

For Iñupiat men, the nature of employment varied little from earlier years. Whether taking positions as unskilled laborers, heavy equipment operators, or carpenters, three out of four found jobs in construction. Overall, approximately 75 percent of the men over 18 worked sometime during 1977. While only 54 percent of women worked that year, their choice of jobs was much

[12] In 1983, the ICC was officially granted Non-Governmental Organization status by the United Nations Economic and Social Council, which enhanced its ability to promote the rights and interests of circumpolar peoples within the international community.

[13] In 1976–77, an extensive research study was undertaken on Alaska's North Slope by the University of Alaska's Institute for Social and Economic Research. Much of the statistical and other data discussed below are drawn from this valuable work. For more details, see Kruse et al (1981) and Kleinfeld (1981), and McBeath (1981).

greater, for along with new clerical and secretarial openings in borough, village, and regional corporations, women were also sought as paraprofessionals in schools and clinics, and in some instances as beginning managerial and professional personnel. Given this breadth of opportunity, it is easy to understand why their participation in the labor force doubled between 1970 and 1977. They also worked for longer periods. Whereas men worked an average of seven months, women's employment averaged 8.5 months. Of the men and women who were employed, approximately 40 percent received at least some on-the-job training—men primarily as machine operators and in the trades, women as clerical workers and paraprofessionals.

As a result of this expanding economic activity, family incomes of borough members rose dramatically. Whereas the 1970 median income of North Slope Iñupiat households was $6,923, by 1977 it had risen to $17,347, an increase of approximately 150 percent. Important, however, were several other factors, some of which followed earlier patterns of occupational and income distribution, and some of which did not.

One item of interest was that between 1970 and 1977 the actual income distribution of borough residents remained the same. That is, *at both time periods*, the poorest 40 percent of the population received approximately 13 percent of the total income whereas the wealthiest 20 percent received 44 percent (Kruse et al 1981:47–8). Thus, there appeared to be no basic change in the composition of the more well-to-do sector, a conclusion supported by other ethnographic evidence.

Other data demonstrated that opportunities for wage employment were more common in larger villages. For example, whereas 50 percent of Iñupiat adults in Barrow held jobs sometime during 1977, in Kaktovik only 20 percent were so engaged. Also, Barrow Iñupiat worked for more hours and more months than Iñupiat in other villages. While personal choice may have played a small factor in this differential—residents in smaller villages chose to spend more of their time in subsistence pursuits—the major reason behind Barrow's higher rate of employment was its location as the administrative center for the borough, the Arctic Slope Regional Corporation, the Ukpeagvik Iñupiat (village) Corporation, and their subsidiaries.

Significant differences were also reflected in the amount of wages received. Construction work, whether skilled or unskilled, brought by far the greatest income. The median level for heavy-machine operators was approximately $600 per week, while for construction laborers it was $500. Service and clerical jobs, held mostly by women, paid much less—$200 to $250 per week according to the 1977 survey results. Thus, although women worked more hours than men, the latter earned more income (Kruse et al 1981:46).

Gender differences, too, were important. Women were drawn to wage work for several reasons. Over the previous several decades, technological advances had reduced their having to fulfill subsistence responsibilities such as skin sewing, once an essential family task. At the same time, vocational training in subjects defined by Euro-Americans as "female-oriented" were receiving greater emphasis in the school curriculum. By the 1970s, one-third of Iñupiat women had been trained in paraprofessional programs and another 20 percent in clerical occupations. Thus, they were now prepared to assume positions in governmental, educational, and other rapidly expanding institutions both within and outside the borough. A reduction in family size further contributed to women's greater participation in wage work, as did their greater involvement in postsecondary education outside the borough—which, in turn, enhanced their competence in English.

Of course, some Iñupiat women chose not to work at all, the most commonly stated reasons being family pressures and responsibilities. Still, that didn't necessarily imply lack of interest. Gender conflict in expected role behavior was also a source of difficulty. As one woman explained, "My husband doesn't want me to work—just take care of the kids. I've been wanting to go to work but he won't let me." Another commented, "As a working mother, I find that even an unreliable baby-sitter is in great demand. There are so many jobs available to anyone that when a working mother or father wants to work, we have problems trying to find a babysitter." (Kleinfeld 1981:9) It was little wonder that a child-care center had become a high CIP priority by 1979.

Iñupiat men, by contrast, viewed their participation in wage employment quite differently. Poor health was a major reason for lack of involvement. More than 50 percent of the men of the North Slope worked only intermittently. The seasonal nature of construction work was partly responsible for this pattern. More significant was personal choice, men wanting to hunt as well as labor for wages, a response not unlike that expressed by Kaktovik Iñupiat seeking work at the Barter Island DEW line site twenty years previously.[14]

How did borough leaders respond to Iñupiat workers' desiring to take time off for such activities? They declared such requests should be honored. Wanting to avoid problems confronting earlier Iñupiat men who had been forced to choose between the two forms of economic endeavor, anyone requesting "subsistence leave" automatically received it. And during the spring whaling season, borough operations virtually ceased while all Iñupiat from the mayor on down took time off to hunt the bowhead. Thus, in the late 1970s, subsistence hunting remained a vital mode of activity for most Iñupiat males.[15] As one young Iñupiat hunter said in speaking about his brother (Kleinfeld 1981:14):

> He's a hunter. He's always hunting. He'd be there surviving. That guy can live on anything. He's all right. He got a fox by running after it. He only works part time when he wants to make money. He's a wise man, smart.

[14] Full-time jobs working on the pipeline and at Prudhoe Bay were also rejected by a large majority of Iñupiat. And those who did accept employment there often quit after a short period of time. "I worked until April 1976," commented one Iñupiat ex-oil worker. "It was whaling time and I came home. I told them they didn't have enough dollars to keep me working."

[15] Interviews with Iñupiat men at this time clearly reflected this commitment. When discussing wage employment they responded in superficial generalities, but when asked to describe their hunting activities, they did so "with involvement and intensity." (Kleinfeld 1981:14)

The contrast between this male view of what constitutes an admirable Iñupiat and that of a Barrow school teacher is striking.

> I've had twenty-three students graduate over the last three years. Except for two working in temporary construction, the others are hanging out. Last year I placed five graduate students in good jobs. They drifted out over the summer. What's the incentive to work? The kids live with their parents. They got food, clothes, some spending money.

This is not to suggest that young Iñupiat were uninterested in receiving vocational training to better prepare them for wage work, or that school teachers lacked respect for those with subsistence skills. Rather, each had a view of the future that drew heavily on his or her cultural past.

Thus, from the perspective of most Iñupiat men, the borough's offering of flex time and subsistence leave was a successful strategy enabling men to work intermittently, thereby earning needed cash income while actively continuing their subsistence pursuits. For Iñupiat women, regular wage labor of more steady duration in offices, schools, and clinics was also appealing. It was hardly a surprise that when borough residents were asked in a survey, "What was the single most positive change occurring in the North Slope since 1970?" the majority responded. "The number of good jobs you can get."

By the close of the 1970s, the borough had more than 800 employees in construction, education, and administration. That was a substantial number considering that the North Slope's Iñupiat population was a little more than 3500, half of whom were children. Non-Natives totaled about 5,000 people, most of them petroleum workers at Prudhoe Bay.[16] A few whites, primarily teachers, lived in outlying villages, and a larger number of teachers, doctors, nurses, government workers, administrators, entrepreneurs, and construction company personnel lived in Barrow.

ECONOMIC PROBLEMS

Although the borough was inspired by the vision of building a modern Arctic community and creating employment opportunities for North Slope Iñupiat, problems quickly mounted. With little experience in such endeavors, Iñupiat leaders had to rely on outsiders, some of whom were eager to make quick profits. Furthermore, the speed with which numerous construction projects were begun raised other difficulties. It wasn't long before costs began to escalate.

The reasons were many. Having to compete for skilled workers and equipment with other companies building the TransAlaska pipeline inflated wages. Contractors, having a relatively free hand, frequently took advantage of the situation. One charged the borough for shipping huge loads of lumber and

---

[16] Temporary oil workers are not considered regular borough residents.

similar materials by air freight when they could have been sent far more cheaply by boat in summer—except that the contractor had already set up his own air freight service. Cheap insulation was used where higher quality had been called for originally. Iñupiat, trained as carpenters and heavy-machine operators, were assigned unskilled jobs as journeymen because unions wouldn't provide the needed waiver. Some local workers whose commitment and skills in construction were inadequate for meeting the needs of the position had to be laid off. Others sat around in quiet frustration doing little; construction foremen neglected to provide adequate on-the-job training but feared letting them go due to signed agreements committing the company to Native hire. Eventually, the turnover rate of Iñupiat workers exceeded all expectations, as did the costs.

One step taken by the borough to deal with the growing financial crisis was to draw on a provision of the state law allowing local governments to tax without limit to pay off bond indebtedness. Challenged in this action by Sohio Petroleum Company, the borough was temporarily blocked in its plan to market additional bonds, thereby bringing to a halt many of its unfinished projects. Through the diligence of the borough's lobbyist, additional legislation was passed enabling municipalities to tax as necessary to finance the interest and bond repayments. Soon, fifty million more dollars became available and the CIP projects resumed.

Then in 1980, Eben Hopson, Barrow's most prominent leader, died of cancer at 57. As construction cost overruns mounted, his elected successor, Eugene Brower, approved even more expenditures. Over the next four years the borough continued its effort to provide citizens with better educational and health services, modern housing, a bus transportation system, and greatly improved water and sanitation facilities. But this was achieved at a devastating financial expense. From an initial projected budget of $60 million in 1975, CIP expenditures had gone to $375 million by 1980. In the next five years, rising interest rates, inflation, and misspending would double that figure.

Concerned over the rapidly escalating indebtedness, the Alaskan Legislature introduced a bill to limit the borough's bonding authority to $25,000 per capita—a dramatic drop from the approximately $130,000 per capita bond debt then existing. In response, the mayor's office mounted its own publicity campaign, taking out full page advertisements that stated: "How much is too much to invest in the American Dream in Rural Alaska?" In press releases, Mayor Brower (1983:29–30) wrote:

> Anchorage papers mimic national newspapers which measure "wealth" by dividing income by the number of citizens in our small population. Resulting per-capita income and spending statistics are used by the press to provoke jealousy and mistrust toward people who are using the income from local resources to develop their communities and provide resources that elsewhere are taken for granted. . . . Without the organization and growth of the North Slope Borough, the billions of dollars we are investing in American Arctic community development would not have been made. Our oil and gas reserves would have been extracted by oil

Photo 34. Modern housing in Barrow.

companies who, like the mining companies before them, left very little behind for Alaskans who live here.

Although the borough's lobbying power was adequate to defeat the bill, the negative publicity resulting from the struggle was formidable. Furthermore, by 1985, the borough's bond indebtedness to Wall Street had exceeded $1 billion. The annual debt service alone exceeded $180 million (Knapp, Colt, and Henley 1986:VI-1). Also, rumors of questionable practices involving conflict of interest, double billing and excessive charging had become rampant.[17]

In the 1985 election, following further reports of corruption and fraud, North Slope voters elected George Ahmaogak as their reform mayor. A well-known whaling captain and community leader, Ahmaogak was committed to a policy of greater fiscal conservatism and closer cooperation with the oil and gas industry. However, accompanying that philosophy was a sharp reduction in the Capital Improvement Plan, which quickly raised the spectre of large-scale unemployment. Additional wage cutbacks were generated by a world glut in petroleum that sharply reduced the price of oil. This, in turn, greatly weakened incoming revenues. A economic crisis was at hand.[18]

[17] After a thorough audit of borough finances, the NSB estimated that many millions of dollars had been lost as a result of these practices, including those that had occurred during the final days of the Brower administration. Eventually, civil and criminal charges were filed against several borough employees and advisors; and in 1989 two of these advisors were convicted in a Federal court of extortion, racketeering and fraud.

[18] The North Slope was not alone in experiencing hardship. The state's revenue department estimated that every $1 drop in the price of oil cost the state $150 million a year in lost revenues. In the summer of 1986, oil prices had dropped from the previous November's high of $32 a barrel to below $10. Alaska's economy tumbled, bankruptcies grew, and many who could, fled the state (Naske and Slotnick 1987:282).

Such a boom-or-bust cycle was hardly new to the North Slope, its residents having experienced similar difficulties following the collapse of the whaling and fur industries earlier in the century. But this latest decline differed in two ways: Not only was there a far greater reliance on commercial products, but Iñupiat subsistence activities and cooperative kin-ties had also been reduced. In addition, the new borough leadership was committed to an entirely different strategy for solving its financial problems, one which shifted the primary responsibility for the region's economic growth from the public to the private sector. To promote this plan, an important meeting was held in Barrow in July 1985. Called a "Private Sector Economic Development Conference," it brought together more than eighty business and community leaders from within and outside the borough, including Native corporation presidents, oil company representatives, economists, community development consultants, educators, and researchers. I, too, participated. It was the first time I'd been back to Barrow in a long time.[19]

[19] The primary reason for my return was to briefly assist anthropologists Rosita Worl and Charles Smythe in their field study of changing socioeconomic and cultural conditions in Barrow, undertaken for the Department of the Interior's Mineral Management Service, Alaska Outer Continental Shelf Region (see: Worl and Smythe 1986).

8/Prospects for the Future

A MODERN BARROW

Coming in for a landing at the Barrow airport, I observed numerous new buildings dotting the long coastal strip of land that defined the community's location 330 miles above the Arctic Circle. In contrast to earlier trips, it seemed like I was entering a new world. Looking for an up-to-date equivalent of the village I had once known, I found instead a modern community. Two large multistoried glass- and metal-enclosed buildings of the most contemporary design dominated the city's center, one housing the courthouse and the other the offices of the Arctic Slope Regional Corporation. Such gleaming facades needed no words to express the symbolic message of the borough's new wealth. Yet, several blocks away, small two- and three-room unpainted houses of much older vintage intermingled with newer ranch-style homes. Dominating one section of the main street was the Ukpeagvik Iñupiat Corporation-owned *stuaqpak* (big store), a popular supermarket and clothing emporium offering its customers the latest food and other commodities ranging from snow peas and Häagen-Dazs ice cream to designer jeans and video cameras. Next door, an even more impressive office building served as the nerve center for the North Slope Borough.

Everywhere I went there was movement, entirely unlike my previous experience on the North Slope. Buses, stopping on street corners to pick up shoppers, were followed by cars, Jeeps, trucks, and ATV three-wheelers. At the nearby Top of the World Hotel, an Iñupiat taxi driver sat in the heated comfort of his vehicle, hopeful that a patron from the hotel's Mexican restaurant would choose his means of transportation rather than walking home. And in clusters of four and five, tourists, their cameras poised, strolled along gravel roadways. These people were distinguished by their brightly colored parkas displaying the logo of the travel agency that had organized their overnight trip from faraway Fairbanks or Anchorage.

Taking a bus out to Browerville on the edge of town, I observed more construction, including several large multiunit dwellings, most of them occupied by whites. Passing a playground, I looked up to see atop one of the houses, stretched like a flag between two poles, the skin and white fur of a large polar bear. Turning to the Iñupiat sitting beside me, I pointed to the bear skin and smiled. "Uh, huh," came the muffled response, followed by a

Photo 35. Barrow's modern courthouse and office building.

clarifying phrase, "That's the house of the new mayor, George Ahmaogak."

Over the next few days, I traced down old friends such as Harold Kaveolook. Vincent Nageak, a respected community elder, had died, but Harold and his family lived in the teacher's apartment building, near the new high school. After retiring from his BIA teaching position at Kaktovik in the early 1970s, he and Mae had returned to Barrow. He was now serving his last year as a village coordinator for the Borough School District before retiring again. All kinds of honors had come his way in recent years. The newly built high school in Kaktovik bore his name, and before long he was to receive an honorary Doctorate in Education from the University of Alaska. Honors aside, it was good just to see him again.

Harold and Mae warmly welcomed me into their living room. Removing a parka from the couch, Harold quickly motioned for me to sit down. Over tea provided by Mae, we shared stories of the past dozen years and then settled into a more serious discussion of recent changes that had occurred on the slope and Harold's view of prospects for the years ahead.

On the positive side, he spoke with enthusiasm of how primary-school children had benefited from the school district's new curricula stressing the use of Iñupiaq in the classroom, and how parents could now actively participate in matters pertaining to their children's education. However, in his quiet way, Harold expressed great frustration with the restraints that had been placed on subsistence activity. Describing the earlier moratorium on caribou hunting and the quota system on whaling, Harold summed up the dilemma: "We can no longer control our lives as we used to."

Photo 36. A typical Barrow street.

Speaking slowly, he mentioned the profound effect of the recently expanded wage economy on the lives of the people and especially how they could purchase many new manufactured goods at large stores such as the stuaqpak. But at the same time, increased dependence on these commodities, when combined with restrictions placed on hunting, was seriously affecting the Iñupiat distribution system.

"There is less sharing now among families than in the past," he said. "It seems that when subsistence and cash are combined, sharing is reduced. People with cash may share their meat but they feel differently about their cash. Of course, hunters will sometime sell meat, too, but that doesn't occur very often."

"What about sharing meat for one's labor?"

"Yes, that happens. Mae does it all the time. She's always helping relatives and friends cut up ugruk or some other animal and she gets a portion in return."

"And whaling?"

"Of course. We always share at whaling feasts and at Thanksgiving and Christmas, too. The church also helps out, letting people know when someone is in need. But at other times when somebody earns money, they don't think so much about sharing."

"Can you give an example?"

"In the past, some people were better off than others. They'd have a big whale boat or umiaq. But today, there are lots of aluminum boats. People buy one and they can travel on their own without having to depend on anybody else. Before, people had to work together, share things, be a member of the crew. There was no power except manpower. If you were a boat owner without a crew, you weren't going anywhere. Now you get an outboard motor and as long as you have money, you can go out by yourself."

During our conversation, it became clear how recent technology and the greater opportunity to use cash as the primary means of providing for one's livelihood had lessened the Iñupiat's need to assist each other. But this was not much different from discussions Harold and I had had in Kaktovik nearly 30 years previously, or for that matter, patterns typifying Iñupiat life a century ago. In times of plenty, there was less pressure for families to share what they had with relatives; and in times of want, they couldn't. Today, a new factor had been introduced. No longer did the Iñupiat have full control over their own hunting and fishing resources, restrictions having been placed on them by external governmental agencies. Thus these limitations, together with greatly expanded reliance on the wage economy, had the effect of seriously eroding the long-held value placed on collective responsibility. Furthermore, by challenging the reciprocity that was the chief bulwark of this relationship, a new ideology was subtly enhanced, one stressing individual achievement, characteristic of the dominant society.

This led to a discussion of cutbacks in CIP employment and the hardship that was causing for families without cash.

"Harold, what's going to happen to those who have lost their jobs? Will they be able to pull together like they did in the past?"

"It's going to be hard on some people. Right now, it's pretty difficult to tell. And the animals, the restrictions on hunting—that's something else. With a lot more people up here, open season comes. That can affect the size of the herd, too. It got smaller several years ago. Maybe, with more people killing caribou, it might happen again. I don't know."

Another question concerned the extent to which younger Iñupiat on the North Slope were still able to acquire the necessary hunting skills. Harold spoke of a "survival school" that had been organized so that problem students could learn how to care for themselves out-of-doors on their own.

"Young people don't know how to survive out there," he said, pointing out the window toward the tundra. "You know, if you are not exposed to outdoor life, spend your time in school, then finish eighth grade and go on for another four years until you're 18, you don't have much time to learn about taking care of yourself. In my time, if parents didn't have enough food, they would take their kids inland rather than leave them at Barrow. Now it's different."

"Two different worlds?"

With a slight smile, Harold nodded his agreement.

Over the next few weeks, I talked often with Harold and other elders about changes in Barrow. Also, I wanted to learn how younger members of the Barrow community—students, construction workers, health aides, subsistence hunters—perceived *their* unfolding world. In undertaking this endeavor, I was reminded of the frustrations felt years ago in Kaktovik while trying to piece together the diverse imagery that came my way through conversations, observations, and interviews. In Barrow, it was the same.

The perspective of a graduating high school student:

I see myself getting an education and growing up in a modern town—not like a village or an uncivilized place. Because of my heritage and culture, I spend a lot of time thinking about that. I try to mix both together and take the best of the two; and try to be myself, too. I don't want to forget about my past culture because of who I am. But I can't go back ten thousand years ago. I've got to go to school and find a job—try to relate it to who I am and what I want to be.

On the future of the Iñupiat:

I think the biggest problem is financing. Because of the introduction of the cash economy, we have become reliant on cash for making things feasible, making things happen, making sure that we have adequate equipment, adequate tools, adequate hunting gear. . . . We can provide food from the store, (but) we still have that inner relationship to our Native food. It makes us feel whole. . . . (Still) in the back of my mind, I am worried.

On dependency:

I can see that burden on the people for not having employment available. On the other hand, it is a threat in that it kind of whittles away the culture, the heritage we are trying to keep up and alive. As Iñupiat people we have been able to adapt; but again, psychologically, the impact of the different social order—it bothers me a little to think about that.

The security and sharing found within Iñupiat culture:

At a time when hardship comes, that is when the Iñupiat people become really close-knit. Especially families that have been separated for awhile. They find the way to come back together. I experienced that in the early 1960s when there were no jobs available and a lot of people were going through hardship. About five or six family members, relatives, would come together and eat as one family. That's when the family unit seemed to strengthen, to come close together.

The economic insecurity faced by a heavy-equipment operator:

I'd like to stay here. I'd rather work in Barrow than anywhere. But if worse comes to worst, I'll go out. (What about hunting?) That's a difficult question. If I owned my own house, I would continue hunting. But since I don't, and because I have to have cash to pay the rent, I must work.

And in the view of several other workers:

Basically, where the money goes, we go.

Non-Native residents, including office managers, city planners, health professionals, scientists, teachers, and small-business owners, also identified themselves positively with Barrow, but with less of a sense of foreboding expressed by their Iñupiat neighbors. On the back of a teacher's blackboard I found the phrase "only four months to go," but for the majority, Barrow was a place they enjoyed living in, working in, and playing in. Thus, from

Photo 37. Even on a foggy day, baseball is a highly popular sport for Native and non-Native alike.

the perspective of non-Natives, most of whom were white, relations between Native and non-Native had a greater sense of common purpose—quite a contrast to the antagonisms of years past. Some, of course, were still drawn by the high wages. Others, seeing numerous opportunities, planned to stay. Still, in the back of everyone's mind was the realization that if the economic problems became too severe, non-Native inhabitants could always go home. For the Iñupiat, they were already home.

Thus, the permanent residents of the North Slope, both Native and non-Native, knew they had to pull together in this latest financial crisis. In keeping with this approach, borough leaders began exploring possible solutions. One effort was the Private Sector Economic Development Conference, held in July 1985.

SEARCH FOR SOLUTIONS

The conference was located in the old Naval Arctic Research Laboratory that had been taken over by the borough several years previously. In his opening address, Mayor George Ahmaogak set the tone for the sessions to follow. He emphasized that the fundamental objective of the borough was to create the most basic facilities of modern community life "so as to enhance the lifestyle of our people." Now, however, the CIP was winding down. Over the next five years borough leaders estimated that between 450 and 900 jobs would be lost. Given these cutbacks, new employment strategies had to be found, including tourism and the development and marketing of Native arts, crafts, and designs associated with Iñupiat culture.

Furthermore, he advised that the borough needed to cooperate much more fully with the petroleum industry, airlines, shipping companies, banking, and financial interests. In a direct criticism of previous policies, Ahmaogak stated that "too often in the past, borough officials have assumed an adversary role in their approach to those industries that do business on the North Slope." Acknowledging that subsistence resources and skills had to be preserved, they also "must be balanced against the opportunities afforded by the development and extraction of natural resources necessary for local, state, and national needs," assuring all the while that such development must not damage the natural resources to such an extent that they will have no value for future generations.

Following the Mayor's talk, a young economist from an Alaskan bank pointed out the "trade-off" between environmental concerns and an increased standard of living, and between that living standard and maintaining one's culture. "A vibrant economy means inevitable change. The more vibrant, the more change," he said. "If you are interested in economic development you must ask yourselves: What does the North Slope have to offer—oil, gas, human resources, and crafts." After encouraging Iñupiat participation in joint ventures with outside businesses, he concluded by emphasizing that it was important to make corporations feel wanted so that there would be a friendly environment for investment. "With the right attitude and perseverance, you can be successful."

Participants then divided into small working groups devoted to local private enterprise, large-scale projects, training and education, and village economic development. Selecting the latter, I joined twenty village leaders, borough officials, economic development advisers, and others in a small room just off the main auditorium.[1] Herman Rexford from Kaktovik was there along with other old friends from earlier days. His son Fenton was the workshop convener. Fenton began by stating, "CIP cutbacks have presented us with a severe problem. Our task is to come up with some creative solutions. How can the village corporations, small businesses, and oil companies take up the slack?"

A representative from Anaktuvuk Pass was quick to respond.

"Why is it that outsiders get so many jobs in the villages? They should be earmarked for us rather than outside workers. In Anaktuvuk, we lost a construction bid and now the job has twelve outsiders and only two local hires. Why can't we hire within the borough?"

Other villagers voiced similar frustrations.

"That's right," one said. "This type of conference should have occurred

---

[1] An irony of contemporary field work in the Arctic is that considerably more time is spent in meetings rather than in analyzing subsistence pursuits and other village activities more commonly associated with anthropological endeavors. The point, of course, is that these undertakings have become an essential feature of Iñupiat political life. Thus, the cultural researcher becomes involved as well.

years ago when the CIP first began. Villages themselves should be doing the contracting rather than having to engage in competitive bidding."

Fenton countered with another question. "Yes, that may be true, but now we're talking about bringing outside income to the villages. How do you do it at Anaktuvuk Pass?"

"We don't. There is no real way to make money there. People mainly exist on unemployment checks. Wages are minimal. Nothing is going on in construction. No jobs. No job training, either. But I have my pride. I don't just want to work. I'm not going to start out on that route. I want to keep on hunting, too."

Leaning forward, the young banker from southeast Alaska who had given the earlier address commented: "In a cash economy, people must learn to compete. Either you accept large-scale development, or an alternative to a cash economy must be found."

Across the room, someone asked, "What about tourism at Anaktuvuk?"

"We have lots of tourists," the Anaktuvuk Pass villager replied. "In summer, planes come in every day bringing people to the Gates of the Arctic National Park. Hikers camp all over the place, but the village doesn't get any real income from it. We can't even hunt and fish like we used to."

The Anaktuvuk Pass Iñupiaq explained that when the park first opened, local villagers were pleased. They had been told that the park would protect their subsistence hunting and fishing from outside pressure. Tourism, too, could bring in a little cash.

"But that's not what happened. The park service told us we had to have a permit to go through their lands and that we couldn't use our ATVs (all-terrain vehicles) to reach our hunting areas because they left tracks on the land. Also, they were not our traditional means of transportation. It was all right on village lands and (regional) corporation land, but not in the park. Then ASRC made a big swap with the Department of the Interior. They exchanged subsurface mining rights on 92,000 acres in the Chandler Lake area of the Arctic National Wildlife Refuge near Kaktovik, for 100,000 acres which is where we travel to do our summer hunting. ASRC was interested in the possible oil and gas around Kaktovik, but they never thought about us at Anaktuvuk. Just the money they might make. And now, we need a permit from the park service to reach our hunting lands, but we can't use our ATVs to get there."

"How about Kaktovik and the Arctic National Wildlife Refuge?"

"We have campers and hikers coming all summer to the refuge. They pitch their tents everywhere. It's a problem for us. We also have two lodges but they are owned by local air carriers, not the village corporation."

"Wainwright is planning to build a hotel to bring tourists to their village. But without a steady flow of visitors, it doesn't work."

"At Barrow, we built a forty-room hotel in 1974, but it is hardly breaking even now. Taking that long just to break even is not good."

"Maybe we should invest in a cruise liner that drops off visitors at each coastal village!"

"Tourism may not be the answer. As soon as someone is successful, outside air carriers come in and take over."

Asking others in the room to share their experiences, Fenton gestured toward the representative from Nuiqsut, the small community near Prudhoe Bay.

Speaking quietly but with feeling, the Nuiqsut Iñupiaq acknowledged his concerns.

"With the CIP projects on the decline, some people say we are fortunate to have the oil interests hiring local people. But most have strong mixed feelings about what will happen five years from now—what will be good for the village and what will not. At our last meeting, one person brought up making gunny sacks to sell to the oil industry. These are things we are beginning to look at. And since a road will be coming north to Nuiqsut sooner or later, that's going to have a big impact, too. So we need to prepare for this by providing training for our young people. We also want to keep our subsistence way of life. People are really worried about that—losing our subsistence. But we are all going to be affected. Whether it is oil, gas, mining, or something else, we can't stop it."

"And Point Lay? What about the coal project there?"

"Engineers are looking the situation over. It's just like Nuiqsut. Some people are afraid it will interfere with subsistence hunting. Others think unemployment is the biggest concern. Everyone wonders whether coal could take the place of diesel fuel. If that happened, everyone would benefit. But now, our people are talking mostly about subsistence. Whether or not we have to make a choice."

An engineer, hired by a subsidiary company of ASRC, added more concrete information.

"Right now, we are halfway through a major state-funded and Alaska Native Foundation-administered effort to determine the feasibility of coal development in the western Arctic between Point Lay and Point Hope. A fair amount of subsurface drilling has already occurred in the area. Investigations of environmental impact have been done. We've had a fair amount of contact with the villagers at the two locations. Studies of transportation out to the rest of the state have been completed. At this point in time, it looks very promising. It might serve as many as 100 villages in both western and northern Alaska, providing a low, effective alternative to fuel oil now used in the region. If the new Red Dog iron mine in the northwest region farther south were to purchase 50,000 to 100,000 tons of coal a year, the cost to the villages would be low and the employment potential would be high, involving as many as fifty to 100 people."

"How do they feel about having a coal mine there?"

"It's about 50-50. Half the folks are all for it and the others worry about hunting. This isn't just an impression. An attitude survey was taken to see exactly how the residents felt and that was the result. But this is just a small effort, not like the Red Dog mine that will eventually involve the sale of millions of tons of zinc. The primary beneficiaries, of course, will be the people in the proposed Northwest Borough."

"How about the environmental impact studies?"

"There are basically two kinds. One involves the environmental agencies— the feds, state agencies, and the North Slope Borough—those are the ones that approve permits for work to go forward. That's one side of it. The other is how the people living in the region feel about it. Do they want it or not. These are two separate issues. But they can be resolved. For example, those most concerned over the impact of the mine on subsistence hunting might be willing to support it if the mine were closed during the migrating season for game or beluga whales."

"That sounds really good. Now, what about Atqasuk?"

"About 70 percent of our labor force is employed on CIP projects. When that's over, most people will be looking for work. To give you an idea of the problem, our new houses built by the borough require between $700 and $900 a month to heat. So cash income is really important. But so is subsistence. The people wonder if they will have to leave Atqasuk and look for work elsewhere. Also, there is only one store in the village. If the cash stops coming in, the store will close and we won't be able to buy things we need."

As the discussion continued into the afternoon, two inter-related questions kept reappearing. Those voiced by villagers focused on how governmental and private agencies and companies could assist them in protecting their subsistence economy. For the public and private agencies, the question was reversed—how could Iñupiat villagers meet the demands of the larger economy? Finally, toward the end of the day, an economic researcher from the University of Alaska placed his pipe on the table and turned toward those present.

"When CIP money dries up, the situation is going to be pretty tough. There aren't likely to be any single answers. People want to keep their pride. You don't want to do anything that doesn't fit your culture. But a lot of people in the villages will have to face not having much money and having to do something that is different from what they are used to. One obvious answer is to work at Prudhoe Bay. Some people have problems with that. But others, including some from Anaktuvuk Pass, are doing it fairly regularly. That's one practical suggestion. It seems that if you want to get money into the villages, more villagers will have to go elsewhere to work. It is either that or adjust to less money. Neither of these options is very attractive, but there seems to be no getting around it."

At the close of the conference the next day, an answer to what could be done about unemployment seemed little closer than it had the day before. The coming together of the villagers, private entrepreneurs, and local borough officials was instructive in enlightening each about the views of the other. And the analysis of the proposed coal mine project at Point Lay was definitely encouraging. But it was also clear that the problems facing the Iñupiat were far larger than could be resolved around a conference table. Yet, if a way couldn't be found, the classic portrayal of a subsistence-oriented people being forced into the lower echelons of a labor force would be played out once again.

Later that year, before an audience of business and oil corporation leaders in Fairbanks, Mayor Ahmaogak announced the establishment of a new training and employment service program "designed to elevate employment within the North Slope Borough." He added that "residents of the NSB hold one in fifty jobs in Prudhoe Bay oil fields." Utilizing a computer databank, residents of the borough could apply through their NSB village coordinator, listing their primary and secondary skills and employment interests. Applicants would then be screened and successful candidates given job training in administrative/office skills, catering/food preparation, electrical maintenance, warehousing/expediting and water/waste water treatment plant operation. After seven to twenty-four months, depending on the training needed, the trainees would be available for hire by the petroleum industry. At a hotel reception prior to the speech, several oil company representatives expressed support for the plan, stating that their corporations looked forward to helping in any way they could. Ethel "Pete" Nelson of Texaco USA was even more explicit in praising the Mayor and his proposal: "The industry has been waiting for someone (like you) to carry the elders to the lifestyle that's beneficial for everybody." (Kakaruk 1985:5)[2]

In conclusion, on the North Slope, the borough had utilized its unique geopolitical advantage to channel a small portion of the enormous wealth created by the extraction of oil at Prudhoe Bay to build a modern community in the Arctic. Some of the funds came from direct taxation of the petroleum industry while other amounts were derived from federal and state transfer payments. Furthermore, rather than concentrating this wealth in the hands of a small privileged sector of the borough population, it had been spread widely throughout the North Slope. All of its residents had benefited from improved education and health care, sanitation, and the establishment of public utilities. From a short-term perspective, the people of Arctic Alaska were the beneficiaries of immense good fortune.

Nevertheless, with the economic downturn, significant income inequalities had begun to emerge, both among Iñupiat and between them and non-Iñupiat. By the summer of 1985, 41 percent of Barrow Iñupiat had jobs compared with 59 percent of non-Native residents. In the villages unemployment figures were much higher. Within the Barrow Iñupiat population itself, those with permanent positions were able to maintain medium to high incomes whereas those without faced serious financial hardship.

In a detailed study undertaken at this time, Worl and Smythe (1987:13) reported that perhaps as many as 15 percent to 20 percent of Native households were near or below the poverty line and that new "institutional jobs," while more permanent, were held by fewer individuals. Summarizing this trend, they concluded: "The resulting economic differentiation will be more

---

[2] By 1987, the borough's training program at Prudhoe Bay's Kuparuk Industrial Center had placed 210 Iñupiat in new jobs.

sustained than earlier periods, and the proportion of the Iñupiat population at lower income levels can be expected to increase." Mediating this trend were the subsistence activities and sharing practices of extended family networks. But whether such efforts could forestall serious problems remained to be seen.[3]

Finally, in the back of people's minds was the fact that while the new consumerism was promoting ever higher expectations for material goods and services, the resource base of oil and natural gas was diminishing. Reductions in the flow of oil at Prudhoe Bay were already being planned for the early 1990s. By the year 2000, other fields perhaps far away would be in production. Would the Iñupiat have to "go where the money goes"?

In a world market dominated by private competition, that appeared to be the primary solution offered by most economic development experts. As the banker commented at the village roundtable discussion, "Either you accept large-scale development by large-scale corporations or an alternative to a cash economy must be found." Or as the university researcher proposed, "If you want to get money into the villages, more villagers will have to go elsewhere to work." And by extension, when the oil runs out at Prudhoe Bay, the Iñupiat must be prepared to move on to other locations where new nonrenewable resources were being developed. But was this the only solution? What about generating a cash economy based on local and regional resources and products? What about reducing the bureaucracy? Somehow, I knew that to be able to address these questions even minimally required getting away from Barrow and back into a village, even if only briefly. As to which one, that was hardly a problem. I'd been looking forward to seeing friends at Kaktovik for quite a while.

RETURN TO KAKTOVIK

The 330-mile flight from Barrow to Kaktovik provided an opportunity to contrast the landscape now with that of my first trip nearly three decades earlier. Halfway between the Colville River delta and Brownlow Point, the plane approached the petroleum complex at Prudhoe Bay. Suddenly, before me lay the town of Deadhorse. Spread over a large area of the tundra, it contained numerous oil rigs, production facilities, a power plant, and housing for 5000 industrial workers. Attached to this complex like a giant umbilical cord was the long thin ribbon of the TransAlaska pipeline, pointing south. Pumping up to 600,000 barrels of oil a day, it flowed through 48-inch diameter pipe on a 789-mile journey across three mountain ranges, beneath 350 rivers and streams, and through several earthquake zones to Valdez on Alaska's

---

[3] Social problems were also a key concern of many Iñupiat who had observed substantial increases in the rates of alcoholism, family violence (most often directed toward women and children), and suicide over the past several decades.

Photo 38. Neruokpuk Lakes, Brooks Range, Arctic National Wildlife Refuge.

southwest coast. It was a technological feat of immense proportions. But so was the cost—$7.7 billion.

I looked down a little later to see Qikiqtaq—Brownlow Point—pass under the wing of the plane. The old weathered log and sod walls of an Iñupiaq house still stood upright as did a segment of the building used by the geologist Leffingwell in his initial survey of the area in the early 1900s. Shortly after passing over the western boundary of the Arctic National Wildlife Refuge, eight musk ox came into view. Reintroduced to the area in 1969 by the U.S. Fish and Wildlife Service, the unique long dark fur, massive heads, and curved horns of these animals quickly set them apart from others in the region. Startled by the sound of the plane, they gathered themselves into a protective circle. Immobile, heads and bodies facing outward like the spokes on a wheel, they stood there quietly, defending themselves and their young from the unknown threat flying overhead.

Turning slightly inland, the plane crossed the Sadlerochit, Hulahula, and Okpilak rivers, all popular hunting areas of Kaktovik hunters. Of the three, the Sadlerochit was my favorite, for it led up to the Kekiktuk fork and then up that river to Neruokpuk Lakes—Schrader and Peters—which, to me, was the most beautiful setting in all of Alaska's northeast wilderness.

Eventually landing at Kaktovik in a brisk wind, I was greeted at the airstrip by friends who had known of my forthcoming arrival. Bundled in a Jeep, and with knapsack and duffel bag thrown in back, I was driven along the sand spit and then up a slight incline to the house of Daniel and Lily Akootchook with whom I was to stay. Kaktovik's physical appearance had changed almost as dramatically as that of Barrow, but since it was much smaller, it was more easily comprehensible. Dominating the landscape was the new school, with its large classrooms, gymnasium, library, crafts room, and small swimming pool. Quite a contrast from years past.

It wasn't long before I was out and around, visiting old friends and being reintroduced to grown Iñupiat I had known as young children. That first evening, I sat down with Isaac and Mary Akootchook, and also brothers Daniel and George, to talk of old times and new. Mary, with a shy smile, commented on the need for repair of my well-worn parka, knowing, of course, that it was the one she had made for me 27 years previously. Isaac had his mind on other matters, not the least of which was whether the winds would abate sufficiently for him and Mary to leave on a hunting trip they had been planning for some time. Whatever I was to learn from Isaac, now was the time to do it for Isaac, as Vincent Nageak had said years ago, was "a real Iñupiaq." When an opportunity arose to go hunting, nothing was going to get in his way.

While Mary sewed busily in a chair across the room, Isaac spoke of the changes that had occurred in Kaktovik since my last visit. Subsistence hunting and fishing were still fundamental to nutrition and culture. More than 70 percent of local Iñupiat relied on the subsistence economy for their major source of protein. Although the small village corporation store did sell commercially canned foods including meat, they were considered a selection of last resort. The one important change that had occurred in hunting and fishing was the means of travel. Today, in contrast to earlier years, villagers could take their three-wheelers out along the beach, check their fish nets, and bring back their catch for dinner. In fall and spring, snow machines served a similar purpose, enabling hunters to reach their animals far more quickly than in the past.

Turning to Daniel, an excellent hunter who prized that activity above all others, I asked what had happened to his splendid dog team.

"They are all gone. I couldn't hunt enough to feed them and us, too. So I had to put them away. All but my lead dog. I couldn't do it. I just couldn't. I finally had to ask someone else. Every time I thought about it, I remembered all the times he brought me home. Once in particular, I was far away. Fog was everywhere. I couldn't see a thing. Damp, too. I kept thinking the village must be off to the right. But that lead dog, he only wanted to go straight. Finally, I lay down in the sled, and sure enough, he brought me home. That dog saved my life several times. I just couldn't do away with him."

After a while, our conversation turned to the Arctic National Wildlife Refuge (ANWR) and the different views of oil and gas exploration. Environmental organizations and developers had been at odds for years, struggling over whether the petroleum industry should be allowed to explore for oil along ANWR's Coastal Plain. Some months previously, the U.S. Department of the Interior under Secretary James Watt had tried to shift responsibility for the management of ANWR from the Fish and Wildlife Service to the U.S. Geological Survey, a move that would have assisted the prodevelopment forces. However, following a lawsuit filed by the village of Kaktovik and a public interest law firm, Trustees for Alaska, the U.S. District Court had blocked Secretary Watt's action. The Interior Department then arranged for an exchange between the federal government and several Native regional corporations whereby the latter could obtain subsurface mineral rights in the reserve for Native-owned lands in other federal preserves. By such federal action, the oil companies were assured of gaining Native regional corporation support for oil development in ANWR. Given past legal efforts undertaken by Kaktovik residents in this struggle, I wanted to learn how Isaac, Daniel, and George viewed the matter.

"Hunting here is good, just like it was before. But I worry about hunting and fishing areas," Isaac said. "I'm not against the oil companies or the government. But they need to take more seriously what the people here say. We know the land and the animals. We know how the animals think, how they live. Outsiders come here all the time. Ask us questions. But then we almost never hear from them again. Only more people coming and asking more questions. We are concerned about posssible damage to the caribou calving grounds and to the fish from seismic work. And the whales, too. If there were an oil spill, that could be the end of whaling for us. That's what I think."

"When I first lived here, there weren't any whales," I reminded him.

"Yes, that's right. They didn't start coming back until 1964. Then, we catch one almost every fall. But now we have a quota. Only two strikes. That's not good. Too many regulations. Same for the sheep. We live pretty good because of the sheep up in the mountains. The mountain sheep. They stay around all the time. But we have to follow the regulations. We do, but it's hard."

"What about your grandchildren? Will they want to hunt?"

"All the kids go to school now. That's very important. To get a good job you have to have a good education. So, that's the first thing, education. I always tell somebody in my family they need to go on in school. Suppose you need a job and can't get one. What are you going to do? How are you going to heat the house? Buy a new rifle? Fix a motorboat? I've been working for almost twenty-five years. I still hunt all the time. Mary, too. But my grandchildren, I don't know. Maybe some of them won't hunt. If the oil people come, there will be jobs, and those kids will at least find work. But we need to hunt, too. Work and hunt. Both."

Daniel and George nodded their agreement and went on to describe their own experiences in the mixed economy. Daniel worked in maintenance at the Kaktovik school while George was involved in construction. But both expressed concern for the animals they hunted and complained about intrusions by low-flying planes coming into the area, and various radio-tracking devices used by Fish and Wildlife Service personnel that frightened the animals. They were concerned, too, of large oil spills and their possible destruction of fish and marine mammals.

Listening to the men discuss the animals and their enthusiasm for hunting,

Photo 39. A modern Iñupiat village is a mixture of old and new.

I was reminded of the formidable amount of scientific wisdom they and other Iñupiat hunters had accumulated over the centuries, each passing down to the next generation what they had learned from their fathers, brothers, and cousins. Mary, too, not only was a capable hunter but a butcher as well. Though sitting quietly while the men spoke, years of exposure to the subsistence way of life had enabled her to master equally important skills with similar competence. In preparing caribou meat for eating, a quick search for placental scars could give evidence of last year's births and signs of possible disease; or, an analysis of the liver would reveal which parasites were present. Sitting in the living room of Isaac and Mary's home, watching the animation in the brothers' faces as they spoke, I was struck by how their subsistence skills, honed on knowledge gained through experience, had provided them with a self-confidence less possible among the younger generation of Iñupiat whose lives were more disjointed.

Over the next few days, other villagers shared similar views, mixing in their minds experiences of the past with the unknowns of the future.

"You can't live anymore without money. If there is no oil around here, people will go hungry."

"Whales are important to us. They come to us. But if there are too many explosive tests or an oil spill, they will go elsewhere and we will never see them again."

"Maybe the oil people won't drive the caribou away. Maybe they will just say you can't take them anymore. I hear that's what happened at Deadhorse. Those animals are everywhere. But no one can take them."

However, similar to my experience at Barrow, the younger generation

Photo 40. An oil painting of Harold Kaveolook.

seemed less concerned about such matters. Kaktovik High School students, recently returned from a trip to Fairbanks, Anchorage, and other Alaska cities, described visiting colleges and universities, the Alaska Vocational Technical School, the Youth Employment Office, and similar institutions. They were shown how to fill out school and job applications and how to respond to employment interviews. "Touring places like this will help us find jobs in big cities," one enthusiastic student said in the high school newspaper. Three former students, having returned to Kaktovik for a summer vacation, spoke of their educational experiences in a beauty school in Anchorage, a trade school in Fairbanks, and a two-year program of study in engineering technology at the Tanana Valley Community College. Some planned to return to Fairbanks or Anchorage permanently. Others hoped they could remain on the Slope. "If the oil people come, more houses will be built, and more jobs will be open up," commented one of the ex-student returnees. "Then, Kaktovik can be a good place to live."

Looking around the village, I saw the impact of oil dollars everywhere, in large-scale housing construction sponsored by the North Slope Borough, in gravel roads, state-supported village fuel oil subsidies, and in the new high school with its fine gymnasium and small laboratory complete with Apple computers. Walking in the front door of the school and down the entry hall, I looked up to find a painting of Harold Kaveolook hanging on the wall above a small plaque describing his accomplishments in the village. How proud he must have been during the dedication of the building. Without these oil dollars and the state transfer payments flowing from them, what kind of educational facilities and opportunities would the Kaktovik students be having today?

But now, oil prices had dropped drastically, jobs had dwindled, and everywhere there was an air of concern for the economic future. Once, it had been fur trapping, followed by a worldwide Depression. Then the DEW line had been constructed, only to become outdated by developments in military technology. And now it was oil, followed by a collapse of the Middle East OPEC cartel, which had forced the price per barrel far lower than it had been in years. For the people of Kaktovik, was this latest boom-and-bust cycle so different from previous ones? Yes, I thought. It was very different.

In contrast to previous decades, the Iñupiat were now, through their regional and village corporations at least, legal owners of the land. And since some of this land was thought to contain large quantities of oil and gas, its owners had become targets of attention from the federal and state governments and the petroleum corporations. For example, one major step undertaken by the federal government to expedite the exploration of oil in the Kaktovik region occurred in 1983 with the 92,000-acre land exchange between the U.S. Department of the Interior and the Arctic Slope Regional Corporation. This swap had resulted in ASRC obtaining subsurface rights to Kaktovik village corporation land on ANWR's Coastal Plain. Soon afterwards, ASRC and the Kaktovik Iñupiat Corporation entered into a joint venture with Chevron Oil Company, allowing the latter to begin exploratory testing for petroleum just east of Kaktovik.

Of course, oil companies regularly sought other ways to strengthen their ties with local Iñupiat. Several years after the Department of the Interior-ASRC trade, a Kaktovik whaling crew was out looking for whales. Spotting one, they gave chase and were able to strike it but then lost it in a patch of fog. An oil company helicopter from Prudhoe Bay was sent over to look for the whale, and after finding it, proceeded to provide the crew with sufficient information that they traced it down and captured it: Technology in service of subsistence, only this time with the compliments of the oil industry. The Iñupiat were deeply appreciative.

In addition, Anchorage-based corporate offices of petroleum companies hire Iñupiat members on their public relations staffs, seeking from them information concerning village leaders and their views on oil development and other matters, village meetings of note, and the like.[4] Small consulting firms give seminars in which Native leaders from key areas of village Alaska are invited at no cost to come to Anchorage and discuss possible common interests with oil company representatives. Out of these meetings have come invitations for more important Native leaders to visit oil fields in Louisiana where they are shown just how safe, clean, and efficient this industrial activity can be. Gifts of choice foods are also sent occasionally by oil companies to whaling captains in northern villages.

---

[4] Needless to say, anthropologists, too, have received their share of offers from such corporations, enabling them to undertake research and write reports on topics ranging from archeological studies of early human sites to historical and cultural surveys of contemporary North Slope peoples.

By such efforts, Kaktovik and other North Slope Iñupiat have come to envision their future as closely intertwined with that of the petroleum industry. It could hardly be otherwise, given a lack of perceived alternatives. Indeed, taking into account the dramatically improved economic conditions of recent years, why would such alternatives even be sought? Nevertheless, thinking back over the past three decades of Kaktovik history, one fact stood out. While the impact of the petroleum industry on the village was momentous, of even greater significance was the transformation brought about by the Alaska Native Land Claims Settlement Act. And due to its corporate economic structure, a new set of social relations had been introduced assuring greater inequality among the Native people. Furthermore, as a result of this historic congressional action, the Native land base faced new threats perhaps even greater than those occurring prior to passage of the act.

PROTECTING NATIVE LAND AND RESOURCES

One major effort to address this threat had begun in 1984 with the formation of the Alaska Native Review Commission (ANRC), led by Canadian Justice Thomas R. Berger. Berger had chaired a similar inquiry for the Canadian government into the possibility of building a Mackenzie Valley pipeline in the Northwest Territories several years earlier (see Berger: 1977). The Alaska Native Review Commission, under sponsorship of the internationally organized Inuit Circumpolar Conference (and having received substantial funding from the North Slope Borough under the leadership of its mayor, Eben Hopson), represented the first serious effort to seek from Alaska's Native people their views on how to resolve problems stemming from the settlement act. Having to rely on corporate structures to protect the land after tax and other exclusions were to be removed in 1991 had caused so much concern among some of Alaska's Natives that it spawned a tribal sovereignty movement designed to "retribalize" the land. In this manner, ancestral lands could always remain in Native hands, though under federal jurisdiction. At the close of their investigation, the Alaska Native Review Commission fully supported this endeavor.

Among other conclusions, the commission recommended the establishment of tribal self-government as an alternative to the form selected by North Slope Borough villages. This option was particularly urged in those regions with diverse ethnic populations and few taxable resources. But even in the NSB, Berger noted (1985:160) that in 1991 when the land became taxable, the borough could be obliged to levy a property tax on all taxable real estate within its boundaries on a nondiscriminatory basis. At this point the vice-president of Barrow's village corporation commented: "After 1991, you might as well turn over all (Native) lands to the borough." Of course, on the North Slope, the borough doesn't own the land. The corporations do. Thus, even on the Slope, active interest has been expressed in having the land placed under a "tribal" government immune from taxation by the borough.[5] Furthermore, if such land were held by a tribal government, then children born after 1971 could be easily designated as common owners of their land. Another recommendation, addressing the issue of subsistence, proposed that Natives exert exclusive jurisdiction over administration of fish and wildlife resources in regions where they lived.

Not surprisingly, Native corporate leaders strongly rejected the Berger Commission's tribal government recommendation. Having predominant influence within the Alaska Federation of Natives, they utilized the resources of this organization to remind everyone that the corporate model freed the Native population from the bureaucratic paternalism of the federal government, an ambiguous relationship of long standing. Now that they had finally achieved that aim, this was no time to turn back. Opponents of the corporate strategy urged that corporations be allowed to transfer their lands to tribal entities without the former having to buy out dissenting shareholders.

Throughout the mid-1980s, amendments were proposed by the AFN and the Native sovereignty movement, the latter composed of a coalition of several regional groupings. But the sovereignty forces did not have the political strength, within the state or outside, needed to achieve a victory. Nor did the Reagan administration or the Alaska state government have any interest in seeing further recognition of tribal powers.[6] The National Rifle Association, too, one of the most influential lobbying groups in Washington, was completely opposed to seeing Native Alaskans managing hunting and fishing lands that might jeopardize the rights of non-Natives to participate. After two years of effort, the AFN-proposed amendment, which left the issue of tribal sovereignty to be settled by the courts, was passed by both houses of Congress and signed by President Reagan in 1988.

The bill included a number of features that helped protect Native lands from possible loss. Specifically, all undeveloped, corporately owned Native lands were placed in a state-regulated "land bank," which protected them from taxation and loss through bankruptcy as long as they remained undeveloped. If the land were developed, leased, or used as collateral, all such protections would be removed. In addition, as an alternative to tribal ownership, the Secretary of the Interior proposed that lands and other assets could be placed in a permanent "settlement trust" with shareholders named as beneficiaries. In such a trust, the beneficiary is separated from trustee

---

[5] For example, in a survey undertaken for the Arctic Slope Regional Corporation in 1985, ASRC shareholders were asked: "Do you think a state-chartered corporation or a tribal entity would best meet the interests of the Natives of the Arctic Slope?" Slightly more than 50 percent chose the tribal entity, whereas only 27 percent thought a corporation would be the best option. Most others either didn't understand the question (11 percent) or were undecided (9 percent) (Hellenthal 1985:12).

[6] As President Reagan expressed it during a discussion with university students on his last trip to Russia just prior to leaving office in 1988: "Maybe we made a mistake" in trying to maintain Indian cultures. "Maybe we should not have humored them in that, wanting to stay in that kind of primitive lifestyle. Maybe we should have said, 'No, come join us. Be citizens along with the rest of us.' "

owners, thereby offering maximum protection of the assets. Futhermore, a trust, and the land placed in it, can last in perpetuity, similar to land held under tribal ownership. However, even though surface land rights can be placed in a trust, subsurface rights had to remain with the corporation.

Trusts offer appeal to those wanting the maximum assurance of protection of Native land. They are far less attractive, however, to corporate directors wishing to maximize profits, for under a settlement trust, no business transactions are allowed. Rather, the trustees are required to pursue the "broader and more amorphous goal of providing the beneficiaries with social and cultural benefits." (Flanders 1989) It is not surprising, therefore, that AFN leaders perceive trust options to be largely unnecessary except for activities such as protecting cemeteries and historic sites.

Tribal sovereignty supporters acknowledged the importance of establishing legal protections over the land. Support, too, is given to another feature of the amendment that allows for the issuance of stock to Natives born after 1971. But this group was deeply frustrated by the government's refusal to offer a way out of the corporate system. They noted also that after 1991, a corporation could terminate existing restrictions by one of two methods. In the first, the articles of incorporation could be amended, following which, shareholder approval would be required. In the second, if 25 percent of the shareholders petitioned for termination for whatever reason, and this petition was then approved by a simple majority, termination of all restrictions could occur. This, in turn, opened the door for a takeover by outside corporations[7] (Anderson and Aschenbrenner 1988).

Finally, rural Native Alaskans feared that because none of these protections applied to developed lands, they could lose the residential core of their villages. That is, as developed land, it could be exposed to loss through taxation, bankruptcy, and other forms of judicial foreclosure. Nevertheless, most agreed that the amendment act implemented in 1988 offered considerable protection at least in the immediate future for both corporations and shareholders. In addition, as Flanders (1989) has noted, for the first time the federal government gave distinct recognition to the view that Native corporations were not just commercial assets, but subsistence and cultural ones as well.

Have rational minds dealt with a difficult problem fairly and with success? In the short term at least, it would appear so. Native lands in Alaska are now relatively well protected within the context of federal and state law. Thus, one could conclude that a way has finally been found for the Iñupiat to draw on "the best of both worlds," utilizing subsistence hunting and fishing for cultural and material sustenance, while accommodating to the necessities of wage labor. Yet, while such a conclusion offers considerable appeal, how realistic it is remains to be seen.

---

[7] However, as a further protection against termination of restrictions, corporations could change their articles of incorporation requiring a majority vote of up to two-thirds of their voting shareholders.

9/Nature, Culture, and Development

Enthusiastic partisans of the idea of progress are in danger of failing to rec-ognize—because they set so little store by them—the immense riches accumu-lated by the human race on either side of the narrow furrow in which they keep their eyes fixed. By underrating the achievements of the past, they devalue all those which still remain to be accomplished.

Claude Levi-Strauss, Anthropologist (1984)

A basic premise of science is that human beings are a part of *nature*. That is, we are an outgrowth of natural, evolutionary processes. Furthermore, we are a tool-making species. Through a long effort to develop technology, we have learned to tap nature's resources to achieve ends we define as nec-essary and desirable. In other words, we don't merely adapt to whatever nature has to offer in the way of gifts or threats. We also transform it by turning raw materials into tools and products in order to satisfy socially defined material needs. This is true of all homo sapiens whether they are Arctic hunters or urban factory workers. It is indeed a unique feature of human evolution that having emerged out of nature, we have acquired the ability to transform the very entity from which we have emerged.

Another important axiom is that human beings are a social species. We are regularly linked with others in relationships involving labor, kin, educa-tion, recreation, and a host of additional shared activities. Of course, we are not alone in being social creatures. But whereas non-human animal behavior is endlessly repetitive—each generation repeating, within limits, the behavior of previous ones—homo sapiens are able to accumulate knowledge and pass it across generations, a capability enabling us to confront nature far more effectively than our nonhuman relatives. The term most often associated with this unique set of interrelations involving language, ideas, social organization, and technology is *culture*. And the utilization of these social linkages and cultural attributes in the process of transforming nature to our own productive use is what makes us truly human.

How are these evolutionary developments related to the events described in this ethnography? In tracing the history of the Iñupiat and their precursors, we have noted how human productivity has been influenced by many factors including the availability of natural resources, the level of technology, and the amount and type of labor input. When the Iñupiat first roamed the Arctic, coastal sea mammals and inland caribou were abundant. However, the level of technology the Iñupiat had achieved in tapping those resources was low, requiring that a considerable amount of time be spent fulfilling basic needs. So, too, the manner in which they organized their labor had its influence on the degree of productivity, kin and kin-like sharing patterns in particular being a vital part of adapting to the vicissitudes of their surroundings.[1]

Finally, although having to confront nature, the Iñupiat also saw themselves as being a *part* of it. Thus, there was an intimate intertwining of humans, other animals, and spirits, all culminating in a commonly perceived bond. This is not to suggest that harmony was the hallmark of such an existence, for both the natural and supernatural worlds were considered fraught with uncertainty. Still, under such conditions, life was not only challenging but productive as well.

IN PURSUIT OF PROGRESS

In the early 1800s, Europeans arrived in the western Arctic led by British explorers such as Beechey and Franklin and the Russian's Kotzebue and A. F. Kashevarov. For these early envoys of European society, the north was something to be conquered rather than shared with nature's creatures. Driven by capitalist-derived economic values, first mercantile and later industrialist backers of these colonial explorers perceived the land and sea as a frozen wasteland traversable in search of greater riches to the east and west. As for its isolated inhabitants, they remained on the outer fringe of culture, and perhaps even beyond. After making contact with the Iñupiat at several northwest Alaskan coastal settlements, Kashevarov wrote (VanStone 1977:91) in 1838:

> The life of the Eskimo, like that of other savages, proceeds regularly, monotonously, like a wound-up machine. He stays within bounds, within the cycle he follows; here now, tomorrow there, and for all the same reasons, for one and the same goal: to live like an animal, as his forefathers existed.

For explorers like Kashevarov, as well as other Europeans of that era, "nature" was seen as containing certain qualities that were in opposition to human virtues. Thus, the moral world of human sympathy was distinguished from the amoral, unfeeling world of nature. Distinctions were also made between the tamed and untamed, cultivated and uncultivated (Barrett 1984:147).[2] Today, nature is viewed in a considerably more positive light by most Europeans and North Americans. Individuals regularly seek the "joys of nature" by planning an outing to the beach, a zoo, city park, or wildlife refuge. Environmental organizations actively encourage their members to

---

[1] In speaking about adaptation, I do not mean to connote a one-sided striving for adjustment and its accompanying corollary of stability. Rather, the productive process always entails continual change and the potential for greater transformation.

[2] The term culture comes from the Latin word *colere*, meaning to till, cultivate, or nurture.

protect local, state and national parks and wilderness areas from encroachment of the forest industry, agribusiness, coal, oil, and gas corporations.

Yet to European forebears of several centuries ago, the idea that human utilization of the land should be restricted rather than encouraged was unthinkable. Throughout the 1800s, the development of European civilization was closely associated with the clearing of forests, cultivation of the soil, and conversion of wild landscape into human settlement. In essence, agriculture's relation to the land was similar to cooking and raw meat—they both converted nature into "culture." Uncultivated land meant uncultivated men and women, and when seventeenth century English citizens moved to New England, part of their argument for occupying Indian territory was that anyone who did nothing to subdue and cultivate the land had no right to prevent others from doing so (Pearce 1965:21).

This sharp distinction drawn between humanity and other forms of life served to accentuate the uniqueness of "man."[3] Not only could humans speak and engage in rational thought, they had a conscience and their soul was immortal. Animals, by contrast, had no conscience, no soul, and, therefore, no afterlife. Hence, the holding of such beliefs offered the best possible justification for exploiting animals as beasts of burden and as food to be eaten. Although Judeo-Christian beliefs stressed as well the responsibility of humans to be kind toward all of God's creatures, the ambivalence of this time was clearly not so significant as to suggest that domination should be replaced by protection.

By such pronouncements, European, English, and North American intellectual and religious elite lay the moral underpinnings for the ascendency of human beings *over* nature as an essential step in the development of civilization.[4] This is not to suggest that religious belief was seen as *the* motivating force behind this development. That responsibility was reserved for those applying newly accumulated capital toward increased industrialization in order to achieve greater profit. Nevertheless, in most respects, *progress* was considered virtually synonymous with the conquest of nature.

The distinction drawn between civilized man and uncivilized animals stimulated an additional form of stereotyping as well: the attribution of "animality" to humans. By definition, if humanity carries with it certain qualities, then those human beings not exhibiting such qualities can be considered subhuman or semianimal. In the late seventeenth century, the supposed animal nature of the Irish was a common target of British stereotyping as typified by Sir William Petty's description of the Irish as living "in a brutish, nasty condition." During the period of American slavery, Africans were regularly seen as having subhuman intelligence and beastlike sexuality. Women, too, were not left unscathed, nor were those living on the margins of society—

---

[3] Although "man" included human beings of both sexes, its usage as an inclusive term suggests that in this period of European history, male domination in intellectual, political, and other circles had the effect of making women's contributions outside the home less visible and, thus, far more difficult.

[4] For a full treatment of this subject, see Thomas (1983:17–50).

the poor, the insane, the vagrants. In each instance, the effort to dehumanize set the stage for maltreatment, domestication, or enslavement. It is in this light that Kashevarov's commentary about Eskimo "savages" who "live like an animal" should be understood.

Hugh Brody (1977:113), a British anthropologist with years of experience in Arctic and sub-Arctic Canada, has described the devaluation of Native northerners in that country with particular succinctness:

> (We regard) the native person (as) at the very edge of, or just beyond, the world of culture. Insofar as he is beyond the frontier and stays outside the economy and society that the frontier is seeking to advance, he remains a part of nature. . . . Peoples in that condition do not know what is best for them (they cannot understand progress) and can only learn by acquiring religion, schooling, housing, money, modern conveniences, jobs. As these are supposed to be the very hallmarks of culture, of civilization, and as they are the indices by which we measure progress, then if the people do not have them, and do not get them, they cannot progress.

Our brief historical analysis of Alaska's colonial encounter suggests that, under the banner of Social Darwinism, Americans, too, were quick to disparage Iñupiat ways. Given this belief, the government had little difficulty defending its commitment to changing Native behavior by instituting educational programs that promoted assimilationist goals and actively denigrated Native language and culture. Nor did Christian missionaries doubt their right to ban the qargi as a symbol of paganism, oblivious to its centrality in Iñupiat social life. Thus, both government officials and religious representatives undertook these actions in the belief that western progress, with its technological advances, industrial growth, capitalist infrastructure, and associated knowledge, had reached the zenith of civilization, and that by implication, such benefits should be passed on to those less fortunate than themselves.[5]

Underlying this paternalistic attitude, and partly hidden by it, was a political relation characteristic of all colonial encounters, one in which the colonizer had an excess of power and the colonized a lack of it. It was not the benefits of improved hunting technology or the introduction of western-based scientific concepts in the classroom that was dehumanizing to the Iñupiat, but the way they were forced to modify their ways of thinking and acting. Denigration of the Iñupiaq language provides a good case in point.

In the colonial era, considerable effort was made to replace Iñupiaq with English—first in the classroom, and eventually at home. Language contains a complex linguistic code, a kind of mental map that gives meaning to experience. By means of this map, children are able to generate phrases of discourse never before encountered. Indeed, they may not even be aware of how their language helps shape their world view. Culture, of course, is reg-

---

[5] In essence, this was the same argument put forward by Juan Ginés de Sepúlveda in his debate with Bartolomé de las Casas over human rights and imperial expansion in 1550. That is, not only was it the responsibility of the Spanish to bring science, written laws, the concept of private property, and other accoutrements of civilized society to the Native population, but that by depriving them of such ideas and products, they would be "greatly retarded in their development" (for Las Casas' opposing argument, refer to the Preface).

ularly expressed through language; and language, in turn, is a significant attribute of culture. Joined together, they are a unique stamp, a "cultural vocabulary" by which people analyze their world and the ecological, social, economic, and political conditions that maintain it, dismantle it, and re-shape it.

However, when this vocabulary is replaced by one prescribed from with-out, school children are deprived of their right to define their experience within their own cultural context. Furthermore, once several generations of students have passed through the school system, they are even divested of the recognition that they have such a right. Thus, as Edna Ahgeak MacLean (1988a:33), an Iñupiat language professor at the University of Alaska, has written: "Parents were indoctrinated with the idea that it was better not to speak Iñupiaq to their children. Although the Iñupiat are no longer subjected to this indoctrination, an entire generation still accepts the belief that speaking Iñupiaq to their children is wrong." The final misfortune occurs when grand-children are unable to communicate with their non-English-speaking grand-parents, thereby sealing off a wealth of cultural knowledge from one generation to another.

It is true, of course, that during the early contact years, given the expan-siveness of the region, reliance on the subsistence economy, and the small number of resident Euro-Americans, the Iñupiat had considerable autonomy. Interested in exploiting the area's natural resources, whalers, traders, and others drawn economically to the Arctic saw the land and its people as largely secondary to their interests. But by the twentieth century, the Iñupiat in-creasingly were having to act in ways defined for them by others. What began with education was followed by the gradual enforcement of federal and ter-ritorial laws that eroded their indigenous forms of social control. Eventually, even subsistence hunting and fishing came under government scrutiny, with accompanying threats of fines and court action. It is in this manner that the Iñupiat became a people burdened by colonialism. It was not an oppression of economic exploitation common to most such encounters, for with the exception of fur trapping, their labor wasn't a significant issue. But living in their own land, they still had lost much of their autonomy.

Even today, school texts frequently present Alaska's colonial experience as an effort by the dominant society to bring the benefits of American progress to its outlying Arctic peoples—and, of course, bring these peoples into the ever-widening expanse of that society. For the Iñupiat, however, one can say that western "progress" represented at least in part an erosion of their history, and with it, a lessened sense of their own self-worth. The tragically high number of young and middle-aged Iñupiat who, through alcohol, drugs, and suicide are destroying themselves in this cultural climate can be adequately understood only by taking into account the fact that many no longer have a sense of who they are.

On the other hand, such threats regularly promote resistance. Today, the North Slope Iñupiat are actively trying to restore their own history. Many of these efforts have already been mentioned. They include the establishment of a Commission on History, Language, and Culture, enhancing utilization of the Iñupiaq language through course instruction from kindergarten through high school, publishing the results of elders conferences, working with archeologists and ethnohistorians to record pre- and early cultural history in specific localities, reintroducing the institution of the qargi, replacing English place-names on Arctic Slope maps with Iñupiat ones (e.g., Qikiqtaq for Beechey Point); and exploring the establishment of a new tribal judicial system to "sustain aboriginal and traditional values."[6]

The lessons to be learned by studying one's own colonial past are many. For the Iñupiat, an especially important one has been that the close of this era did not mean the end of colonial thinking, nor of the economic and political dependence it engendered. Rather, such perspectives and actions took on a new guise. The Alaska Native Land Claims Settlement Act is a good illustration. Although the passing of ANCSA by the U.S. Congress was primarily designed to resolve the aboriginal land claims issue, thereby enabling oil to be extracted from Prudhoe Bay, it also transformed Iñupiat economic and social relations.

EMERGING CLASS RELATIONS

One significant result of this development has been the emergence of an incipient class structure. The social basis for this new structure was formed when, under the terms of ANCSA, the Iñupiat's major financial and natural resources were placed in the hands of a regional corporation. The organizational skills required to run a highly complex multimillion-dollar corporation such as ASRC were considerable to say the least. Eventually, a small elite group of Iñupiat and other non-Native managerial associates ascended to core positions of leadership. These individuals maintained an orientation that set the corporation on quite a different course from that of the borough. As we have seen, borough leaders sought the support of their constituency based on a *shared* distribution of the collective wealth and resources. This was drawn largely from taxation of the Prudhoe Bay oil fields, a policy that reached its heyday during the most active years of the Capital Improvement Program. ASRC leaders, on the other hand, while recognizing that the corporation was created to serve the needs of its Native shareholders, were mandated by ANCSA to be a *profit-making* institution. Thus, the corporation promoted

---

[6] Such efforts not infrequently entail the rejection of that written about them by others, a criticism to which anthropologists are particularly prone. When an anthropologist's ties with others are characterized by a relationship in which the peoples concerned are an "object" to be studied and "known," whereas the investigator is the "knower," with all the power that entails, the latter will always remain suspect by those they seek to work with and come to understand. Only by substituting reciprocity for alienation can anthropologists and other scientists establish a creative intimacy in which subject and object, knower and known, are replaced in a joint effort to create theories and seek solutions that address issues of concern in people's lives. The Iñupiat have strongly urged such collaboration (Brower and Stotts 1984), followed several years later by a response (National Research Council 1989).

the stratification of social relations within Iñupiat society while the borough, by dramatically expanding employment options, had the effect of limiting the formation of these stratified relations.

This difference in orientation was portrayed quite movingly during a 1986 meeting between Arctic Slope Regional Corporation officers and a group of Canadian Inuit from the eastern Arctic. During that spring, three leaders of the Canadian *Nunavut* association, an organization then actively negotiating a comprehensive land claims settlement with the Canadian government, arrived in Barrow. Their purpose in coming was to learn more of the North Slope Iñupiat's experience following implementation of their 1971 land claims settlement fifteen years previously. Information obtained during their stay raised questions of deep concern among the Inuit delegates.

After discussing issues of common concern with the local Utkeagvik Iñupiat Corporation, members of the Alaska Eskimo Whaling Commission, and numerous other borough, city, and village-level organizations, a meeting was held with ASRC officers. At this meeting, the Canadians first sought information about the nature of the corporation's goals and the extent to which they were accomplished. Then a series of questions was raised concerning steps the corporation was taking to assist other Native-run agencies and villages in the borough, such as helping to provide expert advice or organizing joint economic ventures with village organizations. One corporate leader responded: "Our bottom line is profit. We were instituted to make profit and that is what we're doing. All those other things you have been talking about flow from profitmaking; and that's it." When asked the extent to which the regional corporation had been able to enhance ties with Native leaders of the smaller village corporations, the same official replied: "Well, not very much. When they come to town, they aren't very knowledgeable about business practices. And when they open their briefcases, you find smoked fish and maktak."

At the conclusion of their stay in Barrow, at a small gathering with local political leaders, the Inuit were invited to comment on what they had learned. In keeping with the relaxed nature of the meeting, the three delegates expressed appreciation for the hospitality and assistance. One federation representative, however, offered a far more somber message than his two companions, the final summary of which some people in the room not present at the earlier ASRC meeting found difficult to understand. Choosing his words carefully, the Inuk concluded: "I am very concerned about threats to the retention to your lands, and I am also very concerned about people in power— people making decisions who only have money in their briefcases!"

Such an expression of apprehension highlights the *internal* conflicts presently challenging the leadership of the North Slope Iñupiat, conflicts brought on by the conjunction of forces representing industrial, corporate, profit-making interests on the one hand with those of a more kin-based, cooperative, partially subsistence-oriented way of life on the other. Both are powerful features in contemporary Iñupiat life. But in the minds of the people is another fear—co-optation. Might leaders working within the corporate sphere become so imbued with the rewards flowing from their position that they will be trapped into following Euro-American corporate patterns too single-mindedly—and in so doing, lose their concern for the broader interests of the cultural group of which they are a part?

Needless to say, such conflicts are not limited to the North Slope Iñupiat. Other indigenous groups have faced similar problems. In a study comparing the impact of newfound affluence on cultural survival in various societies around the world, Salisbury and Tooker (1984) found that while there was no simple correlation between factors that maintained cultural integrity under conditions of political and economic domination, certain clues were available that could assist a society's members in strengthening their way of life.

Of particular importance in maintaining their cultural integrity was the need to prevent any sharp differentiation from occurring between a newly emerging elite segment of the population and the rest of the population. The second clue concerned the ability of the newly affluent group to creatively incorporate commercial goods into their more traditional activities, including the *conscious* selection of which new goods to adopt rather than a generalized acceptance of all commodities offered. A third clue pertained to the cultural vision of "the good life" brought into clearer focus by these new resources. More specifically, was a wider segment of the society able to achieve this defined good life than had been the case previously when such resources were less easily available? The researchers also found that if the vision became crassly materialistic, then cultural dependence would be encouraged. And, not surprisingly, if a small segment of the society benefited from the affluence at the expense of the rest, then the legitimacy of that segment's enhancement was likely to be challenged by those who had not been so advantaged.

Finally, the anthropologists noted that due to the substantially increased cash flow into the society, newly affluent peoples faced a problem of maintaining their own cultural boundaries intact under conditions that promoted increased dependence on externally produced goods and services. Under these circumstances, it was essential that the members of a society engage in culturally significant activities that reinforced their own cultural integrity and, thus, their own identity.

Given this insight, it is interesting to see the effort undertaken by the North Slope Iñupiat to actively affirm among themselves the cultural as well as material importance of whaling. Comments are regularly made that "whaling is the basis of our cultural way of life." Actually, as people often say to each other, "*sharing* is really who we are," in the sense that it is more representative of what it means to be Iñupiat than any single act such as whaling. Also, as an affirmation of their culture and in their continuing efforts to distinguish themselves from the non-Iñupiat outside world, the whaling complex serves as an excellent designator of cultural distinctiveness.

In conclusion, we can see for the North Slope Iñupiat that following passage of the Alaska Native Claims Settlement Act (with its corporate-based structure) new forces have been set in motion that are enhancing the economic and social positions of the few at the expense of the many. Nevertheless, at the same time that these significant differences in wealth and power are developing, people are engaged in diverse activities to strengthen Iñupiat cultural integrity and identity in ways that reduce the tensions caused by these new stratified relations. One crucial test of whether the cultural glue that joins Iñupiat together will be sufficient to keep in check the corporate infrastructure that threatens to divide them is the commitment made by present and future generations of leaders to ensure, as far as possible through institutional means, that an active kin and partner-based network persists in the people's relationship to their ancestral lands.

COMMODITIES, NEEDS, AND SATISFACTIONS

In the Introduction, I stated that the history of development in Arctic Alaska can be viewed from two perspectives. One, commonly associated with "modernization theory," assumes that capitalist industrialization was a process that emerged in Europe and then spread to other areas and that societies already industrialized served as models for those that had not yet achieved this status. Hence, the less developed sectors of the world entering this arena had to follow a path similar to those that came before. And furthermore, that this same process continues today in those poorer localities that have not yet become industrialized.

The other, so-called "world-system" perspective, challenges the view that industrial capitalism developed separately from the rest of the globe. Rather, in the minds of these proponents, such development occurred in conjunction with it rather than separate from it. Furthermore, beginning with colonial expansion, many so-called undeveloped nations and cultures actually became *underdeveloped* in the sense that their direct involvement with this economic system led to systematically disadvantaged relations where the natural resources of their region became commoditized in world markets and where profits were reaped outside the region.

With these two themes in mind, this book has tried to trace the influence of Euro-American colonial and industrial penetration on the Iñupiat of Alaska's Arctic Slope and highlight their response. In examining this process, we began by tracing early exploratory forays of western colonists into Arctic waters. We then looked at the whaling and trading era, with its introduction of new forms of technology and weaponry, and concluded with an analysis of the Iñupiat's shift to a commodity-oriented economy, with its mixed subsistence and wage labor employment.

Throughout this study, we have seen how the Iñupiat have been active participants in this process as well as, at other times, boldly resistant. They were actively drawn to the benefits brought during the colonial encounter such as improved technology, better health care, and material advantages in standard of living. Many also found in their new commitment to Christianity a belief in a more benevolent deity that released them from the threatening supernatural world envisioned by aboriginal shamans.

We have also taken note of the severe loss in human lives, especially stemming from the importation of western diseases during the early colonial era. We have seen how, in that same period, the Iñupiat and other Alaska Natives were basically treated as part of the natural environment—if they could be used in obtaining the particular resource being sought, all well and good. If not, they were simply pushed aside and their resources taken, sometimes bringing severe hardship.

With the emergence of the wage economy in the late 1940s, a different pattern emerged, one in which an active attempt was made to maintain a mixed subsistence *and* wage economy, the degree of emphasis on one or the other depending on fluctuating markets, Cold War conflicts, and the exploitation of nonrenewable resources such as oil and gas. As a result of this process, there was an increased occurrence of large-scale geographical, economic, and cultural dislocations, with their accompanying psychological trauma, even though the region benefited from the inflow of sizable revenues.

An overall review of this history provides the contemporary observer with numerous examples of advantages and disadvantages, positive and negative features, from which to evaluate the patterns of change. The orientation one brings to bear on the question of what constitutes development and social change will color the final summation. But with these elements acknowledged, one nevertheless must recognize that given the technological advantages and material improvements in their style of living from colonial times to the present, the cultural life of the North Slope Iñupiat has been seriously eroded. As for the wealth contained within their land, by far the largest portion ended up being appropriated by the state. In turn, the land was leased to private corporate oil companies that exploited its mineral wealth, with relatively little being returned to improve the material and social well-being of the people from whence it came.

Acknowledging this history, the Iñupiat have nevertheless moved on and are now trying to gain a measure of control over their continually shifting circumstances. In doing so, they are having to face a most difficult question: Given that their remaining land in northeast Alaska may contain considerable amounts of marketable oil, gas, and other minerals, is that nonrenewable underground wealth of greater value than the surface land that has sustained them so well until now? Those Iñupiat in charge of making that choice have already made their answer known. But it will be several decades before all the Iñupiat learn the consequences of that decision.

Of course, this question is being raised in other quarters too. Increasing numbers of people throughout the globe are becoming concerned about the natural environment of the Arctic. In the 1960s, a large public outcry opposed Project Chariot's proposed atomic blast at Cape Thompson in northwest Alaska, one which threatened both the land and its people. In the early 1970s, nuclear bomb tests conducted by the People's Republic of China resulted in an eight-fold increase in radioactive pollution of Alaskan lichens, affecting the caribou that ate them, and a year later, the region's Iñupiat subsistence hunters. In the 1980s, international research was initiated to study the growing problem of Arctic haze, a form of atmospheric pollution that absorbs light from the sun and thereby alters the temperature of Arctic air, a significant determinant of weather conditions throughout the globe. In the spring of 1989, the worst oil spill in American history occurred in Alaska's Prince William Sound when the tanker *Exxon Valdez* went aground spilling more than 10 million gallons of North Slope crude oil in the sea and surrounding shoreline. For the 1990s, even greater concern is being expressed over the production of humanmade chemicals that have affected the Arctic's atmospheric ozone layer, which is so vital to protecting organisms from lethal ultraviolet rays. Such threats to the Arctic environment carry implications not only to those living in the north but for peoples throughout the world. By the year 2000, how will such matters have been dealt with?

Perhaps one approach will be to re-examine the basic premises that have led us to our present dilemma, premises addressing the relation between human societies and nature. At the beginning of this book, it was suggested that today nature is largely viewed as a commodity among other commodities to be protected as long as it doesn't impede the achievement of material fulfillment or national defense. Underlying this message is the view that once nature is subjugated, it becomes an object of human satisfaction. And finally, that whatever problems are raised about the environment, they can be solved by our advanced knowledge of science and technology. Thus, through science, nature becomes an object of control for our benefit. If one holds to such a belief, the only remaining question has to do with how effective science will continue to be in *supplying* us with these satisfactions.

Yet the problem of supply is not meaningful in and of itself. It only becomes so when seen in relation to demand and need. In the high material consumption world of industrial capitalism, a world that frequently equates freedom with consumer products and exalts this lifestyle as the highest goal of human existence, human beings can easily be trapped by their own compulsions. As William Leiss (1975:x) has so aptly put it, "individuals are led to misinterpret the nature of their needs and to misunderstand the relationship between their needs and the ways in which they may be satisfied." The only way to break out of this vicious circle of expanding production and expanding wants is to reorder the high-consumption lifestyle of industrial nations in a direction more in keeping with our redefined needs. To do otherwise is to promote increased competition over increasingly scarce resources, in which ever greater environmental risks are taken, only to generate greater differences between those who have and those who do not.

Therefore, as initially raised in the Introduction, the two major problems facing humankind today—one concerned with the formidable unequal distribution of productive wealth among the world's peoples, and the other with ecological deterioration—are conjoined. In trying to seek a resolution of these problems we face the ultimate challenge of development: How to reconceptualize the relationships between our societies and our utilization of nature.

Bibliography

Alaska Health Survey Team
  1954 Alaska's Health: A Survey Report to the U.S. Department of the Interior.
    Graduate School of Public Health. University of Pittsburgh.

Alaska Native Review Commission
  1984 Summary Report of the Overview Roundtable Discussions. Anchorage:
    Alaska Native Review Commission.

Alaska Native Woman's Statewide Organization (Barrow Local Chapter).
  1982 Tagiugmuit Agnani: Seminar for Arctic Slope Iñupiat Women. Barrow.

Anderson, Bob and Lare Aschenbrenner
  1988 1991 Provides Protections. ANC (Alaska Native Coalition) News. 1(3). May/
    June. 1,7–8.

Arnold, Robert D.
  1969 Characteristics of the Economy of Village Alaska and Prospects for Change.
    Paper presented at the 20th Alaska Science Conference.
  1976 Alaska Native Land Claims. Anchorage: Alaska Native Foundation.
  1978 Alaska Native Land Claims. Anchorage: Alaska Native Foundation (2nd
    Edition)

Asch, Michael I.
  1983 Native Research and the Public Forum: Implications for Ethnological Theory.
    In Frank Manning (ed) Consciousness and Inquiry: Ethnology and Canadian
    Realities. National Museum of Man. Ottawa: National Museum of Canada.

Barker, F. A.
  1870–71 Journal. (Typescript) Turnball Library. Auckland, New Zealand (cited in
    Bockstoce 1986:136).

Barrett, Richard A.
  1984 Culture and Conduct: An Excursion in Anthropology. Belmont: Wadsworth.

Beechey, F.W.
  1831 Narrative of a Voyage to the Pacific; 2 v. London: Henry Colburn and Richard
    Bentley.

Berger, Thomas, R.
  1977 Northern Frontier, Northern Homeland. The Report of the Mackenzie Valley
    Pipeline Inquiry. Volumes I and II. Ottawa: Supply and Services Canada.
  1979 Native Rights in the New World. Northern Perspectives VII:4.
  1985 Village Journey: The Report of the Alaska Native Review Commission. New
    York: Hill and Wang.
  1987 Alaska Natives: Subsistence and Self-determination. Cultural Survival Quar-
    terly 11:1. 65–69.

Berry, Mary Clay
  1975 The Alaska Pipeline: the Politics of Oil and Native Land Claims. Bloomington: Indiana University Press.

Bigjim, Frederick Seagayuk, and James Ito-Adler
  1974 Letters to Howard: An Interpretation of the Alaska Native Land Claims. Anchorage: Alaska Methodist University Press.
  1985 We Talk: You Listen: A Discourse on Education in Alaska. Portland: Press-22.

Blackman, Margaret B.
  1989 Sadie Brower Neakok, an Iñupiaq Woman. Seattle: University of Washington Press.

Bockstoce, John R.
  1986 Whales, Ice and Men: The History of Whaling in Western Alaska. Seattle: University of Washington Press.

Bodfish, Waldo Sr.
  1981 Testimony. Puiguitkaat. (The 1978 Elder's Conference.) Barrow: The North Slope Borough Commission on History and Culture.

Bodley, John H. (ed)
  1988 Tribal Peoples and Development Issues: A Global View. Mountain View: Mayfield Publishing Company.

Borbridge, John Jr.
  1970 Native Organization and Land Rights as Vehicles for Change. In G. Rogers (ed) Change in Alaska. College: University of Alaska Press.

Brewer, Max C.
  1975 Land Commitments in Alaska. Arctic 28(4) 263–274.

Brody, Hugh
  1977 Testimony before the Canadian Mackenzie Pipeline Inquiry (cited in Thomas R. Berger, Northern Frontier, Northern Homeland, Volume One. Ottawa).
  1987 Living Arctic: Hunters of the Canadian North. London: Faber and Faber.

Brooks, Paul
  1971 The Pursuit of Wilderness. Boston: Houghton, Mifflin Company.

Brower, Charles D.
  1942 Fifty Years Below Zero. New York: Mead and Company.

Brower, Eugene
  1983 A Message to All Alaskans. Alaska Native News. 1:(8). 28–31.

Brower, Eugene and James Stotts
  1984 Arctic Prospects: Problems and Opportunities. In United States Arctic Interests: The 1980s and 1990s. William E. Westermeyer and Kurt M. Shusterich (eds.) New York: Springer-Verlag.

Burch, Ernest S. Jr.
  1971 The Nonempirical Environment of the Arctic Alaskan Eskimos. Southwestern Journal of Anthropology. 27(2). 148–165.
  1974 Eskimo Warfare in Northwest Alaska. Anthropological Papers of the University of Alaska 16:2, 1–14.

1975 Eskimo Kinsmen: Changing Family Relationships in Northwest Alaska. American Ethnological Monograph No. 59. St. Paul: West Publishing Company.
1978 Traditional Eskimo Societies in Northwest Alaska. *In* Alaska Native Culture and History. Y. Kotani and Wm. Workman, eds. 2 53–304.
1981 Traditional Eskimo Hunters of Point Hope, Alaska:1800–1875. Barrow: North Slope Borough.
1988 The Eskimos (with photographs by Werner Forman). Norman: University of Oklahoma Press.

Burch, Ernest Jr., and Thomas Correll
1972 Alliance and Conflict: Inter-personal Relations in North Alaska. *In* Alliance in Eskimo Society. D.L. Guemple (ed). Proceedings of the American Ethnological Society, 1971. Seattle: University of Washington Press.

Chance, Nancy F.
1988 Gender and Culture: North Slope Iñupiat Women in Historical Perspective. Ann Arbor: University Microfilms.

Chance, Norman A.
1960 Culture Change and Integration: An Eskimo Example. American Anthropologist 62:1028–1044.
1965 Acculturation, Self-Identification, and Personality Adjustment. American Anthropologist 67:372–396.
1966 The Eskimo of North Alaska. New York: Holt, Rinehart and Winston.
1970 Directed Change and Native Peoples. *In* Change in Alaska. G. Rogers (ed). College: University of Alaska Press.
1984 Alaska Eskimo Modernization. *In* Handbook of North American Indians: Arctic. D. Damas (ed). 5:646–656. Washington: Smithsonian Institution.
1987 Subsistence Research in Alaska: Premises, Practices, and Prospects. Human Organization 46:1. 85–89.

Chapman, Oscar L.
1951 Public Land Order 715. Reserving Public Lands for the use of the Department of the Air Force for Military Purposes. Washington, D.C.: Department of the Interior.

Conn, Stephen
1985 Inuit Village Councils in Alaska—an Historical Model for Effectuation of Aboriginal Rights? Etudes/Inuit/Studies 9 (2). 43–59.

Cornell, Peter G. and Gerald McBeath
1982 Alaska's Rural Development. Boulder: Westview Press.

Correll, Thomas
1972 Ungalaqlingmuit: A Study in Language and Society. Ann Arbor: University Microfilms.

Davis, Nancy
1979 Social implications of ANCSA. Commission Study 44. Alaska Native Claims Settlement Act 1971–79. Anchorage: Federal-State Land Use Planning Commission for Alaska.

Davis, Robert and Mark Zannis
1973 The Genocide Machine in Canada: The Pacification of the North. Montreal: Black Rose Books.

Dryzak, John S.
  1983 Conflict and Choice in Resource Management: The Case of Alaska. Boulder: Westview Press.

Dryzak, John S. and Oran Young
  1985 Internal Colonialism in the Circumpolar North: The Case of Alaska. Development and Social Change. 16. 123–145.

Edwardsen, Charles, Jr.
  1974 The New Harpoon. *In* Etok: A Story of Eskimo Power, H. G. Gallagher. New York: G. P. Putman's Sons. 251–257.

Engler, Robert
  1969 New Frontier for Old: Alaska and the Politics of Oil. Abstracts. 20th Alaska Science Conference.

Ennew, Judith
  1976 Examining the Facts in Field Work: Considerations of Method and Data. Critique of Anthropology. 7:43–66.

Ervin, Alexander
  1976 A Review of the Acculturation Approach in Anthropology with Special Reference to Recent Change in Alaska. Journal of Anthropological Research.

Fagan, Brian M.
  1987 The Great Journey: The Peopling of Ancient America. New York: Thames and Hudson.

Federal Field Committee for Federal Planning in Alaska
  1968 Alaska Natives and the Land. Washington, D.C.: U.S. Government Printing Office.

Feldman, Kerry D.
  1981 Anthropologists Under Contract: Two examples from Alaska. *In* Anthropologists at Home in North America. E. Messerschmidt (ed). New York: Cambridge University Press.

Fienup-Riordan, Ann
  1983 The Nelson Island Eskimo. Anchorage: Alaska Pacific University Press.
  1984a The Spirit of ANCSA: Native Expectations and the Alaska Native Claims Settlement Act. Overview Papers, XIV. Anchorage: Alaska Native Review Commission. 1–34.
  1984b Overview Roundtable Discussions. Volume I. The Spirit of ANCSA. Testimony before the Alaska Native Claims Commission. Anchorage: Alaska Native Claims Commission.
  1987 Robert Redford, Apanuugpak, and the Investigation of Tradition. Études/Inuit/Studies 11(1) 135:148.

Flanders, Nicolas E.
  1987 Tuberculosis in Western Alaska, 1900–1950. Polar Record 23(145) 383–396.
  1989a The Alaska Native Corporation as Conglomerate: The Problem of Profitability. Human Organization. 48.
  1989b The ANCSA Amendments of 1987 and Land Management in Alaska. Polar Record (25).

Foote, Don Charles
  1959 The Economic Base and Seasonal Activities of Some Northeast Alaska Vil-

lages: A Preliminary Study. Report for the Bioenvironmental Studies of Project Chariot. Washington: U.S. Atomic Energy Commission.
1961 Project Chariot and the Eskimo People of Point Hope, Alaska. Report to the U.S. Atomic Energy Commission. Contract No. AT (04–3)-315. March 1961.

Forbes, Jack D.
1984 Native Americans and Nixon: Presidential Politics and Minority Self-Determination, 1969–72. Los Angeles: University of California, American Indian Studies Center.

Frank, André Gunder
1971 Capitalism and Underdevelopment in Latin America. New York: Penguin.

Franklin, Marvin
1973 Department of Interior news release 5546–73, May 7 (cited in Jack Forbes (1984:120)).

Gallagher, H. G.
1974 Etok: A Story of Eskimo Power. New York: G. P. Putnam's Sons.

Garvin, C. C. Jr.
1986 The Search for Solutions. The Lamp (winter issue).

Giddings, Louis
1967 Ancient Men of the Arctic. New York: Alfred A. Knopf.

Governor's Commission on Cross-Cultural Education.
1970 Time for Change in the Education of Alaska Natives. Juneau: State Department of Education.

Gregory, Albro
1960 Editorial. Jessen's Weekly (Fairbanks, August 1st).

Gubser, Nicholas J.
1965 The Nunamuit Eskimo: Hunters of Caribou. New Haven: Yale University Press.

Guemple, Lee
1986 Men and Women, Husbands and Wives: The Role of Gender in Traditional Iñupiat Society. Études/Inuit/Studies 10(1–2). 9–24.

Hall, Edwin S., Craig Gerlach, and Margaret B. Blackman
1985 In the National Interest: A Geographical Based Study of Anaktuvuk Iñupiat Subsistence Through Time. Barrow: North Slope Borough.

Hanke, Lewis
1959 Aristotle and the American Indians. Bloomington: Indiana University Press.

Heinrich, A. C.
1955 An Outline of the Kinship System of the Bering Strait Eskimos. Unpublished M.A. Thesis. University of Alaska.
1963 Eskimo Type Kinship and Eskimo Kinship: An Evaluation and a Provisional Model for Presenting Data Pertaining to Iñupiaq Kinship Systems. Ann Arbor: University Microfilms.

Hellenthal, Marc E.
1985 Shareholder Attitude Survey (prepared for the Arctic Slope Regional Corporation by Hellenthal & Associates, Inc., Anchorage).

Helmericks, Constance and Harmon
    1952 The Flight of the Arctic Tern. Boston: Little, Brown and Company.

Herbert C.
    1970 Statement of the Alaska Miner's Association before the Subcommittee on
        Indian Affairs on Alaska Native Land Claims. House of Representatives. 91st
        Congress. Washington: U.S. Printing Office.

Hickok, David M.
    1982 Letter to the Editor (by David M. Hickok, Director, Arctic Environmental
        Information and Data Center, and Chairman, Alaska Council on Science and
        Technology). Alaska Native News. 1 (1):36.

Hippler, Arthur E.
    1969 Barrow and Kotzebue: An Exploratory Comparison of Acculturation and
        Education in Two Large Northwestern Alaskan Villages. Minneapolis: Uni-
        versity of Minnesota Training Center for Community Programs.

Hoffman, David, David Libbey, and Grant Spearman
    1988 Nuiqsut: Land Use Values Through Time in the Nuiqsut Area. North Slope
        Borough and Anthropology and Historical Preservation section of the Co-
        operative Parks Study Unit. Fairbanks: University of Alaska.

Hopsen, Eben
    1977 Iñupiaq Education. *In* Cross-Cultural Issues in Alaskan Education. R. Bern-
        hardt (ed). Fairbanks: Center for Northern Educational Research. University
        of Alaska. 3–6.

Hughes, Charles C.
    1960 An Eskimo Village in the Modern World. Ithaca: Cornell University Press.
    1984 History of Ethnology after 1945. *In* Handbook of North American Indians:
        Arctic D. Damas (ed). 5:23–26. Washington: Smithsonian Institution.

Ingstad, Helge M.
    1954 Nunamuit: Among Alaska's Inland Eskimos. London: Allen and Erwin.

Jackson, Sheldon
    1896 Annual Reports (I to XVI) on Introduction of Domestic Reindeer into Alaska,
        1890–1905. U.S. Bureau of Education. Washington: Government Printing
        Office (1891–1908).
    1890–91 Annual Report of the General Agent of Education for Alaska to the U.S.
        Commissioner of Education, Department of the Interior. Washington. Cited
        in R. L. Stewart, Sheldon Jackson. New York: Fleming Revel, 1908.

Jacobson, Michael J., and Cynthia Wentworth
    1982 Kaktovik Subsistence: Land Use Values Through Time in the Arctic National
        Wildlife Refuge Area. U.S. Fish and Wildlife Service. Northern Alaska Eco-
        logical Services. Fairbanks.

Jorgensen, Joseph G.
    1971 Indians in the Metropolis. *In* The American Indian in Urban Society. J.
        Waddell and M. Watson, eds. Boston: Little Brown.
    1984 Native Rights and Rural Anglos: Conflicts and Cultural Responses to Energy
        Developments. Human Organization. 43:2 178–185.

Kakaruk, Steve
   1985 NSB unveils new employment/training program. Tundra Times. November
        11.

Kerekoper, Fred G.
   1937 Dogsled Trip from Barrow to Demarcation Point, April 1937. Barrow: North
        Slope Borough Commission on History and Culture (reprinted 1977).

Kisautaq, Leona Okakok
   1978 Puiguitkaat. The 1979 Elders Conference. Barrow: North Slope Borough
        Commission on History and Culture.

Kleinfeld, Judith
   1973 A Long Way from Home: Effects of Public High Schools on Village Children
        Away from Home. Center for Northern Educational Research. Institute of
        Social, Economic, and Government Research. Fairbanks: University of
        Alaska.
   1981 Different Paths of Iñupiat Men and Women in the Wage Economy: The North
        Slope Experience. Alaska Review of Social and Economic Conditions.
        XVIII(1).

Knapp, Gunnar, Steve Colt, and Troy Henley
   1986 Economic and Demographic Systems and Base Case Projections of the North
        Slope Borough. Diapir Field Lease Offering (June 1986). Volume 1. An-
        chorage: Institute of Social and Economic Research. University of Alaska
        (draft).

Kruse, Jack, Judith Kleinfeld, and Robert Travis
   1981 Energy Development and the North Slope Iñupiat: Quantitative Analysis of
        Social and Economic Change. Institute of Social and Economic Research.
        Anchorage: University of Alaska.

Kuhn, Thomas
   1962 The Structure of Scientific Revolutions. Chicago: University of Chicago Press.

Langdon, Steve J.
   1986 Contradictions in Alaskan Native Economy and Society. In Steve Langdon
        (ed) Contemporary Alaskan Native Economies. Lanham: University Press of
        America.

Langdon, Steve J. (ed)
   1986 Contemporary Alaskan Native Economies. Lanham: University Press of
        America.

Lantis, Margaret
   1957 American Arctic Populations: Their Survival Problems. Arctic Biology. Cor-
        valis: Oregon State College.
   1973 The Current Nativistic Movement in Alaska. Circumpolar Problems: Habitat,
        Economy, and Social Relations in the Development of Alaska. G. Berg (ed).
        New York: Pergamon Press. 99–118.

Larson, Helge, E., and Froelich Rainey
   1948 Ipiutak and the Arctic Whaling Culture. Anthropological Papers of the Amer-
        ican Museum of Natural History. 42.

Lauritzen, Philip
  1983 Oil and Amulets: Inuit, A People United at the Top of the World. Breakwater
       Books, Ltd.

Lee, Molly
  1983 Baleen Basketry of the North Alaskan Eskimo. Barrow: North Slope Borough
       Planning Department.

Leiss, William
  1974 The Domination of Nature. Boston: Beacon Press.
  1976 The Limits to Satisfaction: An essay on the problem of needs and commodities.
       Toronto: University of Toronto Press.

Levi-Strauss, Claude
  1984 Tristes Tropique (English edition). New York: Atheneum.

Maclean, Edna Ahgeak
  1980 Iñupiallu Tannillu Uqalunisa Ilanich (Abridged Iñupiat and English
       Dictionary). Alaska Native Language Center, University of Alaska, Fair-
       banks, and the Iñupiat Language Commission, North Slope Borough, Barrow,
       Alaska.
  1988a Elders as Teachers: As an Educational Unit of the Iñupiat Community.
       Alaska Native (Summer). 32–33.
  1988b Quest for Iñupiaq Knowledge and Truth. Alaska Native (Summer). 30–32.

Malinowski, Bronislaw
  1915 The Natives of Mailu. Transactions and Proceedings of the Royal Society of
       South Australia, XXXIX.

McBeath, Gerald A.
  1981 North Slope Borough Government and Policymaking. Institute of Social and
       Economic Research. Anchorage: University of Alaska.

McBeath, Gerald A. and Thomas Morehouse
  1980 The Dynamics of Alaska Native Self-Government. Lantham: University Press
       of America.

McElroy, Ann
  1975 Canadian Arctic modernization and change in female Inuit role identification.
       American Ethnologist: 662–686.
  1977 Alternatives of Modernization: Styles and Strategies in the Acculturative Be-
       havior of Baffin Island Inuit. Vol. 3. New Haven: Human Relations Area
       Files.

Mikkelsen, Ejnar
  1909 Conquering the Arctic. London: W. Heinmann.

Milan, Frederick A.
  1964 The Acculturation of the Contemporary Eskimos of Wainwright, Alaska.
       Anthropological Papers of the University of Alaska. 11:2.

Morehouse, Thomas A.
  1984 Alaska Resources Development: Issues for the 80s. T. Morehouse. Boulder:
       Westview Press.
  1987 Native Claims and Political Development. Institute of Social and Economic
       Research Occasional Paper No. 18. Anchorage: University of Alaska.

Morehouse, Thomas, Gerald A. McBeath, and Linda Leask
1984 Alaska's Urban and Rural Governments. Lantham: University Press of America.

Murdoch, John
1892 Ethnological Results of the Point Barrow Expedition. Ninth Annual Report of the Bureau of American Ethnology, 1887–88. Washington: Government Printing Office. 1–441.

Nash, Roy
1934 Report adverse to the Lomen Reindeer Corporation. U.S. Department of the Interior, Director of Investigations, Seward Peninsula, Alaska Region.

Naske, Claus M. and Herman E. Slotnick
1987 Alaska: A History of the 49th State (2nd edition). Norman: University of Oklahoma Press.

National Research Council
1989 Arctic Social Science: An Agenda for Action. Committee on Arctic Social Sciences, Polar Research Board. Washington: National Academy Press.

Neakok, William
1984 Transcript of Proceedings (Barrow). Volume 27. Alaska Native Review Commission.

Nelson, Richard K.
1980 Shadow of the Hunter: Stories of Eskimo Life. Chicago: University Press.

Nielson, Jon M.
1977 Kaktovik, Alaska: An Overview of Relocations. Barrow: North Slope Borough Commission on History and Culture.

Northern Frontier Reindeer Company
1941 Annual (cited in Sonnenfeld: 1957. Record is in Barrow)

Ostermann, H.
1952 The Alaskan Eskimos as described in the posthumous notes of Dr. Knud Rasmussen. Report of the 5th Thule Expedition of 1921–24. Volume X, Part 3. Gyldendalska Boghandel, Nordisk Forlag, Copenhagen.

Oswalt, Wendell H.
1963 Napaskiak: An Alaskan Eskimo Community. Tucson: University of Arizona Press.
1979 Eskimos and Explorers. Novato: Chandler and Sharpe.

Paul, Fred
1984 Statement by Fred Paul. Transcript of Proceedings. Alaska Native Review Commission. Volume II. Anchorage.

Pearce, Roy Harvey
1965 Savagism and Civilization. Baltimore.

Pospisil, Leopold
1964 Law and Societal Structure Among the Nunamuit Eskimo. In Explorations in Cultural Anthropology: Essays in Honor of George Murdock. Ward Goodenough (ed). New York: McGraw Hill.

Puxley, Peter
1977 The Colonial Experience. In Dene Nation: The Colony Within. Mel Watkins (ed). Toronto: University of Toronto Press.

Ray, Dorothy Jean
  1967 Land Tenure and Policy of the Bering Strait Eskimos. Journal of the West.
       6(3):371–394.

Rearden, James
  1982 Subsistence—Alaska's Agony. Alaska (October) 7–9 60–66.

Richards, Eva Alvey
  1949 Arctic Mood. Caldwell: Caxton Printers.

Rintoul, William
  1986 Looking for Oil in Alaska. The Lamp. 18–23.

Rock, Howard
  1962 Editorial. Tundra Times (November 1).

Rogers, George
  1970 Change in Alaska. College: University of Alaska Press.
  1972 Impact of economic conditions on Cross-cultural Education in Alaska. Edu-
       cation in the North. F. Darnell (ed). Fairbanks: University of Alaska Press.

Rostow, W. W.
  1960 The Stages of Economic Growth. New York: Cambridge University Press.

Salisbury, Richard R.
  1984 Affluence and Cultural Survival: An Introduction. *In* Affluence and Cultural
       Survival, Salisbury, Richard F. and E. Tooker (eds). 1981 Proceedings of the
       American Ethnological Society. Washington: American Ethnological Society.

Sater, Beverly F. (ed)
  1970 A Report of the Conference on Arctic Research and Resource Development.
       Washington: Arctic Institute of North America.

Scovel, S. F.
  1879 Historical Sketch of the Women's Executive Committee on Home Missions.
       (cited in R. L. Stewart, Sheldon Jackson. New York: Fleming Revel.
       1908:257).

Senungetuk, Joseph
  1971 Give or Take a Century: An Eskimo Chronicle: San Francisco: The Indian
       Historical Press.

Simpson, John
  1875 Observations on the Western Eskimo and the Country They Inhabit (from
       notes taken during two years at Point Barrow). London: Royal Geographical
       Society. Arctic Geography and Ethnology.

Sonnenfeld, Joseph
  1957 Changes in Subsistence Among the Barrow Eskimo. Ph.D. dissertation. Johns
       Hopkins University.

Spencer, Robert F.
  1959 The North Alaskan Eskimo: A Study in Ecology and Society. Washington:
       Bureau of American Ethnology, Bulletin 171.
  1984 North Alaskan Coastal Eskimo. *In* Handbook of North American Indians,
       Vol 5. (Arctic). David Damas (ed). 320–337.

Stefansson, Vihjalmur
  1913 My Life with the Eskimo. New York: MacMillan Company.
  1914 The Stefansson-Anderson Arctic Expedition of the American Museum: Pre-

liminary Ethnological Report. Anthropological Papers of the American Museum of Natural History. XIV.

Stocking, George
1968 Race, Culture and Evolution: Essays in the History of Anthropology. Madison: University of Wisconsin Press.

Stotts, James
1984 Transcript of Proceedings (Barrow). Volume 27. Alaska Native Review Commission.

Sullivan, James W.
1969 Personal Income Patterns in Alaska. Alaska Review of Business and Economic Conditions. IV:1. Fairbanks: University of Alaska.

Tetpon, John
1988 Between Two Worlds: Growing Up in Alaska. Alaska Native (summer).

Thomas, Keith
1983 Man and the Natural World. New York: Pantheon.

Thompson, Morris
1973 Department of the Interior news release, 2695–73.

U.S. Bureau of Education
1898 Education in Alaska. Report of the Commissioner of Education. Washington: U.S. Government Printing Office.
1910–11 The Work of the Bureau of Education for the Natives of Alaska. U.S. Department of the Interior. Annual Reports. Washington: U.S. Government Printing Office. (cited in Sonnenfeld 1957:321–2).

U.S. Department of the Interior
Curriculum Planning Guide for Bureau of Indian Affairs Teachers.
1957 Washington: Department of the Interior, Bureau of Indian Affairs.
1893 Annual Report (Regulations for Teachers).
1985 ANCSA 1985 Study (Draft). Bureau of Indian Affairs.

Upicksoun, Joseph
1971 Statement before the Hearings of the Local Boundary Commission, Barrow, Alaska, December 2nd and 3rd. Juneau: Governor's Office, State of Alaska (cited in McBeath and Morehouse 1980:78–79).
1984 Alaska Native Review Commission. Transcript of Proceedings, February 29, 1984.

Upicksoun, Joseph and Charles Edwardsen, Jr.
1971 Letter to Honorable Richard M. Nixon (reprinted in Alaska Native News September 1984 16–18).

Van Ness, William
1984 Testimony. Transcripts of Proceedings. Overview Roundtable Discussions. IV. ANCSA Institutions and Legal Regimes. Anchorage: Alaska Native Review Commission.

VanStone, James W.
1960 A successful Combination of Subsistence and Wage Economies on the Village Level. Economic Development and Cultural Change. 8 (2) 174–191.
1962 Point Hope: An Eskimo Village in Transition. Seattle: University of Washington Press.

1977 A. F. Kashevarov's Coastal Explorations in Northwest Alaska, 1838 (edited by James W. VanStone and translated by David H. Kraus).

Vaudrin, Bill
1974 Native/non-Native Communication: Creating a Two-Way Flow. *In* James Orvik and Ray Barnhardt (eds), Cultural Influences in Alaska Native Education. Fairbanks: Center for Cross-Cultural Studies, University of Alaska.

Watkins, T. H.
1988 Vanishing Arctic: Alaska's National Wildlife Refuge. New York: Aperture.

Wallerstein, Immanuel
1974 The Modern World System. New York: Academic Press.
1986 The World System: Myths and Historical Shifts. The Global Economy: Divergent Perspectives on Economic Change. E. Gondolf, Irwin Marcus, and James Dougherty (eds). Boulder: Westview Press. 15–25.

White, William
1986 Borough Gets Money Back. Anchorage Daily News. April 22.

Wilimovsky, Norman J. (ed)
1966 Preface. Environment of the Cape Thompson Region, Alaska. U.S. Atomic Energy Commission. Washington: Government Printing Office.

Will, Anne
1984 Alaska History for Local Historians: The North Slope. Fairbanks: University of Alaska (Rural Education).

Wolf, Eric
1974 Anthropology. New York: Norton.
1982 Europe and the People Without History. Berkeley: University of California Press.

Woodbury, Anthony C.
1984 Eskimo and Aleut Languages. *In* Handbook of North American Indians: Arctic. D. Damas (ed). Washington: Smithsonian Institution.

Woolfe, Henry D.
1893 The Seventh District. *In* Report on Population and Resources of Alaska at the Eleventh Census: 1890, House of Representatives, 52nd Congress, 1st session. Washington, D.C. (cited in Bockstoce 1983:141).

Worl, Celeste
1988 Nusunginya wins day in court for whalers. Alaska Native (summer).

Worl, Rosita and Charles W. Smythe
1986 Barrow: A Decade of Modernization. Technical Report No. 125. U.S. Department of the Interior. Minerals Management Service. Alaska Outer Continental Shelf Region. Alaska OCS Socioeconomic Studies Program. Anchorage. 1–455.
1987 Barrow: A Decade of Modernization. Alaska Native Magazine. 5:2.

Wright, Don.
1984 Overview Roundtable Discussions. Volume I. The Spirit of ANCSA. Alaska Native Review Commission. Anchorage.

Glossary

Aanigutyak: A special parturition lodge.

Aipariik: The term used by female partners in a co-marriage.

Angatqaq: An Iñupiat shaman, skilled in magical practices and supernatural knowledge.

Arigaah: Good! An expression of satisfaction or pleasure.

Ataniq: Hunting group leader.

Eskimo: The word once used by the Indians of eastern Canada to describe their enemies to the north. The term was universally adopted by western scholars and is only now being replaced by *Iñupiat* (north and northwest Alaska), *Yup'ik* or *Yuit* (southwestern Arctic Alaska and Siberia), *Inuvialuit* (western Canadian Arctic), *Kallalit* (Greenland), and other (regional) terms preferred by those living in the areas concerned. *Inuit* (*Inuk* sing.) is also commonly used in Canada particularly.

Iñupiat: Real or genuine people.

Iñuqun: Monsters

Iñuqugauzat: Little spirit people.

Kamik: Skin boots.

Ki: "Go ahead."

Makkiligaarok: A ten-legged polar bear.

Maktak: Whale meat and blubber, a delicacy among the Iñupiat.

Nalukatak: Spring whaling festival.

Nanuq: A polar bear.

Niuviriik: Trading partner.

Nuliaqatigiit: Co-marriage or "spouse exchange."

Nuliaqatigiit: The term used to describe the four partners in a co-marriage.

Nuliaqpak: Primary wife of a *umialik.*

Nunamiut: The aboriginal inhabitants of the Brooks Range, Colville and Kobuk River drainages. They were primary hunters of caribou who traveled to the coast each summer to trade, hunt, and gather.

Qargi: Family gathering place and ceremonial house.

Qatangutigiit: The reciprocal term used by children from a co-marriage.

Qatizut: Annual village-wide social gathering in the larger villages with several local families.

Qatnut: Trade fair.

Qayaq: One-person skin-covered kayak.

Tanik: White person (from the Iñupiaq word *tanikhlugo* (to wash)).

Tareumiut: The aboriginal inhabitants of the Arctic coastal and adjacent river drainages

Tundra: The treeless Arctic plain.

Tuunraq: A helping spirit.
Ugruk: Bearded seal weighing several hundred pounds.
Umialik: Boat captain, "boss," or "rich man."
Umiaq: A large skin boat used for hunting in the open sea.
Yuit: A term similar to *Yup'ik* referring to southwestern and Siberian Arctic peoples.

Acronyms

AEWC	Alaska Eskimo Whaling Commission
AFN	Alaska Federation of Natives
ANCSA	Alaska Native Claims Settlement Act
ANRC	Alaska Native Review Commission
ANILCA	Alaska National Interest Lands Conservation Act
ANWR	Arctic National Wildlife Refuge
ASNA	Arctic Slope Native Association
ASRC	Arctic Slope Regional Corporation
BIA	Bureau of Indian Affairs
CIP	Capital Improvement Program
ICAS	Iñupiat Community of the Arctic Slope
ICC	Inuit Circumpolar Conference
IRA	Indian Reorganization Act
IRA's	A particular form of government set up under the IRA
NARL	Naval Arctic Research Laboratory
NSB	North Slope Borough

Index

Page numbers in italics refer to photographs or maps.